EARLY
MEDIEVAL SOCIETY

EARLY
MEDIEVAL SOCIETY

Edited by

SYLVIA L. THRUPP
The University of Michigan

APPLETON-CENTURY-CROFTS
EDUCATIONAL DIVISION
New York MEREDITH CORPORATION

720—2

Library of Congress Card Number: 67–12835

PRINTED IN THE UNITED STATES OF AMERICA

390—88035—3

ACKNOWLEDGMENTS

SELECTION 1. From Bertha Phillpotts, *Kindred and Clan in the Middle Ages* (Cambridge, England, Cambridge University Press, 1913). Reprinted by permission, with some abridgement.

SELECTION 2. Lorraine Lancaster, "Kinship in Anglo-Saxon Society," *The British Journal of Sociology*, vol. 9, nos. 3 and 4 (1957), pp. 230–233. Reprinted by permission, with some abridgement.

SELECTION 3. From Lujo Brentano, essay in *English Gilds*, E.E.T.S., Original Series 40 (1870, reprinted 1963). Reprinted by permission of the Council of the Early English Text Society, Oxford, England, with some abridgement.

SELECTION 4. Gabriel Le Bras, "Sociologie de l'église dans le haut moyen âge," *Le Chiesi*, Settimane di Studio del Centro italiani di studi sull'alto medioevo (1960). Reprinted by permission.

SELECTION 5. From Imbart de la Tour, a series of articles in the *Revue historique* (Paris, 1896–98), printed by the Presses universitaires françaises in book form as *Les Paroisses rurales dans l'ancienne France*, 1898. Translated and printed by permission.

SELECTION 6. William A. Chaney, "Paganism to Christianity in Anglo-Saxon England," *The Harvard Theological Review*, LIII (July, 1960). Copyright 1960 by the President and Fellows of Harvard College. Reprinted by permission.

SELECTION 7. Karl Bosl, "Ueber soziale Mobilität in der mittelalterlichen Gesellschaft," in *Vierteljahrshrift für Sozial und Wirtschaftsgeschichte* (1960), reprinted in Karl Bosl, *Frühformen der Gesellschaft im mittelalterlichen Europa* (Munich, R. Oldenbourg Verlag, 1964). Translated and printed by permission, with some abridgement.

SELECTION 8. From Pierre Bonnassie, "Une famille de la campagne barcelonaise et ses activités économiques aux alentours de l'An Mil," *Annales du Midi*, t. 76, no. 68 (1964). Translated and printed by permission.

SELECTION 9. From Jacques Boussard, "La vie en Anjou . . . ," *Le Moyen Age* (1950). Translated and printed by permission with some abridgement.

SELECTION 10. From Edouard Perroy, a lecture not originally intended for publication, appearing in mimeographed form as Chapter VIII of *Les Carolingiens* (Les cours de Sorbonne, Centre de Documentation Universitaire, 5, Place de la Sorbonne, Paris 5e, France, 1961). Translated and printed by permission.

SELECTION 11. From Aidan W. Southall, *Alur Society*, published for the East African Institute of Social Research (W. Heffer and Sons, Ltd., Cambridge, England, 1956). Reprinted by permission.

SELECTION 12. From Phyllis Kaberry, "Primitive States" *The British Journal of Sociology*, vol. VIII, no. 3 (1957). Reprinted by permission.

SELECTION 13. From E. Ewig, "Résidence et Capitale dans le haut Moyen Age," *Revue historique* (1963). Translated and printed by permission.

SELECTION 14. Edith Ennen, "Les différents types de formation des villes européennes," *Le Moyen Age* (t. LXII, 1956). Translated and printed by permission.

SELECTION 15. Fernand Vercauteren, "La circulation des marchands en Europe occidentale du VIᵉ au IXᵉ siècle," *Centri e Vie di irradazione della civiltà nell'alto medioevo*, Centro italiano di studi sull'alto medioevo (1964). Translated and printed by permission.

SELECTION 16. Marc Bloch, "Economie de nature ou économie d'argent . . . ," *Annales d'histoire sociale*, t. XI (1939). Translated and printed by permission.

SELECTION 17. Gino Luzzatto, "Mutamenti nell'economia agraria italiana," *I Problemi comuni dell'Europa post-carolingia*, Centro italiano di studi sull'alto medioevo (1955). Translated and printed by permission.

SELECTION 18. Pierre Riché, "Les Foyers de culture en Gaule franque du VIᵉ au IXᵉ siècle," *Centri e Vie di irradozione della civiltà nell'alto medioevo*, Centro italiano di studi sull'alto medioevo (1964). Translated and printed by permission.

SELECTION 19. Mary Catherine Welborn, "Lotharingia as a center of Arabic and Scientific Influence in the XI century," *Isis*, Vol. 16 (1931), pp. 188–98. Reprinted by permission with some abridgement.

SELECTION 20. From Karl W. Deutsch, "Medieval Unity and the Economic Conditions for an International Civilization," *The Canadian Journal of Economics and Political Science*, Vol. 10, No. 1 (February, 1944). Reprinted by permission with some abridgement.

THE COVER. Used in the design is a reproduction of a copy, made *circa* 1109, of a map of the world originally drawn in the last quarter of the eighth century by St. Beatus, a monk of Valcavado, in Spain. Britain and Scotland are shown as separate islands. By permission of the trustees of the British Museum.

Preface

The stretch of time known as the early middle ages—viewed here as running from the disintegration of Roman power in its western provinces into the mid-11th century or in some regions later—presents a special kind of challenge. For a Westerner faces here, with pride, or embarrassment, or scientific curiosity, the fumbling origins of his own culture. It was in these centuries that Western Europe, through accepting the common impress of Latin Christianity, became for the first time a distinctive and active area of civilization. Yet that civilization seems more diverse than unified, its people more strange and exotic than Western.

Over the years historians have held widely different views of the early middle ages, whether they concentrated on their own country or tried to see the whole civilization in perspective. Often their controversies have generated more heat than light, and although nowadays there is more constructive international cooperation among medievalists, new problems turn up as fast as the old ones are resolved. One excuse for disagreements lies in the fact that records are naturally thinner than for the later centuries of the middle ages, when writing came into more general use. This leaves room for speculative interpretation. However, when one thinks of the occasions there must have been for accidental or deliberate destruction of manuscripts over so long a lapse of time, it is astonishing how many have survived. We have a vast quantity from the hands of ecclesiastics, including personal letters. Legal sources, which have been the best worked, let us know at least the wishes of the main lawmakers, both secular and religious. In addition, there are several bodies of sources which are still far from fully exploited in any systematic way for the purposes of social history: numerous records of property transfers, which often contain economic and genealogical detail; the literary sources, the art and iconography; the uses of languages; and—most abundant of all—the archeological finds. Much early digging was done by amateurs who damaged or disarranged their finds irreparably, but excavation has for some time now been expertly controlled. The royal treasures, the warrior's weapons, the ornaments and other personal possessions found in the pagan graves, never fail to excite popular curiosity: finds concerning Vikings and Anglo-Saxons are perennially in the news. Examined with skill, not only the more spectacular finds but the very disposition of graves in a burial site, or the alignments and groupings on a building site, can be a clue to social organization and to the mentality of the people who designed these arrangements.

The sources are not so poor, then, as to justify any longer the amount of guesswork that entered, as late as Pirenne's time, into controversy over the character of early medieval civilization. The early controversies were in fact mere battles between rationalist and romantic ideologies. Rationalist writers saw the age as "dark" with superstition, dirt, and ferocity; to romantic writers the self-same facts signified a happy release from Roman rationality and discipline, a resurgence of free poetic imagination, of "natural" loyalties between lord and man, and so on. Other distortions arose out of racial theory. That great scholar and magnificent writer, Henri Pirenne, wishing to stress the emergence of the North and the Northwest as a rival or complement to the Mediterranean area, misread, a little, the changes that occurred in the slow rhythm of early medieval economic life. His work helped to spur new economic research, and controversy over his "thesis" lives on only in American classrooms.

Controversy is sometimes mere intellectual pugilism, attracting attention because it steps up the incisiveness of writing. Or it may create schools which for a time pursue divergent lines of research. Rationalist writers on the early middle ages were attracted by the passage of the Graeco-Roman-Judaic tradition, the "passing of the torch" of elite rationality and humanism. But dispassionate Catholic scholarship has done far more to build a rounded view of intellectual and religious development. Romantic schools in the 19th century did valuable descriptive and narrative work, especially on political events and institutions. But deeper research, going beyond the blood-and-thunder chronicles they loved, has radically revised the pictures they drew. Too biased a writer, though he may avoid the sin of pallid writing, is likely to misread his sources now and then, even in just trying to tell what happened; and if he moves on to the question of why events took a given trend he will give only the *a priori* explanation of which he was convinced beforehand. Aldous Huxley in an early essay on *The Future of the Past* made great fun of historians for perpetually discovering, in the middle ages, the ideals of one or other school of thought of their own day.

The writers whose work is represented in this book demonstrate rather well how an historian can guard against falling into this trap. They test, openly and honestly, both the descriptions and the explanations that they offer. They test them in the first place by the professional rule of looking for bias and possible error in the documents relevant to their subject; they use a wide range of types of evidence. They test their explanations also by comparing the evidence as to a course of development in one part of early medieval Europe and another, and in later periods. Further, several of them demonstrate the usefulness of tools borrowed from the analytical disciplines of anthropology, economics, sociology, and political science, and of comparison with other societies whose thought and habits and forms of organization have more in common with those of early medieval men than our own have.

The book deals throughout with the reasons for the shifting division of power between kingship, lordship, Church authorities, and popular associations, which has been so many times described in political and legal terms. If one thinks, instead, of individual people and the social relationships and the loyalties in which they were most immediately engaged, it seems more natural to look first, with Bertha Phillpotts, whose book through going out of print has been in danger of oblivion, at the extent to which customs of mutual help among relatives might have limited or even removed, people's need to turn for help and protection to lords or patrons. These circles of relatives were not, as she shows, permanently organized groups: the kindred were merely the people who recognized one as kin and who materialized as a group, as it were, only when one was in trouble. Bertha Phillpotts' conclusions as to the effectiveness of such help in preventing the development of economic dependency or of political feudalism, as she herself pointed out in 1913, need further testing. Yet Lorraine Lancaster's work published in 1957 (here slightly abridged), was the first to test them carefully for England, and the methods she devised have not been applied with similar care, yet, anywhere else.

This negative approach to the growth of lordship in northern areas is complemented by two positive approaches: Karl Bosl's, which would make personal service—in household and court, on estates and in administration—the primal organizing principle both of Celtic and of Germanic society; and Pierre Bonnassie's unique analysis of how ecclesiastical patronage of laymen operated, and of how economic dependency ultimately developed, among the enterprising free peasantry around Barcelona.

Another novel feature of the book which calls for an introductory note is the section following Professor Perroy's lucid exposition of the weakness of Charlemagne's empire, of how tenuously it held together and of how constantly and easily parts of it could fall away. The discussion on the analogy of the earthworm which illustrates the French sociologist Durkheim's classic definition of a segmental state—one that can be segmented, like an earthworm, without being destroyed, because each part is virtually a self-sufficient political organism—of how well the parts of various early African kingdoms and medieval European kingdoms could survive independently, may be suggestive. Certainly it is more directly applicable to the 9th century than the political theory of Charlemagne's clergy which Professor Perroy recalls, and more applicable also than 19th-century theories of sovereignty.

The concluding essay is a final invitation to think along lines that have been little used in historical work. If we can explain why Latin Christian culture won the West, we should be able to explain by the inverse of this reasoning, why the four other rival civilizations on the early medieval scene, though each had shown itself capable of penetrating other cultures, or of conquest, failed to win it. Professor Deutsch's question is not the ancient one of whether or why Charles Martel kept France from turning to Islam; it is a challenge to use history in one's thinking about nations and international community and to bring questions of major importance to bear on history.

For kind permission to translate or reproduce the essays in this book I owe thanks to all of the living authors, especially to Professor Edouard Perroy, whose essay is a lecture not originally intended for publication; to Professor Edith Ennen for offering slight revisions; to Professors Fernand Vercauteren and Pierre Riché for taking the trouble to check my translations of their work and to Signora E. Polacco for checking my translation of the article by her uncle, the late Professor Gino Luzzatto; to Professors Karl Bosl and Karl W. Deutsch and Monsieur Pierre Bonnassie for permitting me to abridge their articles slightly; to Professor W. Chaney for bringing his final note up to date. I am greatly indebted also to Professor Giuseppe Ermini, President of the *Centro italiano di studi sull'alto medioevo,* for permission to translate three articles from the Center's publications. My thanks are due further to the editors of the following journals—*The British Journal of Sociology, The Harvard Theological Review, Le Moyen Age,* the *Annales: Economies, Sociétés, Civilisations* (for permission to translate the article of Marc Bloch from the *Annales d'histoire sociale), Isis,* and *The Canadian Journal of Economics and Political Science*—and to the following publishers—Cambridge University Press, R. Oldenbourg Verlag, the Presses universitaires françaises, Wm. Heffer and Sons, Ltd., and the Clarendon Press.

S.L.T.

Contents

xi

Forms of State

Towns

Economic Life

Humanism and Science

Medieval Unity

Kinship, Lordship, and Association

I

The Germanic Kindreds

BERTHA PHILLPOTTS

The Influence of the Kindreds on Social Conditions

The importance of the *pre*-historic kindred-system is constantly recognized by historians, and has often been credited with more power than it can ever have possessed; but it is no less constantly implied that such features of the system as survived into historic times had little or no influence on the body politic, and are only worth mentioning in connection with criminal law. It is true that the shifting nature of the Teutonic kindred precluded its ever having a chief, and asserting itself as a permanently compact body, so that its workings are bound to be obscure. Yet such organizations as existed in Denmark and Friesland, the Netherlands and Picardy, cannot have been without influence on the social conditions of their times. A man who can at any moment surround himself with a large group of persons, all of whom are willing to make sacrifices for him, is in a very different position to one who has to depend on his own efforts and on those of his immediate family for protection against aggression.

Not only would his position be better from the social and political point of view: it would also be far better from the economic point of view. It is generally agreed that the isolation of the small landowner was his undoing, since it rendered him unable to withstand adverse circumstances, such as a bad year, a fire, a plague among his beasts, or a piratical raid on his homestead. "In such an emergency the simplest and best expedient was always to surrender one's land, getting it back as a benefice, and now at least to have the social support of the patron, which had also an economically useful side." [1] This is all quite true of the isolated small landowner, but we cannot believe that it was at all true of the small peasant proprietor who was surrounded by a kindred. We have seen evidence to show that the cohesive kindred would rally round a member threatened with a lawsuit, and that it probably performed the functions of an insurance society, besides keeping a jealous watch on the inherited land belonging to its members. In regions where the kindred preserved its solidarity it would thus be far less easy for a wealthy landowner, or even for ecclesiastical foundations, to exploit the financial and social difficulties of a poor neighbor, by acquiring his lands or by extorting rights over him at periods of want. In such regions we might reasonably expect to find few great territorial lords, and few seignorial privileges, together with a preponderance of free peasant proprietors. This is exactly what we do find in Schleswig-Holstein. The "nobles", up to the 12th century, are peasant proprietors who perform certain military services to the king, and who receive certain immunities in return, but they are little wealthier than their fellows, and have no seignorial rights. This class of noble disappears in the 13th century in Schleswig-Holstein, and somewhat later in the rest of Jutland, largely owing to poverty. The later class of nobles also sprang from the peasant farmers, but has a different history. In order to encourage colonization, the Count of Holstein granted fiefs in Eastern Holstein to persons of the peasant class, who thus became rich and powerful, with feudal rights over their dependents. Almost the whole of the later nobility of Denmark, as well as of Schleswig-Holstein, can be traced back to these colonists. Except in the colonized districts, the peasant farmers possessed their own lands, and continued to enjoy a high degree of local autonomy up to the 16th and 17th centuries. This independence is also character-istic of the Old Saxon peasants, until the country was overrun by coloniz-ing nobles; and for a much longer period of time of East and West Friesland. . . . In non-Frisian Holland, too, free peasant proprietors con-tinued to flourish until the rise of the towns, when it would seem that the free kindreds flocked thither, preserving their independence throughout the whole of the Middle Ages, and abandoning agriculture to a lower class.

In France, owing to the need for cavalry occasioned by the Saracen invasions, an immense impulse was given to feudalism, which naturally resulted in depressing the status of the ordinary freeman. Yet of the early Frankish kingdom it has been observed that "the prevalence of lordship is by no means so clear as in England".[2]

Of our own country, on the other hand, Professor Vinogradoff has said that "in a sense, the feudal law of England was the hardest of all in Western Europe". The dependent state of the ceorl in the greater part of England (before the Norman Conquest) has been commented on by many authorities, and is so marked that Seebohm found himself forced to con-template a serf origin for the English village community. Maitland at-tributes the ceorl's loss of independence to the exhausting efforts made by Wessex to keep off the Danes.[3] This would account for his poverty, if poor he was, but would it account for manors and seigneurial rights? We must observe that the Viking raids (together with ecclesiastical influence which should surely have been effective in England if anywhere) have been recently adduced as paving the way to an "elevation of the lowest elements of the population" in Friesland.[4] Friesland suffered more than England at the hands of the Northmen, and it shakes our faith in the Vikings as the agents of social change to find them adduced in England as the chief cause of the prevailing serfdom, and in Friesland as contributing towards the rise of the agricultural classes.

Moreover even in Northern and Eastern England the only form of independence granted to free sokemen is the right to choose their own lord. Lords, it seems, they must have; and not only must they have lords, but for purposes of administration and police supervision they must be dragooned into groups (tithing groups), whose function it is to guarantee their orderliness and produce them when required. In Wessex, too, feudal lords are frequently mentioned in Ine's laws,[5] before the Danish invasions. Of course England was a military kingdom, won at the point of the sword, but it has been maintained that it was not until some time after the conquest that status of the ceorl begins to fall, and in any case it is strange that the rigors of feudalism should be more pronounced in England than in the Frankish kingdom, which was also won by force of arms.[6]

The real reason why the burden of the small landowner so soon proved too heavy for him to bear in England was not that the burden became so much heavier, but that it was a burden calculated for the backs of many individuals, not for one. Wergild for instance became a crushing imposition, leading to debt, serfdom, poverty, when the price was paid out of the cattle and household goods possessed by the individual slayer and his immediate family:[7] when dispersed among a whole kindred it was comparatively little felt.

Now let us compare England with a country that was not gained at the power of the sword. In Iceland individuals, not associated in kindreds, took peaceful possession of their land, and at the outset all landowners were on an equal footing. There were no Viking raids to repel, there was no national army whose officers might obtain over-lordship over their fellows; and yet, within a few years of the settlement, every landowner, unless himself a chief, had a lord to whom he owed military and other service, and the courts of justice were more seignorial than popular in character. By the 12th century the small landowners were so crushed that the few powerful families could demand what services and dues they liked. No resistance was ever made, despite the fact that the chiefs were always at war among themselves. Now if there is any fact agreed upon by all authorities, it is that these Icelandic settlers were no servile class accustomed to tyranny, but men with an extreme independence of character and traditions. Many of them, we are told, left Norway because they would not acknowledge Harold Hairfair's right to tax their ancestral lands, which they declared to be their own absolute property. And yet this is their history in Iceland, where they only needed protection against each other! If they had had kindreds to protect them, should we have found this absolute and speedy decline into dependence on a lord? It is not entirely the absence of a central executive which reduces them to this pitch, for in the commonwealth of Ditmarschen, which till the middle of the 15th century was governed by its kindreds, the noble class disappeared in the 13th century, and when Holstein nobles pressed in, in the 16th century, after the subjugation of the country, the peasants united to buy them out.

As in Iceland, the chief feature of medieval Norwegian history is the enormous power wielded in the 12th and 13th centuries by the nobles and their followings, until the class was practically annihilated in their protracted civil wars against Sverri.

In Sweden, on the other hand, the aristocratic class does not make its appearance until the end of the 11th century,[8] and when it reaches the summit of its power, in the 15th century, it admittedly owes much to its sense of kinship-solidarity, as the extensive genealogical tables in Swedish history-books testify. Even then, however, the Swedish commons are still powerful enough to play a leading part in the struggle between king and nobles.[9] As late as 1608, justice is still administered in rural courts, with 12 doomsmen, and even cases of manslaughter are within their competence.[10]

We must note how very few traces of a hereditary class of nobles there are in the earlier period of the Viking Age, and indeed in the literary traditions from the Age of National Migrations. Kings there are in bewildering plenty, and it is they who lead migrations and Viking expeditions of every kind. Such nobles as there are seem to be officials of the king. Round him are gathered an aristocracy of fighting men, often, it would seem, foreigners, to the wealth of whose equipment archeological finds testify. When these *comites,* as Tacitus calls them, reach a certain age, the king grants them land and they settle down. Professor Chadwick has shown us that in England this class soon formed a hereditary nobility, which early gained rights over the neighboring freemen in return for protection. But if we suppose strong cohesive kindreds among these neighboring freemen, for instance in the Jutish peninsula, is it so certain that the retired *comes,* unsupported by a kindred of his own,[11] would obtain or maintain rights over his neighbors? The absence of seignorial rights among the nobility of Jutland, Schleswig, and Friesland may thus well be due to the strength of the kindreds; just as the growth of these rights in England and in Iceland has to our mind a common cause, and is bound up with the absence of cohesive kindreds in those countries, the military nature of the settlement in England having only a subsidiary influence.

These may be said to be hasty generalizations, and indeed the subject deserves a more exhaustive inquiry, but it seems that we must acknowledge this much: where cohesive kindreds persist into the later middle ages, there the peasant or townsman tends to be free. Where, on the other hand, the solidarity of the kindred disappears early, there the liberty of the individual suffers, and seignorial rights make their appearance. Further evidence pointing in this direction is not entirely lacking. Thus it is highly significant that wherever the kindreds survive the blood-feud remains a privilege of all classes, recognized, if deplored, by the law.[12] It is the unquestioned right of the slain man's kin in the Swedish law-books of the 13th century. In France and the Netherlands it persisted until the same period and later, in spite of well-governed towns and powerful kings or nobles. In Namur we have seen a slayer acquitted in the 15th century, on its being shown that he committed the deed in a legitimate feud, the slain man's *cousins* having killed his father. In England, on the other hand, there is no trace of legitimate blood-feuds after the time of Eadmund (c. 943). But the true significance of the survival of feud in France and the Netherlands is not fully apparent until we remember that in Iceland the blood-feud was never legally recognized, and that even the heir avenging himself on the slayer of his kinsman was as liable to penalty as the original aggressor unless he succeeded in killing his man before the next Althing. There is only one way of accounting for this extraordinary discrepancy between the laws of anarchical Iceland and the comparatively well-policed Frankish towns and territories. In the latter, large cohesive kindreds could stand on their rights, however disturbing to the community at large; in England and Iceland the feud was a matter between a few individuals only, and it was easy to override their wishes in the interests of the general public. . . .

It thus seems safe to admit that the kindreds of the early middle ages played no negligible part in the making of history. The countries where the kindreds did not survive—England, Norway, and possibly the States of Central and Southern Germany—avoided, it is true, a problem of government which gave other states some trouble, since among the difficulties in the way of a central government they did not have to reckon with the obstinate, if passive, resistance of the kindreds. Is it not possible, however, that they paid a heavier price for this immunity than their historians have ever quite realized?

In Iceland, it is true, there was no problem of a central executive, for in lacking a king, Iceland lacked also a nucleus round which a central executive could grow up. But since they further lacked the main cohesive principle of the ancient Teutonic State, the bond of kinship, the political efforts of the Icelandic settlers may be likened to the making of bricks without straw, and indeed the frail structure of their constitution, in some ways the most wonderful achievement of the middle ages, crumbled and fell through inner disintegration, before it was seriously threatened by enemies from without. But it is important to realize that theirs was a barren experiment, *not* because their constitution was an antiquated survival of a pre-historic Teutonic polity, but because it had lost both the factors, the kindred and the king, which made for permanence and cohesion in the ancient order, and had found no sufficient substitute. We must therefore beware of regarding the Icelandic commonwealth as a new Germania of Tacitus, miraculously appearing in the Northern seas to show us what the original condition of the Germans was really like. Anglo-Saxon England is almost equally suspect from this point of view, for, if it has kept the king, it too has lost the kindred, probably a much more integral part of the ancient Teutonic State. In fact, if we want to seek after the original German condition, would it not be safer to turn our attention to those regions where its two main elements remained longest in something like their ancient equilibrium, namely in Denmark and the old Danish provinces, and in Southern Sweden?

We may summarize what seems to have been the tendency of the kindreds by describing it as democratic,[13]—that is to say that in discouraging the rise of petty local chiefs they tended to keep the status of all freemen equal, but we must believe that they achieved this result by refusing opportunities to the strong, as well as by protecting the weak against outside aggression. They were not democratic in the sense that the medieval Church was democratic. But though it seems that we must concede this quite reasonable degree of influence to the kindreds, we must be careful to note that it implies no active organization, no conscious political aim, on their part. It was achieved as it were anonymously, by what we may call passive resistance. We still have no right to think of the Teutonic kindreds as "organizing" themselves in any but the most temporary manner, or as combining for aggression. A kindred can only be said to exist at the moment when it groups itself around a given kinsman, and a large proportion of this group must merge into some other groups if some other individual is in need. So long as kinship was recognized through both male and female—i.e., during the whole historic period—these characteristics of the kindreds must have set very definite bounds to their political power.

We need only compare the kindred with its offshoot, the gild, to realize the deficiencies of the earlier group in this respect. The gild is definite, organized, transplantable—everything that the kindred is not. Yet it is a question whether the very indefiniteness of the kindred, its anonymity, its shifting outline, what we may call its Protean attributes, did not qualify it for its obscure workings towards social equality better than a fixed organization, open to attack, could ever have done. There can be no question that the kindred, through a long course of centuries, clung far more closely to the democratic ideal than the gild. The gilds did a great deal for the towns and the craftsmen, but did they achieve more than the kindreds, wherever they survived, accomplished for the rural districts or for the agricultural classes?

Causes of the Decline of the Kindreds

We must now set ourselves to consider the causes of the disintegration of the kindred, but it is a task of unexpected difficulty, owing to the failure of the commonly-received explanations when confronted by the facts we have observed. For instance, the influence of Roman law has been considered to be the disintegrating factor: where the Roman law first took hold in Southern Germany, there, it was declared, did the kindreds first disappear. So long as the history of the kindreds in Germany was considered without reference to the history of the institution elsewhere, this explanation seemed sound enough. But if Roman law was the solvent, how was it that the kindreds were so tenacious of life in Northern France, the Netherlands, and North-West Germany—conquered by Romans, or by partly Romanized Franks, and during the later middle ages steeped in an atmosphere of Roman ideals of law—while in Norway and Iceland they disappeared before Roman law was even a name?

Then again the influence of Christianity has been invoked, and indeed the doctrine of the responsibility of the individual must to a certain extent have acted adversely on the kindreds, though perhaps not so much as has been sometimes assumed. For the result of impairing the sense of corporate responsibility was too often the temptation to take summary vengeance. That there was a tendency to sporadic and ill-disciplined acts of vengeance wherever the kindred was early shattered may well prove to be the case: Frauenstädt's collection of instances in South Germany,[14] and the Icelandic Sagas, might go far to establish such a theory. So that the early Church in Northern Europe probably took the better part in profiting by the sense of corporate responsibility rather than in weakening it. Almost everywhere the Church mediates between the kindreds, and few would criticize her role.[15] But whatever the effect of the medieval Church in urging the acceptance of wergild rather than recourse to arms, it is obvious that neither Christian doctrine nor ecclesiastical influence can be the determining factor in the decay of the kindreds, when once we admit that they survived many centuries of Christianity in France and Germany, while their disintegration was complete in heathen Iceland by the year 1000 (the year of the introduction of Christianity).

A similar objection applies to the theory that a strong executive was the force which finally pulverized the kindreds. France and Denmark, at least, had as strong a line of kings as any medieval Teutonic State, yet in France the organized feuds of the kindreds were with difficulty checked in the 14th century, and in Denmark the kindred clung together for two centuries more. In Iceland, on the other hand, where the kindreds might have been a substitute for a strong executive (as they actually were in Ditmarschen and in Wursten), those ancient Teutonic organizations had but the feeblest hold.

Yet there can be no doubt that though Roman law, Christianity and strong executives cannot be made to explain the decline or predominance of the kindreds in the various parts of Teutonic Europe, they were nevertheless factors which had a mighty influence in pulverizing the kindreds in those regions where the institution had survived the earlier middle ages. It is the recognition of this fact which makes our task so difficult, for we have to account, not only for the disparities we have already noticed in the duration of the system, but also for the resisting-power exhibited by the kindred-organization all through the middle ages in just those regions where these three destructive influences were brought to bear on it, in strong contrast to its early disappearance where it had apparently nothing to contend against.

Our survey of the evidence in those countries where the kindreds showed marked vitality seems to suggest that the 14th century was the first in which their cohesion was really seriously threatened, and the date leads us to infer the possibility that the Black Death, which ravaged Northern Europe in 1349–50, may have had a more adverse influence on the kindreds than has been suspected. By killing off a very considerable proportion of the population, it may have helped to disintegrate the kindreds, both by encouraging migration and by causing individuals to look to themselves instead of having recourse to the help of a wide group of kinsmen. There may well be an element of truth in this theory, but of course its uses as an explanation of the phenomena just described are but limited. It cannot, for instance, be made to account for the disappearance of the kindreds in Norway, England, Iceland, or even in Central and Southern Germany, since kinship-solidarity as a social factor of importance had entirely disappeared in these regions long before the visitation of the Black Death. Yet other explanations which have been put forward are no more satisfactory.

It has been maintained that the Teutonic kindreds broke down as a result of their recognition of cognates. This theory, however, seems untenable in the light of our recent survey, for those regions where the most absolute equality between agnates and cognates prevails are the very strongholds of the system, while in Norway and England, where we trace a discrimination in favor of agnates, it disappears early. But we shall deal with this question again later.

Another suggestion is that the village-community form of settlement was favorable to the formation of kindreds, while a system of solitary homesteads tended to weaken them. This suggestion is attractive at first sight, since solitary homesteads are characteristic of Iceland and of most of Norway. But unfortunately they are equally characteristic of Friesland and the Netherlands, where the kindreds show strong vitality, while the village-community system is prevalent in England, where the kindreds languished.

As far as the Norwegian kindreds are concerned, emigration, in the form of Viking expeditions, might be considered to have had an adverse effect upon kinship-solidarity, but this suggestion again is contravened by the fact that the kindreds were especially strong in the Jutish peninsula, whence emigration must at one time have taken place on a very large scale, and in the rest of Denmark, which took its full part in Viking expeditions. It would of course also fail to explain English conditions.

The disappearance of kindreds has also been ascribed to an increased density of population. "Kin economy", it has been said, fails in intensive culture where that becomes necessary, and has consequently survived where the population is of no great density.[16] This may be true in certain cases, though it is hard to reconcile with the fact that the wasteful system of strip-holding survived in Teutonic countries long after the equal partition of land among the kindred, supposed to be its justification, had disappeared. But in any case, if there is a connection to be traced in Northern Europe between density of population and the survival of kindreds, it is of an almost opposite kind to that suggested. Probably the marsh-lands of Schleswig-Holstein, where the kindred survives longest, would be found to offer the best example of intensive culture, as also of density of population, while the sparsely inhabited Iceland and Norway, with their absence of kin-solidarity, do not encourage us to pursue this line of investigation.

There seems to be a growing tendency to regard the southernmost part of Sweden, Denmark, Schleswig-Holstein and the old Danish duchies as the original home, at any rate from the Stone Age onwards, of the Teutonic race. Certainly no other theory can be so well reconciled with the facts, both archeological and philological. Now it is exactly these regions where the solidarity of the kindred persisted longest. The kindred-system of those tribes whose migration did not lead them far afield, as the Frisians, shows a not very much reduced vitality. It is easy to imagine that the tribes which met with little resistance on their migrations, or who overcame it speedily, and settled down comparatively soon, would preserve the organization of the kindred almost unimpaired. Such a fortunate tribe were the Frisians; such, to an even greater extent, the Salian Franks, most of whom remained in the south-west regions of the basin of the Scheldt. On the other hand, many of the South or Middle German peoples must have been in an unsettled condition for centuries, liable to the necessity of frequent migration, and constantly at war.

Yet the disintegration resulting from years of wandering and of warfare would not be very great except in extreme cases. But the analogy of the Icelandic settlers will incline us to accept the idea that a migration involving transport by sea was especially likely to impair the sense of kin-solidarity among those who venture on it,[17] though the organization of those who remained behind might not be appreciably affected. It is extremely unlikely that each group of kindred would build a vessel and man it exclusively, or even mainly, with their own kinsmen; on the contrary, all analogies show us that any individuals wishing to join an expedition would rally to the first ship that was sailing, and probably remain permanently associated with its crew in the new country. Professor Vinogradoff has pointed out that in the ancient Teutonic tribal system, which involved an equal claim to the ancestral estate on the part of a number of coheirs, the danger of excessive subdivision of land was avoided by the renunciation of their claim on the part of the supernumerary heirs, who received an indemnity, calculated not according to the value of their shares, but to the ability of the estate to bear the outlay.[18] Where this system of coheirs (the sons and daughters) still persists, in the moorlands of Schleswig-Holstein, these supernumerary heirs often leave home, permanently or for a time, to settle in the towns, since they have not the means to marry if they remain on the land. . . .

In prehistoric times in Denmark these supernumerary heirs no doubt went to swell the military followings of kings, who like themselves were very often in a landless condition.[19] The historical sagas of Iceland and Norway give us the clearest insight into this process in Norway, and it is just these "supernumerary heirs," encouraged to seek other means of livelihood than agriculture, who join with others in the same position, and leave their country on permanent or temporary Viking raids; in the earlier period under the leadership of a king, later under a noble. A classic example is afforded by the sons of Earl Hrollaug of Norway, one of whom, Göngu-Hrolf, is declared by Snorri to have founded the Duchy of Normandy; one lost his life in the Western Isles of Scotland on an expedition with Harold Hairfair; another became Earl of the Orkneys, while yet another settled in Iceland. It seems more than probable that the peoples of Schleswig-Holstein lived under similar conditions in the 5th century, with Viking expeditions, and finally the permanent conquest of England, as the result.[20] The settlers in England might therefore be almost as lacking in full kindreds as the settlers in Iceland a few centuries later. Before we make certain that the invaders must have come over *en masse,* in full kindreds, in order to achieve such a vast result as the conquest of England, we shall do well to remind ourselves that the feat was all but paralleled in a much shorter time and in the teeth of a resistance at least equally obstinate, by the Vikings of a later period; yet no one thinks it necessary to assume a wholesale emigration of kindreds in this case, or to postulate that the organization of the Vikings, when they arrived in England; was on a basis of kindreds.

If we are to adopt the Danish theory that the Normans are mainly of Danish, and not of Norwegian origin, we can point to Normandy also as offering corroborative evidence for the disintegrating influence on the kindred of a settlement by sea. According to this theory the invaders of Normandy came from the highly cohesive kindreds of Denmark. Yet the traces of kinship-solidarity in thirteenth-century Normandy are far fainter than in other districts of Northern France, which the Teutons reached by land.

So far as it goes, too, the evidence available for the easternmost and westernmost of Teutonic settlements bears out our contention. The laws of the Swedish kingdom in Russia, won by naval expeditions, show but a feeble conception of kinship: the slayer alone pays for his deed, and the right of vengeance is limited to brother, father, son and nephew.[21] On the other hand, West Gothic custumals in Spain show division of wergild between kinsmen, definitely organized blood-feuds between kindreds, and oath-helpers of the kindred: in fact, as Professor de Hinijosa observes: "The Spanish family of the first part of the middle ages shows in the sense of solidarity that animates it, the same bent as the German *Sippe*."[22] The West Goths travelled a long way, but they travelled by land.

This particular instance suggests that the earlier the migration, the greater the cohesion of the kindred, and it is very probable that some connection of the kind might be traced. But there is hardly enough difference in time between the Frankish settlements in Gaul and the Anglo-Saxon conquest of Britain to account, on this theory, for the strength of the kindreds in the one country and their weakness in the other. Moreover the Vierlande, settled by Dutch immigrants at a late date, and Lübeck and other towns not founded until the 12th century, yet show considerable kin-solidarity. So do the records of the Silesian towns investigated by Frauenstadt, yet these only became German in the late middle ages.

Thus we are driven to the conclusion that the main disintegrating factor in the case of the Teutonic kindreds was migration, and especially migration by sea. Denmark and Schleswig are the strongholds of the kindreds: those of Friesland, the Netherlands and Northern France had vitality enough to withstand centuries of highly adverse influences, whereas the Icelander stood alone from the moment he set foot on Icelandic soil; and it may be questioned whether the Anglo-Saxon settler was in much better case in this respect. Here, too, we should find an explanation of the weakness of the kindreds in Norway, for much of the settlement of that country must have been accomplished by sea, and at a very late period (the Trondheim district and northwards does not seem to have been settled by the Teutonic invaders before the Iron Age). No doubt the character of the country and the consequently often individualistic nature of the settlements were unfavorable to kinship-solidarity, and it may be that the small numbers of the invaders and their relations with the aboriginal race were a partial cause of the weakness of the kindreds.

. . . it is useless to seek for the original bounds of the Teutonic kindred. If the original group was of the nature of a clan, recognizing kinship through the female only, it is easy to account for the divergences in estimating the limit of kinship among the Teutonic races, for there would be

no primitive model to follow. A group organized on patrilinear or matrilinear lines will probably include much more distant degrees of kinship
than a kindred recognizing descent through both parents. In the former
case the whole group will have a name by which its members can distinguish one another, and the right to this name, i.e., descent, is the main
factor determining kinship, rather than the actual degree of relationship
between any two members of the group. But once kinship is reckoned
through both sexes, we have to take into account the fact that the various
branches of a man's kindred will no longer share a common name, will in
fact no longer be related to each other as well as to himself, and the un-
wieldiness of the kindred will increase in proportion to the number of unrelated groups in it. This circumstance obviously sets a limit to the size of
the shifting kindred. Thus it is easy to account for the divergences among
the Teutonic races with regard to the extent of the kindred, for the necessity for limiting the group would arise naturally, and would depend in the
last resort on the extent to which men took wives out of their own district.
Where marriage within the district prevailed to any extent, the various
branches of the kindred would be likely to be at hand and could be readily
assembled; where this was not the practice the kindred would be unwieldy
and its limits would tend to shrink. (This refers only to the kindred as an
effective and cohesive group: for purposes of inheritance kinship was frequently acknowledged as far as it could be traced.) On this theory, Öster-
götland and Vestergötland in Sweden, with kinship recognized to the sixth
degree as late as the 13th century, must have been the home of very much
localized kindreds.

It has occasionally been stated that while kindreds organized on
matrilinear or on patrilinear lines are to be found in various parts of the
world, a cohesive kindred which should reckon kinship through both
male and female not only did not exist, but was inherently impossible. It
is true that permanently organized kindreds on the double basis are un-
thinkable; but our researches have shown that the shifting kindred can
persist for hundreds of years—probably it would not be an over-statement
to attribute a thousand years of life to it in Schleswig—and that in spite of
its lack of organization, of local habitation and name, it was able to exercise no small influence on the history of the nations which harboured it.

We have seen it manifest its solidarity in various ways: it appears in
law-courts, now to support a kinsman by oath, now to pledge wergild or
peace, now to sue the slayer or to insist on the proper distribution of wergild. Or again, we have seen it refuse to submit its internal affairs to
judicial control, and this is perhaps its most characteristic and most primitive side. We have seen it maintain its own poor, and cling through centuries to the right to avenge its own wrongs. We may well doubt whether
agnatic clans could have achieved more towards securing the independence
of the settled agricultural classes. . . .

But it must be admitted that protracted migrations were likely to prove fatal to a group for whose continued existence it was necessary that the families of all the women who had married into it should be close at hand and willing to cooperate with one another. Moreover the shifting kindreds were totally unfitted to serve as the organization of a migrating people. Everything would depend on the king and on his following of professional warriors, and in prolonged migrations this group would tend to increase very greatly at the expense of the disintegrating kindreds. Yet as long as the latter had not been entirely annihilated, they would tend to rally when a final settlement was made, the need being more urgent than before in view of the increased strength of the *comites* or nobles. Where however the migrating group is not a tribe, but a collection of warriors, as in the case of a migration by sea, there will be no nucleus round which a kindred can grow up, so that England and Iceland will lack the influences which the institution brings to bear on the social and political order. Yet even in these countries, the laws will still show clear traces of a system which had been the keystone of the social fabric before migration.

NOTES

1 Inama-Sternegg, *Die Ausbildung der grossen Grundherrschaften in Deutschland* (1878), p. 54.

2 H. M. Chadwick, *The Heroic Age* (1912), p. 351.

3 W. F. Maitland, *Domesday Book and Beyond* (1897, and reprint, New York, Norton, 1966), p. 339.

4 Ph. Heck, *Altfrieslandische Gerichtsverfassung* (1894), p. 238.

5 Laws of Ine, cc. 21, 27, 39, 50, 76. Note also the *manbot*, fine paid to the lord for a slaying, as against the fine paid to the inhabitants of the district in Sweden.

6 It must be remembered that large seignorial estates need not necessarily put an end to the ownership of land by groups of free peasant proprietors: in Russia the two have co-existed for centuries.

7 K. Lamprecht, *Beiträge zur Geschichte des französischen Wirtschaftslebens im llen Jahrhundert* (Leipzig, 1878), pp. 74, 94.

8 See *Sveriges Historia*, vol. I, ed. O. Montelius, 1st ed. (1877), p. 461. It is to be noted that in the provincial laws fines are paid to the king, to the hundred or härad (district) and to "all men", i.e., the neighborhood. There is thus no trace of seignorial justice.

9 *Ibid.*, vol. II, ed. H. Hildebrand (1877), p. 244.

10 See G. O. Berg, *Huru rätt skipades i Sveriges för trehundra år sedan*, Upsala, 1908.

11 There is a Danish document of the 12th century which appears to represent the nobles of the kingdom organized, in groups, in an artificial brotherhood—a very significant fact. See Steenstrup, *Studier over Kong Valdemars Jordebog* (1874), chapter 22.

12 It is noticeable that continental state-craft attempts rather to obviate blood-feuds by *asseurement* and similar devices, rather than to abolish them.

13 It is perhaps worthwhile to note that various observers have commented on the unusual degree of social equality between the families of farmers and of day-laborers in villages in Ditmarschen at the present day. In Wursten, where the kindreds were powerful, no native succeeded in obtaining seignorial rights until 1673, when the king of Sweden granted them to one family.

[14] Frauenstadt, *Blutrache und Todtschlagssühne im deutschen Mittelalter*, Leipzig, 1881.

[15] We even find the Church paying compensation on behalf of the delinquent: see Gregory of Tours, *Historia Francorum*, book VII, chapter 47 (in 585).

[16] E. Grosse, *Die Formen der Familie* (Freiburg, 1896), pp. 211–12.

[17] The above does not apply with the same force to the case of clearly defined clans, each of whose members bears the same name as all the others, and regards himself as kin to him, however distant the actual relationship may be. Not only is such a clan more capable of undertaking a common venture, such as the building and manning of a vessel, but all the migrating members of the clan recognize each other and would tend to form a nucleus for a clan-group in the new country. In the case of the ordinary shifting kindred of the Teutons, the groups of kindred on the paternal and maternal side respectively are not in any way related to one another, still less have they a common name. There is no reason why my father's first cousin should consort with my mother's first cousin in a new country, if I am not there to form a connecting link.

[18] P. Vinogradoff, "Village Communities", *Encyclopaedia Britannica*, 11th ed., vol. 28, pp. 69–73.

[19] Among royal families the centrifugal force must have been even stronger, for every member of a royal family was a king, and if he could not rule over the ancestral kingdom he was very likely to seek to obtain another kingdom for himself—a state of affairs of which Snorri seems to have preserved the tradition for Norway. Hence perhaps the absence of any suggestions of solidarity within the kindred in the oldest traditions of the period of national migrations—a phenomenon to which attention has been recently directed. See Chadwick, *op. cit.*, pp. 347–8, 373–4, 391.

[20] I do not see any reason to suppose that all the adventurers who won England were actually from Schleswig-Holstein, though the leaders were. We know that the invaders called "Danes" by the English included Norwegians and probably Swedes, and that the "Norman" conquest was largely effected by non-Norman mercenaries.

[21] Jaroslav's *Pravda* (from first half of 11th century), c. XXVII and I–II, in Ewers, *Älteste Rechte der Russen* (1826), pp. 264, 306.

[22] E. Grosse, *op. cit.*, and see article on *Sippe* in Schrader's *Reallexikon*.

2

Kinship in Anglo-Saxon Society (7th Century to Early 11th)

LORRAINE LANCASTER

The Tracing of Kinship in Anglo-Saxon Society

Anglo-Saxon kinship systems, like those of modern England, belong to the class of non-unilineal kinship, in which every individual has, in general, the option of tracing affiliation to a set of persons through both his parents (and their descendants) and his parents' parents (and *their* descendants) and so on. The first problem set by such a system concerns the limits of this set of persons recognized as one's consanguines. The living members of this set may or may not be a group in the most common sociological sense of the word.

It is clear that the extent of the recognition of living kin depends on the conventions existing in a society of counting certain cousins in or out. Studies so far carried out into kinship in South and East London, for instance, do not suggest that third cousins are regularly included as members of a set of recognized kin, but there are no formal rules of inclusion or exclusion.[1] In other bilateral systems, as in one Melanau sago-producing community, fifth cousins are usually considered to be included in the recognized kin set, but not sixth. . . .[2]

. . . A number of Old English words may roughly be translated as "family", "kinsmen" or "kindred", including *sibb, cynn, maegsib, maegburg, maeg, maeg* (ð)*lagu* and *magas*. But none appears before the time of Edward the Confessor, in a context which makes clear either the limits of the set of people to whom the term refers or even that such limits were of significance. No legal definition accompanies the use of any such term. The word *sibb* was not widely used in those Anglo-Saxon laws which refer to the rights and duties of a kin group in its solidary aspects: it is used in Ethelred's laws at the end of the tenth century and in Cnut's laws at the beginning of the eleventh, fairly late in our period. The term *cynn* has the meaning of "kind" or "species", and is in no way precise. The words related to and derived from *maeg* (a kinsman) are particularly important where kin groups are referred to, but even here there is no record whatever of which relatives were considered to constitute the *maegð*. . . . There are no references in contemporary data to second, third, fourth, fifth or sixth cousins as particular categories, and consequently, as analysis of kinship terminology shows, there are no specific terms to apply to these categories of relatives. . . .

It is possible to argue that the complete lack of reference to the furthest extent of the set of kin concerned with the payment for wergild (indemnity for slaying) is a result of the fact that limits were common knowledge and unquestioningly adhered to. But it seems more reasonable to assume, in the light of other legal statements about what kin should or should not do, that such reference was not made because it had little meaning in practical situations: it seems more likely that a circle of kinsmen, variable according to many factors, including biological chance, patterns of residence, ease of communication and possibly personal preference, made up the group defined by the ties of kinship.

. . . It seems as if rules were not precise, and that it would be a mistake to assume that the form of any continental system is directly applicable to England. There is, however, rather more information as to the nature of the inner circle of kinsmen . . . . Throughout the Anglo-Saxon laws there are references to the plight of the kinless man, for example, Ine 23.1 (688–94); Alfred 31 (871–99); VIII Ethelred 24 (1014) repeated in I Cnut 5.2c (1020–3). There were probably many men in Anglo-Saxon England far from the place of their birth—immigrants and followers of a distant lord—and thus far from the relatives with whom they had been brought up. There were, too, illegitimate or unrecognized children. But unless a local man were descended on both sides from long lines of only children, the likelihood of his being without anyone *at all* whom he could call kinsman does not seem great, in the light of the large potential size of bilaterally reckoned kin sets. References in the laws, then, may sometimes equate kinlessness with the lack of an inner group of close kin willing to take up a kinsman's responsibilities. It is significant that where there is reference in Anglo-Saxon poetry to the sad fate of a man without kin or friends, it is a very near kinsman who is thought to be missing:

> Hapless is he who must needs live alone . . . .
> . . . it were better for him had he a brother . . . .[3]

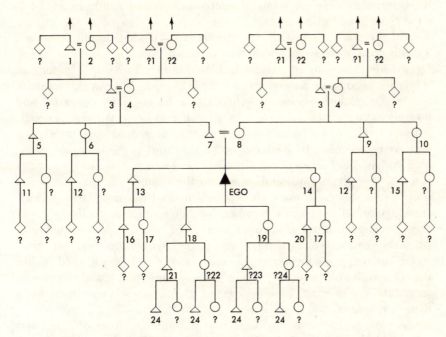

Figure 1. Old English consanguineal kinship nomenclature.

△	male	11 swor, geswiria, fæderan sunu
○	female	12 swor, geswiria
◇	male or female	13 broðor, broður
=	marriage	14 sweostor, suster
?	term not certain	15 swor, geswiria, modiran sunu
1	þridda fæder	16 nefa, genefa, suhterga, suhtriga
2	þridde modor	17 nefena, nift
3	ealda fæder, yldra fæder	18 sunu, barn, bearn, eafora, maga,
4	eald modor	magu-timber, tudor, ciid
5	fædera	19 dohtor
6	faðu, faðe	20 nefa, geswiria, sweostor sunu
7	fæder	21 nefa, genefa, sunasunu
8	modor	22 nefena
9	eam	23 nefa, genefa
10	modrige, moddrie, modrie	24 nefena, nift

What is known of Old English kinship terminology substantiates the importance of a group of close kin, and at the same time throws light on the relationships within it. . . . Figure 1 gives a sketch of consanguineal kin terms in Old English, apparently current in the whole period in which we are interested, from the seventh century to the accession of Edward the Confessor. They are terms of reference; it is impossible to recover a set of terms of address.[4]

(a) *Nuclear Family*. O.E. *fæder* represented modern English "father". To this basic term slightly different shades of meaning could be given, e.g. *ærfæder,* referring to a late or deceased father. The words *ealdor* and *ildra* could also be used to refer to a father. The general term for "mother" was *modor*. Other specific meanings could be given by *cennestre* and possibly *sunu-cennicge,* referring to a mother in her quality as genetrix. A usual term for "kinsman", *maga,* may have been used for a father, but we have no record of it. We have, however, record of the feminine, *mage,* used for "mother". In *Beowulf,* Grendel's mother is referred to as *Grendles magan.* This gives additional weight to the assumption that the set of people who may be considered as kinsmen need not necessarily include anyone more distant than members of Ego's nuclear family.

Old English terms that could be applied to a son proliferated: *cild* (with the sense of young child); *barn, bearn, byre; maga,* used for "son" as for "mother"; *magorinc, magu-timber, tudor* and *eafora,* used within the context of "offspring", "progeny", "issue" and "son"; and the precise term *sunu* (= "son"). There appears to have been only one term for a daughter, *dohtor.*

A sister or half-sister was known as *sweostor* and a set of sisters was collectively known as *gesweostor.* A term for half-brothers in general is not noted by Bosworth and Toller, but where brothers shared both parents, the relationship could be denoted by *æwe gebroðor,* translated by Campbell[5] as *germani fratres.* If the same father was shared, a brother could be called *fæderenmæg,* which seems to have referred particularly to an agnate, and could be used of a brother. The terms *broðorgefædred* and *broðorgemedred* also referred to the relationship in which the father or the mother, respectively, was shared. There was a collective term for brothers (*gebroðor*) but there does not seem to have been one for siblings of both sexes.

(b) *Lineal Ascendants and Descendants*. The Old English terms for lineal ascendants were based on those for the nuclear family. Ghurye[6] sees in this the primacy, even in Anglo-Saxon times, of the nuclear family as against any wider kin group. A grandfather was referred to as *ealda fæder* or *yldra fæder* (i.e. "old father" or "elder father"), with the sense of "second father" being understood, since a great-grandfather was termed a *þridda fæder* (i.e., "third father"). Further male lineal ascendants could be traced, linguistically, to the distance of "great-great-great-great-grandfather", who was known as *sixta fæder.* Similarly, "grandmother" was *eald modor,* "great-grandmother" *þridde modor,* and an upper limit of "great-great-great-grandmother" *fifte modor.*

A grandson could be known as a *nefa* or *sunsunu* (i.e., "son's son").

A great-grandson could be referred to as a *þridda sunu,* on the same principle as *þridda fæder.* A granddaughter was spoken of as *nefena,* which also did duty to refer to a brother's or a sister's daughter.

(c) *Collateral Kin.* There was a distinction drawn between "father's brother" and "mother's brother" which is not preserved in the modern English "uncle" (< Latin *avunculus*). A father's brother was *fædera* and a mother's brother, *eam.* Similarly, "father's sister (*faðu* with variations) and "mother's sister" (*moddrige* with variations) were distinguished from each other. The terms *nefa* and *genefa* seem to have been general ones, applicable both to a brother's and a sister's son, but *suhterga* and *geswiria* served to specify a brother's son and the term *swustorsunu* was, as its form suggests, only applicable to a sister's son.

It is most significant that a term existed (*suhter-(ge)fæderan*) to refer to the relationship between a man and his father's brother. There was no special term to refer to the corresponding relationship on Ego's mother's side.

The words *nift* and *nefena* appear to have applied to either a brother's or a sister's daughter, in the same manner as we use "niece". But the more specific terms *broðor-dohtor* ("brother's daughter") and *sweostor-dohtor* ("sister's daughter") were also used.

There was a remarkable dearth of special O.E. terms for the relationship of cousins of various degrees, although certain terms with other uses did duty to cover cousins as well. Words denoting a kinsman or kinswoman, applicable to anyone within the orbit of the *mægð,* could also refer to a male or a female cousin, whether first or more distant. Thus we find *mæge, mage, nidmæge, nidmage* used. *Suhterga,* which we have already noted in the context of brother's son, could also express the relationship of those whose fathers were brothers, that is, parallel cousins on the father's side. Another term for this relationship was *fæderan sunu* (i.e., "father's brother's son"). The corresponding relationship of parallel cousins on the mother's side could also be specifically denoted: The word *sweor* (also used for "father-in-law") represented a cousin german, probably on the mother's side, while such a cousin could be more accurately described as *gesweostrenu bearn* ("child of sisters") or *moddrian sunu* ("mother's sister's son").

The general characteristics of the system suggest three points: firstly, our belief that the *mægð* need not have been an extensive group is borne out by the restriction of specific terms to a relatively small set of kin; secondly, the complete lack of specificity in terms for cousins of various degrees, which would be all-important in the operation of a wide-ranging bilateral system, suggests that these kin and the distinctions between them were not regularly of major significance. Lineal ascendants could be traced back to *sixta fæder,* and in fact were traced back further in the historical and mythical genealogies of the *Anglo-Saxon Chronicle.* Nevertheless, the cousins who would share so remote an ancestor are not put in any particular linguistic category. Thirdly, the Anglo-Saxon naming system was remarkably flexible in that it contained many synonymous terms for one relationship, while the same term sometimes did duty for different relationships. The number of terms existing to refer to the father-son relationship provides an example of the former case, and the variety of the uses of the word *mæg* (in its different forms) provides an example of the latter. Where we see the linguistic equation of grandson and nephew and granddaughter and niece, we cannot immediately jump to the conclusion that a man would be expected to act in an exactly similar way towards kin so associated. Nevertheless, the relatives concerned are of the same degree of genealogical distance, and it is not unreasonable to suppose that the intensity of the implementing of rights and duties may have been roughly similar in both instances. This serves only to underline the impression already received that there was interchangeability rather than strict rigidity in the formal modes of behaviour outside the nuclear family.

As we might expect from the bilateral nature of the Anglo-Saxon kinship system, there was a balanced distribution of terms for both one's father's and his mother's siblings and their lineal ascendants and descendants. There was, however, a clearly defined differentiation on the basis of sex, which ran through the whole pattern of terminology. Radcliffe-Brown has pointed out the value of the notion of the unity of the sibling group: "The bond uniting brothers and sisters together into a social group is everywhere regarded as important, but it is more emphasized in some societies than in others." [7]

Elements of this important tie are linguistically evident in the O.E. terms. The words for "father", "father's brother" and "father's sister" are all linked (*fæder, fædera* and *faðu*). Similarly, the words for "mother" and "mother's sister" are linked (*modor* and *moddrie* or *modrige*). But overriding this is a strong division on the basis of sex: the words for "father's brother" and "father's sister" are, in fact, different, while the words for "mother's brother" (*eam*) and "mother's sister" are quite separate terms.

*   *   *   *   *

This type of differentiation is compatible with the fact that there were phrases to cover the relationship of parallel cousins, but none to cover that of cross-cousins.[8] Since there was certainly no preferential cousin marriage, this fact is not linked with marriage regulation but rather with a tendency to associate siblings of the same sex. There was an elaboration of terms for male kin compared with those for female kin. This evidence, by itself, is too shadowy to prove that male kin were more important or appeared in more varied contexts than female kin, although the emphasis on the paternal uncle relationship is suggestive. In a society in which the keystone was a man's association with a lord—in war, administration and economic life—some emphasis on agnatic links is not surprising, and it appears not only in terminology, but, as we shall see, in many other aspects of the kinship system.[9]

The web of Anglo-Saxon kinship, of which we have attempted to sketch the formal pattern, was extended in various ways by institutions we may speak of as semi-kinship, quasi-kinship and ritual kinship. Semi-kinship refers merely to the number of "half" relatives resulting from remarriages (marriage was, ideally, monogamous). A half-brother, whether sharing father or mother, was usually just called *broðor*. (A full brother could be emphasized as *æwe gebroðor*.) A half-sister was *sweostor*, but a term to distinguish full from half-sisters is not recorded. A stepfather was referred to as *steopfæder* and a stepmother as *steopmodor*. Not only could a stepson be referred to as *steopsunu* but also as the ubiquitous *nefa* (used for nephew or grandson). A stepdaughter could likewise be a *steopdohtor* but also *nift*.

Quasi-kinship in Anglo-Saxon society applied particularly to fostering: a foster-father was a *foster fæder* and a foster-mother *foster* (*fester*) *modor*. A foster-son or child could be a *foster cild, fosterbearn* or *fosterling*, but there was no word solely for foster-daughter. The terms *fosterbroðor* and *foster sweostor* were used for siblings.

Ritual kinship set up a series of relationships within the orbit of a nuclear family. Anglo-Saxon society after the advent of Christianity recognized a godfather as a male sponsor for a chlid in religious matters, termed *godfæder* or *godfædera* (the similarity of the latter to the word for father's brother may be significant). An Anglicized Latin term, *cumpæder*, was also used late in the period. A godmother (*godmodor* or *gefædere*) was recognized to have similar duties of sponsorship. A godson was *godbearn*, *godsunu* or *bisceopsunu*, while a goddaughter was *goddohtor*. The godparents of a child stood in a particular relationship of mutual respect towards each other and towards the parents of the child, but this relationship was confined to those immediately concerned and did not extend throughout the kin group.

Marriage and Affinity

It is clear that the question "To what extent is the *mægð* an exogamous group?" is one without much reality. Since we can set no precise limits to the *mægð*, generally or in particular situations, we cannot speak of marriage within it or outside it. Furthermore, we completely lack data on the prevalence of types of marriage, and such material as we do possess on ideal forms of marriage for various periods and areas in Anglo-Saxon

England provides only a very vague picture. The confusion lies not only in our records, but in the situation itself, especially where foreign immigrants were concerned. As early as 695, Wihtred of Kent found it necessary to try to unify different norms,[10] while in 1020–3 King Cnut was again attempting to settle the problem in the same way: "Foreigners, if they will not regularize their marriages, are to depart from the land with their goods and their sins."[11]

Some little information concerning marriage between members of an inner group of intimate kin can, with caution, be derived from marriage prohibitions. The Church early interested itself in the problem of proscribed marriages. In answer to St. Augustine's questions, Pope Gregory, in 601, forbade marriage *within* the third degree of kinship, that is, first cousins.[12] Whitelock writes that "the later Church forbade it within the sixth degree, and with the widows and widowers of kinsmen within the same degree, and between co-sponsors".[13] The last phrase refers to those ritually related. Since we cannot be certain that Gregory's pronouncement was framed to fit Anglo-Saxon customary marriage rules, it throws no light on previous behaviour, but only on subsequent norms. The gap between ideal and real is nowhere so clearly documented as in the material concerned with marriage. We have frequent Church reminders as to what was acceptable. The proceedings of the Synod of Hertford in 673 stressed the fact that only lawful marriage should be allowed and uttered a warning against incest, although degrees of consanguinity concerned were not specified. Boniface, in a letter to Nothhelm, Archbishop of Canterbury, written in 736, was exercised by the authenticity of Pope Gregory's reply "in which among other chapters it is stated that the faithful are permitted to marry in the third degree of relationship",[14] and in such a context as to suggest that the question was one in which he had a practical interest in making judgment.[15] The frequency of defection from ecclesiastical rulings on marriage with near kin was a cause of warning and complaint. In 874, Pope John VIII wrote to Burgred, king of Mercia, saying that fornication was rife and that men "presume to marry women of their own kindred".[16] About sixteen years later, Fulk, Archbishop of Rheims, wrote to King Alfred in much the same strain.[17] Allowing for its fire-and-brimstone character, we may also suppose that Wulfstan had some definite cases in mind when in his *Sermo Lupi ad Anglos* (?1014), he castigated, among other sins, widespread incest or marriage within permitted bounds.[18] Still later, Cnut legislated against incest thus:[19]

51. If anyone commits incest, he is to pay compensation according to the degree of the relationship, whether by wergild or by fine or by all his possessions.
51.1. It is by no means on a level whether a man has intercourse with his sister, or with a more distant relation.

The Law of the Northumbrian Priests of 1020–3 forbids "that any man should marry a nearly related person, [any nearer] than outside the fourth degree. And no man is to marry anyone spiritually related to him."[20] Any couple considering marriage, according to the short text on the betrothal of a woman,[21] probably written towards 1030, should take care to note that intending spouses are not "too closely related". This reminder immediately suggests the possibility of laxity in common observance.

There were certain elements in failure to observe the forms of marriage laid down by the Church which at first sight seem to derive from pre-Christian forms of marriage. The question of marriage with a deceased father's widow (stepmother) comes up twice at least in the Anglo-Saxon records, and was specifically condemned by Gregory in his letters to St. Augustine. Early in the seventh century, Eadbald of Kent married his stepmother. Bede wrote that he was "defiled with fornication of such a kind as, the Apostle testifies, was unheard of even among the Gentiles, that one should have his father's wife." [22] And in 858, Æthelbald, son of King Æthelwulf, married Judith, his father's widow, of whom Asser wrote, "his son Æthelbald, contrary to God's prohibition and Christian dignity, and also against the usage of all pagans, ascending the bed of his father, married Judith, daughter of Charles, king of the Franks, earning much infamy from all who heard of it".[23] Whitelock says that this form of marriage was "the Germanic practice",[24] but since both Bede and Asser seem, judging by the terms in which they refer to the events, to have been surprised as well as shocked by them, we cannot then assume that a particular form of the widow inheritance that exists in some primitive societies was familiar in England, whatever may have been the continental custom.

Quite elaborate precautions were taken by Anglo-Saxon lawgivers to mitigate the plight of a widow. No doubt many widows were able to fend adequately for themselves, but the position of others may have been difficult. It was early felt that the widowed mother had the right to keep her children by her, as the laws of Hlothhere and Eadric (Kent, ? 673–85) indicate, but a paternal kinsman was to be the child's "willing protector" until the child was ten years old. Thus we know that at this place and time there was, ideally, some association between a widow and her affinal kin. We may assume also that she was the direct responsibility of some members of her mægð. This is the significance of the early laws of Ethelbert (Kent, ? 602–3) penalizing breaches of the guardianship of widows.[25]

The text concerning the betrothal of a woman,[26] whether maiden or widow, shows that, late in the period, the arrangements for marriage were only to take place "if it so pleases her and her kinsmen", but her wishes were often disregarded, as Wulfstan's sermon indicates.[27] In addition, she was not permitted to remarry within a year after her spouse's death. King Ethelred's code of 1008 states:

21. And every widow who conducts herself rightly is to be under the protection of God and the king.

21.1. And each [widow] is to remain unmarried for twelve months; she is then to choose what she herself will.

This law was repeated twelve or fifteen years later in the laws of King Cnut, with some riders. The widow was warned that if she married within the twelvemonth she forfeited her morning-gift (a gift from husband to wife after the consummation of the marriage). All the possessions that came to her through her former husband were to go to her nearest kinsman, while her second husband had to pay a fine. This was to happen even if the woman had been married by force, unless she repudiated the man. These variations make this an interesting law, coming, as it did, after a notorious event in 1015,[28] when the atheling Edmund married the widow of a certain thegn Sigeferth, against Cnut's will, "after a short interval", and took possession of her former husband's estates.

Cnut's law[29] reading "A widow is never to be consecrated [as a nun] too hastily" suggests a possible fate for a dazed widow, whether she had a vocation for monastic life or not. On the other hand, the position of an abbess could be one of high achievement for an able Anglo-Saxon woman, open to widows, as well as to the unmarried. . . .

Marriages followed certain customary forms. We are fortunate in having fairly detailed statements in the early laws (Ethelbert, Kent, 602–3) and in a late text ("Concerning the Betrothal of a Woman", already mentioned) which reveal some interesting changes in interpretation. Ethelbert's laws (77–84) are rather obscure, but provide for the payment of brideprice, safeguard the wife's rights if she bore a child, and seem to have allowed a remarkably easy separation on the wife's initiative. Although the expression of the laws appears to have implied the purchase of the wife, studies made by anthropologists [30] warn us that this is not a legitimate interpretation of brideprice in primitive societies, nor does it seem appropriate here.

The later text on betrothal [31] put little emphasis on brideprice but a great deal on the assuring of the bride's future. A man wishing to marry should, with the agreement of the woman herself and her kinsmen, promise her "advocates" that he intended to support her honourably. His "friends" (note not necessarily kinsmen) were to stand surety for his intention. "Next, it must be known to whom belongs the remuneration for rearing her." The groom was supposed to pledge this, again with his friends' surety. A contract was to be drawn up, granting her certain goods as his wife and as his widow. She was entitled to all these goods if they had a child, half if they did not, and, by implication, nothing if she married again. The "leader of the betrothal" was to receive the security on the final agreement between both parties. The woman's friends would wish to be assured that no wrong would be done to her if the man wanted to transfer to another thegn's district, and be allowed to pay any compensation she was unable to pay. The text states that a priest should officiate at the ceremony, checking, apparently, on the closeness of consanguinity of the couple, but this was not indispensable.

We may assume, by analogy with what we know of present-day Western and primitive societies, that the ceremony of marriage was one which gathered kinsmen for its celebration. The kinsman of the bride most likely to be concerned with contractual and ritual arrangements was her father, or, in his absence, her brother. A late marriage agreement from Kent [32] (1016–20) reads:

Here in this document is made known the agreement which Godwine made with Brihtric when he wooed his daughter; first, namely, that he gave her a pound's weight of gold in return for her acceptance of his suit, and he granted her the land at Street with everything that belongs to it, and 150 acres at Burmarsh and in addition 30 oxen and 20 cows, and 10 horses and 10 slaves.

An agreement between Wulfric and the sister of Archbishop Wulfstan, belonging to the same period, shows that a brother, particularly an important one, could be his sister's legal representative. Such was also the case when King Athelstan, after his father's death, gave his sister in marriage to Sihtric of Northumbria. This marriage was frankly a political one, and other alliances between important families brought similar advantages in power and property. It is impossible to know to what extent there was marriage up or down in the ranking system, or how many marriages were contracted between former slaves and freemen, but it does appear, from a law of Ethelbert (Kent, 602–3, Law 85), that marriage between unfree labourers (? slaves) was sanctioned.

Before going on to discuss the stability of Anglo-Saxon marriages we must examine, as far as possible, expectations of behaviour in the roles of husband and wife. Some light is thrown on these by the ideal forms of marriage that we find reflected in the laws and other records. Throughout the period, marriage was monogamous. This is clear, by implication, in all the early laws. Later, however, perhaps because it was being overlooked, especially in the north, it was felt necessary to specify this norm. In the Laws of the Northumbrian Priests (1020–3) we find: "61. And by virtue of God's prohibition we forbid that any man should have more wives than one; and she is to be legally betrothed and wedded." There is a reference by Wulfstan, also early in the eleventh century, to a practice which he appears to think widespread but which cannot be considered polyandry: "And it is shameful to speak of what has happened too widely, and it is terrible to know what too many do often, who commit that miserable deed that they contribute together and buy a woman between them as a joint purchase".[33] Two important expectations of marriage, then, were those of having one wife and of faithfulness in marriage. Although these norms were formally stressed, there must have been others taken for granted. A division of labour operated, in Anglo-Saxon as in every society, between spouses, the wife being particularly concerned with the running of the household and possibly some gardening and livestock raising, while the husband was concerned with ploughing and similar heavy labour or supporting his lord's undertakings. But failure to fulfil such practical expectations is not mentioned as a cause of marital instability in any Anglo-Saxon records. Husband and wife were not taken to form one unit of legal responsibility, although the husband was clearly considered in most cases to have authority over his wife. A law of the West Saxon king Ine (688–94) provides an example of this:

57. If a husband steals any cattle and brings it into his house, and it is seized therein, he is guilty for his part, but without his wife, for she must obey her lord; if she dare declare with an oath that she did not taste of the stolen meat, she is to receive her third portion.

(The last phrase means that the wife is to receive her due if her husband's possessions are forfeit.) The same principle operates in the laws of the bishops and reeves of the London district in the tenth century (VI Athelstan 1.1). And Cnut's laws made it even more precise:

76. And if any man brings home stolen property to his cottage, and he is found out, it is right that he [the owner] should have what he has tracked.
76.1. And unless it has been brought under the wife's lock and key, she is to be clear.
76.1a. But she must look after the keys of the following: namely her storeroom, her chest and her coffer; if it is brought inside any of these, she is then guilty.
76.1b. And no wife can forbid her husband to place inside his cottage what he pleases.

The legal responsibility of the husband's acts were borne by him and his kinsmen and of the wife's acts by her and her kinsmen, but the mere fact of marriage did not involve either spouse in the wrong-doing of the other. Both were involved, however, in legal responsibility for a child, since parents were nearest kin in the child's mægð. The early laws [34] suggest that ten years was the age at which a child was considered to have discretion, but later the age rose to twelve years,[35] and Athelstan even felt "that no man younger than fifteen should be killed unless he tried to defend himself or fled".[36] The laws of Ine state that if a man stole with the knowledge of his wife and children, they were all to go into slavery; but if they had no knowledge of the act, retribution fell on him alone. During the latter part of our period, abuses of this principle grew up, since it was to the advantage of the injured party to assume a child's shared guilt and to claim him as a slave. A more humanitarian approach thought it illogical that a young child or baby should be party to a father's theft. This is the background to the law of Cnut (1020–3,

76.2) which reads: "Up till now it happened that the child which lay in the cradle, although it had never tasted food, was reckoned by avaricious folk as being guilty as though it had discretion."

This clear separation of roles and responsibilities was accompanied by what appears to have been a recognized instability in Anglo-Saxon marriages, although we have no quantitative measures. The existence of extra-marital unions is frequently referred to in the records. The *Anglo-Saxon Chronicle* for 755 (actually 757) describes the widely known incident in which King Cynewulf was surprised and killed by his enemy Cyneheard, while the former was visiting his mistress at Meretun. There was frequent legislation against adultery and fornication, not only among the clerics, but also among the lay. Ethelbert's laws [37] reveal an attempt to convert an act of adultery into an acceptable marriage. Wihtred of Kent (695; Law 3) remonstrated against illicit cohabitation. In 746-7, an illuminating letter was written by Boniface [38] (and seven other missionary bishops) to Æthelbald of Mercia, urging him among other things to take a wife:

For if the race of the English—as it is noised abroad throughout those provinces and is cast up against us in France and in Italy, and is used as a reproach by the pagans themselves—spurning lawful marriage, lives a foul life in adultery and lasciviousness after the pattern of the people of Sodom, it is to be expected that from such intercourse with harlots there will be born a degenerated people, ignoble, raging with lust.

Boniface also contrasts Anglo-Saxon laxity in the face of open adultery with a strict continental ideal, where punishment was quite violent.

Subsequent laws provided some severe penalties, although we do not know how strictly they were enforced or their results. Alfred (871-99) made provision for a man to fight without precipitating a blood feud if he found his wife, daughter, sister or mother (not other kin) with a supposed adulterer.[39] The Laws of the Northumbrian Priests, early in the eleventh century, legislated against bigamy, while Cnut, about the same time, drew up the following laws:

50. If anyone commits adultery, he is to pay compensation for it in proportion to the deed.

53. If a woman during her husband's lifetime commits adultery with another man, and it becomes known, let her afterwards become herself a public disgrace and her lawful husband is to have all that she owns, and she is to lose her nose and her ears.

54.1.1. And if anyone has a lawful wife and also a concubine, no priest is to do for him any of the offices which must be done for a Christian man, until he desists and atones for it as deeply as the bishop directs him, and desists from such for ever.

The evidence points to the possibility that Anglo-Saxon marriages were frequently unstable as far as relations between spouses were concerned, but divorce as a *complete* severance of the marriage tie was not approved legally or ecclesiastically. A legal separation was permitted on certain grounds, including adultery. In the laws of Ethelbert already quoted (Law 79) separation appears in a remarkably casual light. Some seventy years afterwards, however, a canon promulgated by the Synod of Hertford (presided over by Archbishop Theodore) and quoted by Bede [40] was more specific:

X. Relating to Marriages: "That nothing but lawful wedlock be allowed to any-one. No one shall commit incest, no one shall leave his own wife, unless on ac-count of fornication, as the holy gospel teaches. And if anyone divorces his own wife, joined to him by lawful wedlock, he shall take no other, if he wishes truly to be a Christian; but remain as he is, or be reconciled with his own wife."

In his later Penitential, Theodore broadened his concept of separa-tion, bringing into account the impact of misfortunes on marriages. Where a spouse was indefinitely in captivity, he thought that remarriage should be possible after five years; and where a man had been abandoned by his wife for five years, he thought the man should be allowed to re-marry. A woman whose husband had been penally enslaved should be able to remarry after a year.

The high value placed by the Church on chastity and morality in marriage led to another type of separation available to a married couple. It was possible for either spouse to vow himself or herself to chastity and enter a monastery. The Law of the Northumbrian Priests (? 1020–3) reads:

64. If anyone abandons a living legal wife, and wrongly takes to wife another woman, may he not have God's mercy, unless he atones for it.
65. But each is to keep rightly his legal wife as long as she lives; unless it comes about that they both choose to separate with the bishop's advice and wish thence-forth to preserve chastity.

It may have been frequently the wife who initiated this arrangement since it could be a method of achieving status and even saintliness, as the following story shows: [41]

King Ecgfrith married a wife called Æthelthryth, daughter of Anna, King of the East Angles. . . . Another man had had her to wife before him, namely a prince of the South Gyrwe called Tondberht. But as he died soon after he had married her, she was given to the aforesaid king. Although she lived with him for twelve years, she yet remained in the glorious integrity of perpetual virginity, as Bishop Wilfred of blessed memory informed me, when I questioned him, since some doubted whether this was so; and he said that he was an undoubted witness of her virginity, in that Ecgfrith promised to give him many lands and much money if he could persuade the queen to fulfill her marriage duty, for he knew that she loved no man more than him . . . A divine miracle, by which the flesh of this woman when buried could not suffer corruption, is a sign that she had not been defiled by familiarity with man.

Marriage in Anglo-Saxon society, as in almost all societies, set up some relationships with affinal kin. In modern English society, this

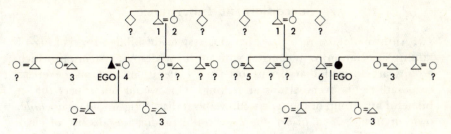

Figure 2. Old English affinal kinship nomenclature.

1 sweor
2 sweger
3 aðum
4 wif, cwene, beweddod wif, æwe

5 tacor
6 bonda, ceorl, etc.
7 snor, snru

relationship may be an important one. From Anglo-Saxon data, however, no clear picture emerges of expectations of behaviour, or of rights
and duties. Some little aid in examining the problem may be derived
from affinal kinship terminology (Figure 2). It may immediately be seen
how few terms for husband's and wife's affinal kin appear. The word
sweor ("father-in-law") we have already noted as possible translations
for "cousin", particularly a parallel cousin. On the other hand, *sweger*
("mother-in-law") had no additional meanings. In Ego's own generation,
a man could refer to his wife by one of several synonymous terms: *wif,*
which also meant "woman", "female", "widow" or "separated woman";
cwēn, which could have a less exalted meaning then than now; and
æwe, which meant particularly "married woman".

A husband could be known as a *bonda,* or possibly *hus-bonda* (which
had more specifically the meaning of the "man of the house"), and also as
ceorl. A brother-in-law, in the sense of a husband's brother, had a special
O.E. term, *tacor;* but we have no record of this term used in the sense
of wife's brother or sister's husband, who was referred to rather as
aðum. This word could also be used for a daughter's husband by both
a man and a woman. A son's wife could be referred to, again by both,
as *snoru.*

In a bilateral system, a man's affinal kin are the consanguineal kin
of his child: through this relationship legal ties may be set up. But the
relative insignificance of affinal links in Anglo-Saxon society, compared
with that of modern England, is suggested by our lack of information
on the subject and the sparseness of affinal kin terms. The most significant kinship unit was comprised by the group of close consanguineal
kin who took up responsibility for, and in turn demanded their rights
of the focal kinsman.

Succession and Inheritance

. . . Anthropologists recognize that this system [of bilateral reckoning of kinship association] is in contrast with unilineal descent systems, in which groups are formed that persist over the generations and may exercise corporate rights over persons and things. One would not expect that a bilateral kin group of the type we have been discussing would, *as a whole,* own anything . . . *A priori,* then, we could predict the absence of clear evidence in Anglo-Saxon records of the pre-eleventh century showing that a kin group could be a landowner. Nevertheless, despite lack of evidence . . . the theory has been put forward that some form of communal tenure existed . . . .[42]

If a kin group as a whole was not an heir, who, out of a set of recognized relatives, was likely to succeed to an estate? . . .

In unilineal societies, the channels of inheritance are usually fairly clear, but in bilateral kinship systems, patterns may become extremely complicated. In the case of the Anglo-Saxons they are of particular interest, since they may throw some light on the extent of kin recognition and effectiveness. . . .

The earliest rulings on inheritance are to be found in the Kentish laws of Ethelbert at the beginning of the seventh century. . . . a wife leaving her husband and taking their children with her was entitled to half the goods they possessed. Similarly, if she was widowed, and had a child, she was entitled to inherit half the goods. . . .[43]

Ine (Wessex 688–94) was also concerned with the problem of the widow with the child . . . .

If a husband and wife have a child together, and the husband dies, the mother is to have her child and rear it; she is to be given six shillings for its maintenance, a cow in summer, an ox in winter; the kinsmen are to take charge of the paternal home, until the child is grown up. (Law 38)

We are not told the origin of the six shillings and the cattle, but it seems likely that they were to come from the estate of the husband.

. . . Alfred nowhere ruled who should be a man's heirs but he supported the legality of restrictions on the granting of land held by book or charter:

The man who holds bookland, which his kinsmen left to him—then we establish that he may not alienate it from his kindred if there is a document or witness [to show] that he was prohibited from doing so by those men who acquired it in the beginning and by those who gave it to him. . . . (Law 41)

This is relevant to the limiting of heirs to a certain kin range . . . and must not be taken to mean that the land was to be bequeathed to any group as a whole.

... In VI Athelstan I. 1 we read that the wife of a convicted thief was to have one third of his property (less the value of the theft) if she were not implicated. ... In the laws of Cnut (1020–23) there is a clause that suggests that by this time a person would regularly leave directions as to the disposal of his property after his death (Laws 70, 70.1):

And if anyone departs from this life intestate, be it through his heedlessness, or through sudden death, the lord is then not to take more from his possessions than his legal heriot.[44] But by his direction, the property is to be very justly divided among his wife, the children and the close kinsmen, each in the proportions which belongs to him.

It is difficult to know whether the last phrase means that accepted rules existed to govern the relative size of these proportions. Possibly it merely implies that some sort of equitable division was to be made, under the supervision of the lord.

... In II Cnut 77 a man who had satisfactorily carried out all obligations on an estate during his lifetime was permitted to give it to whomever he pleased after his death. Formal rules, then, suggest that wife, children and close kin were expected to be the chief heirs of a man's property, but that considerable freedom in disposal existed. Conspicuous by its absence is any suggestion in the laws that the kin group had a right, after the land had been sold or given away (legitimately and not in contravention to any charter) to claim the land again or even to exercise a right to pre-emption. ...

The scarcity of precise formal rules in the laws is in itself of significance, and makes the patterns of inheritance that emerge from an examination of Anglo-Saxon wills particularly important. ... There are in existence more than fifty wills dating from the Anglo-Saxon period together with a number of medieval Latin documents which probably are based on Old English wills. I shall first analyze as a set the thirty-nine wills edited by Professor Whitelock. ... .[45] As usual, it is only with some reservations that the sources can be used for our purposes: the set of wills we are examining do not represent a random sample but only a haphazard one; probably only a proportion of people (and no peasants) made written wills; ... Our main expectation is to be able to find, in the wills, some indication of the range of possible heirs.

There is no doubt as to the most frequent beneficiary under these wills: all mention the Church. Twenty-four specify what shall be given to the lord.[46] Twenty-eight wills mention kinsmen and half-kinsmen as heirs, one mentions a ritual kinsman, one mentions a quasi-kinsman and eighteen mention friends and servants. The importance of lord and Church is to be expected; what is of particular interest here is the relationship of heirs to the maker of the will. Of all kinsmen mentioned as heirs, one alone was not left land; ten kinsmen were left movable property and five were left money. Women as well as men could inherit and bequeath property: ten of the thirty-nine wills were made by women, twenty-five by men and four by husband and wife. The property handed on by women was by no means limited to household property; all the ten had land to give, and only the will of Wynflaed (950) contains very detailed references to gifts of household goods to kin, friends and servants: a bracelet, a brooch, two buffalo-horns, a horse, a red tent, chests, cups, bed-clothing, gowns, her best dun tunic, a black tunic, a holy veil, a cap and headband, a little spinning box, a long hall-tapestry, seat coverings, books and so on. Wynflaed also gave instructions that all penally enslaved men on her estates and some of her bondsmen should be freed, while others were to go as servants to some of her kin.

. . . Husbands left estates to wives, but frequently the estates were not to be disposed of freely: widows were to have the usufruct of estates later destined to go to the Church for the benefit of the souls of both husband and wife. . . . An estate might also be granted to a wife with the proviso that the land . . . "is to revert to my kindred, those who are nearest." [47] Possibly to avoid subsequent litigation, a wife's right to dispose of an estate could be made quite explicit: Thurketel Heyng said, "And my wife's portion is to be for ever uncontested, for her to hold or to give where she pleases" . . . .[48] From the wills, it appears that estates could be left to sons, daughters (and daughters' husbands), sons' sons, sons' daughters, daughters' sons, brothers (and brothers' wives), sisters, brothers' sons, sisters' sons, nieces, nephews' children, mother, husband's mother, mother's brother (the last case is to be found in late wills, is perhaps twenty years or so out of our period) and father (a special case since the father was the king). Estates could also be left to a variety of kin who . . . may have been more distant genealogically and who are referred to merely as "kinsman". No *exclusive* preference can be observed for sons as heirs rather than daughters, or for older over younger sons, so that formulation of patterns of inheritance in terms of primogeniture or equal division amongst sons or any similar legal rule seems out of place. . . .[49]

. . . Among Anglo-Saxon charters is one that refers to a case in which a man sued his mother for land, at which she was, quite understandably in view of the circumstances, "strongly incensed".[50] Another charter gives a masterly summary of a complex dispute (964–88) between a man and his brother, which continued until it involved the man and his brother's son's wife's second husband.[51] The contingencies of actual inheritance in operation, here and in other cases, are such that we should hardly be surprised to find them in a modern series of wills, and they emphasize the unreality of assuming that in any given area throughout the whole of the Anglo-Saxon period a single rigid rule of inheritance prevailed.

Although inheritance is an aspect of succession, the term succession, used by itself, is sometimes employed by anthropologists to apply to the taking-over of a predecessor's legal and social position. The lines of succession in Anglo-Saxon society are difficult to determine, since legal

rules cover few situations and other material is complex and its interpretation is far from clear. In the ranking system, a man regularly succeeded to the same status as his father, with certain rights and duties
pertaining to it. A 1002–3 compilation on status, *Gethyncðo,*[52] says that
if a thegn prospered, he could attain the status of an earl but in the
Norðleoda laga it is stated that even if a *ceorl* prospered, he was still a
ceorl, but that if his son's son prospered, then the offspring entered hereditary ranks of the *gesith.* Here, as in other fairly rigidly stratified societies,
there was a certain amount of upward mobility.[53] Succession to particular
positions through kinship is hard to trace, except for the kingship which
by its nature is exceptional and moreover demands a discussion that
would involve much of Anglo-Saxon political history. The only general
conclusion that can be arrived at is that kinship with the holder of the
throne was a first requirement for regular succession, and that although
the king's appointment by election was in the hands of the *witena gemot,*
a tendency towards the acceptance of primogeniture grew up over the
period.[54] Succession along a line of brothers, however, is clearly apparent in the genealogy of the house of Wessex.

Succession to the chief position in a monastery could follow family
lines: in 736–7, a case [55] was decided in which the rightful succession as
abbess in a certain monastery was to go from a nun to her daughter's
daughter.

More pertinent information can be obtained about legal succession
to a man's position in regard to the fulfilment of certain obligations.
The laws of Ine [56] state that if a man sold some property and then died,
his heir and successor was in a position either to declare the purchase
incontestable or declare that the dead man never owned that property.
Ethelred later tried to limit this type of responsibility in saying that
if a man lived free from claims on his property while he was alive, no one
could bring an action against his heirs after his death.[57] Cnut also emphasized this law, but added the proviso that if a man had had claims made
against him during his lifetime, then his heirs could be made to answer
the charges.[58] But despite these adumbrations of the taking-over of a legal
personality, it is clear that we have here nothing like the "universal succession" that existed in Roman law, or that exists in a somewhat similar
form in some primitive societies.

Rights and Duties

. . . The rights the members of one's kin group could exercise over one
were limited.[59] One . . . was that of not being overlooked as heirs to bookland if this provision was written into the charter. Certain sectors of a kin
group could demand rights. Early in Kent, as the eighty-first law of
Ethelbert shows, a childless woman (who had left her husband?) had to

hand over her possessions and her "morning gift"—the present from her husband after the consummation of the marriage—to her paternal kin.

What duties did one's kin group owe one? First and foremost, they owed the duty of avenging one's death, either by prosecuting a feud, or by exacting wergild payments. On the other hand, if one had killed or injured a man, one could expect some support from kinsmen in helping bear a feud or pay a wergild. I discussed above, which persons were likely to represent the effective kin in a crisis like this. Additional backing for the hypothesis that the kin concerned might comprise only the nearest relatives may be found in records of what actually happened. For example:

Then Earl Brihtnoth asked Athelstan for his wergild, because of the failure of the vouching. Then Athelstan said that he had nothing to give him. Then Edward, Athelstan's brother, spoke up and said, "I have the title-deeds of Sunbury which our parents left me; give me possession of the estate and I will pay your wergild to the king." Then Athelstan said that he would rather that it perished by fire or flood than suffer that.[60]

Athelstan thus refused to let his brother (and no other kin seem to be involved) pay the wergild.

Members of a kin group also owed one guardianship. Early Kentish laws (Hlothhere and Eadric, Law 6) state that a fatherless child had the right to expect a paternal kinsman to look after him and his property until he reached ten years of age. . . . Members of a kin group had the duty of supporting one at certain *rites de passage,* rudimentary though our information on these is in the Anglo-Saxon period. . . . A child probably had the right to the presence of kin and of ritual kinsmen at baptism. The ritual relationship had its own rights and duties. Ine's Law 76 reads: "If anyone kill the godson or godfather of another, the compensation for the (spiritual) relationship is to be the same as that to the lord. . . ." Of funerals we hear surprisingly little in Anglo-Saxon records so that an assumption of the regular presence of kin here, as at marriages, is only a reasonable guess.

. . . Alfred's Law I.2 states that a man in prison for forty days for breaking his oath was to be fed by his kinsmen if he himself had no food. Under certain circumstances he could be freed, after his kin had paid his wergild as a fine (II Athelstan 6.1). By II Athelstan 8, landless men who had been serving in another shire were on their return to be harbored by a kinsman on condition that the latter should be responsible for their misdeeds. A man who had sought sanctuary from pursuers in a church, according to Alfred's Law I.2, could hand over his weapons to those who were in pursuit of him and await his kinsmen's help in settlement. The pursuers had the duty to let the kinsmen know their help was needed.

Similar considerations applied to the man who was besieged in his own home (Alfred's Law 42).

. . . Kinsmen also had a duty to stand surety for one. In II Athelstan I.3, we read that the kinsmen of a thief redeemed from prison by a fine were to stand surety that he would desist from thieving for ever. When an alleged thief had been slain, the man who was demanding his wergild could come forward with three others, two from the paternal and one from the maternal kin, and swear that their kinsman was innocent. . . .

If compensation for deliberate harm done was not settled, a feud could be prosecuted. In feuding the legal solidarity of the kin group is demonstrated by the fact that one member of the slayer's kin group is as good a victim for vengeance as the slayer himself. One could imagine a feud spreading among overlapping kin groups in a bilateral system. Edmund wished [61] that a slayer should alone bear the feud (and thus stop it spreading from kin group to kin group) or, with the help of others, pay the wergild. But if the slayer's kin were to abandon him, and not even help him pay compensation, then they would not be considered part of the feuding system and the bereaved kin had absolutely no right to revenge themselves on anyone but the delinquent. But Ethelred's code of 1014 (Law 23) reverses Edmund's decision as far as men in holy orders accused of feuds were concerned. Cnut, in his laws, appears to be willing that feud and wergild payments shall operate as means of social control, but that manifest murder (which to the Anglo-Saxons was concealed killing) required the handing over of the murderer by his kinsmen to the kin of the slain man.

Evidence suggests that the claims of kinship were likely to be weaker the further distant a kinsman was, genealogically and perhaps physically, but that this characteristic was not so regular in its operation as to be a structural principle of the kin group. It is possible that there were circumstances in which *all* kin could set aside their regular duties. . . .

Bilaterality and the Patrilineal Principle

. . . Emphasis on patrilateral kin, though not making the system patrilineal, was significant in a society in which physical force was at a premium, in battle and feud. The "spear side" was more important than the "spindle side." Ancestry, where it was traced back in a single line, was usually traced agnatically; we have many examples of this in the *Anglo-Saxon Chronicle,* which abounds in genealogies. . . .

In the laws, the emphasis on patrilateral kin is clear. It is a paternal kinsman who is appointed to be a child's protector in Hlothhere and Eadric's law 6. In Alfred's laws [62] it is said that if a man without paternal kin kills a man, then his maternal kin are to pay a third of the wergild. Later, Athelstan's laws [63] at Grately preserve the 2:1 ratio when they say that a man demanding payment for a slain kinsman shall be supported by three oath givers, two from the paternal and one from the maternal kin. We cannot assume in a simple way that paternal kin were just twice as important as maternal—this in fact would have little meaning in view of the *ad hoc* nature of Anglo-Saxon effective kin—but merely that in some contexts an agnatic emphasis existed.

The Importance of Kinship

. . . If one could solve the problem of the relationship between kin groups and local organization, this would throw much light on the limits of effectiveness within the set of recognized kin, since day-to-day cooperation as a group depends on constant communication. Preserved records, however, give few answers. It is not possible to know the patterns of residence, but hints suggest they may have been predominantly virilocal, a wife coming to live with her husband on marriage. A marriage agreement of 1016–20 [64] speaks of bringing the bride from Sussex to her future husband's family in Kent. If a man's sons all continued to live on his property after their marriages, the results would be to gather groups of agnatically related kin. Lack of data leaves the matter uncertain, but some forms of land inheritance, with possible scattering of estates in different areas and land-holding by women, suggests that such local groups of kinsmen were unlikely to have existed everywhere. . . .

There is no doubt that emotional identification with kin was close. Throughout Anglo-Saxon poetry, people are characterized by their kin relationship to others. . . . The plight of men far from home is often expressed as the distress of being far from kin. . . .

A kinless man was similarly deprived, and negative instances of the importance of kinship are given by provisions made in law for a kinless man; not he who had forfeited the rights of kinship, but the man who was born illegitimate, or who was a foreigner, or who had lost or renounced all relatives who were willing to take up the duties of kinship. Ine's laws state that the wergild of a kinless foreigner was to go half to the king and half to the *gesith,* probably his protector.[65] In Alfred's laws, a man without any kin was supported by the king, and by his associates, if he was killed. If he himself slew someone, his associates were to pay half, and for the other half he was to flee. . . .[66]

The two substitutes for kin, then, who were especially significant were a person's lord and his associates. It would provide a pattern easily grasped if we could find a man's ties to his lord becoming stronger over the period, as his ties to his kin group became weaker, but this does not seem to be the case. Early, in the *Chronicle* for 757 (755) one may see that men who chose lord above kin were highly regarded, while in the earliest laws concerning slaying [67] the emphasis on what is owed the lord as compensation is almost as great as that owed the kin. Internal evidence alone warns us against assuming constant change in the balance between these two ties. It is possible, on the other hand, that friends and associates became constantly more valuable as supporters. But here a problem is set by determining the meaning of Old English *freond* or *frynd*. It may even mean "kinsman," as it appears to in V Ethelred 31.1. Most uses are late, and "friends" do not appear in the earliest laws. During the period they gained continued importance as oath-helpers.[68] After the end of the tenth century, it was even permissible for a feud to be prosecuted or wergild claimed by a man's associates or guild-brothers.[69] If murder was done *within* the guild, kinsmen again played a part.

The only function of kin for which there is material to trace changes over time is that of feud and wergild. Phillpotts has examined aspects of this question in relationship to Anglo-Saxon and continental Teutonic systems, and, in general, her analysis holds. It is possible, however, that her tendency to see a pattern of constant steady decline in Anglo-Saxon kin functions leads her to some exaggeration. She states, for instance, that "there is no trace of legitimate blood-feuds after the time of Eadmund (c. 943)" [70] which is a misapprehension, as Ethelred's 1014 [71] code shows. At certain stages and in certain areas there were high points of kin strength in the taking of vengeance: King Athelstan hoped by one of his laws [72] to quell unruly kin groups, and King Edmund, feeling (as we have seen) that the spread of feuding was getting out of hand, legislated against it.[73] We also know that in Wulfstan's time, early in the eleventh century, it was possible to deplore, as he did, the lack of protection of kin by kin—"how too often a kinsman does not protect a kinsman any more than a stranger."[74] Nevertheless, in the compilation on status, dated by Whitelock between 1002–23,[75] the implication is clear (and made explicit in the case of the king's wergild in the *Mircna laga* and the *Norðleoda laga*) that wergild could still be claimed by kin. Kinship certainly tended to decline in importance over the period, but an irregular movement seems most faithfully to represent the scanty facts.

. . . I have tried to examine Anglo-Saxon kinship within a framework of ideas that will bring it into line with some current kinship studies. . . . The picture that emerges is complex: the system appears to have been less rigid than has frequently been thought; the circle of effective kin smaller; the lack of descent groups probable, despite patrilateral bias; the stability of marriage uncertain; and the corporateness of kindreds as landholding and residential units unproven. But at the same time we cannot posit a neat scheme of regular disintegration in the function and structure of kin groups; right up until the accession of Edward the Confessor, the kinship system remained a potent force of social control.

NOTES

1 R. W. Firth, ed., *Two Studies of Kinship in London*, 1956; Michael Young and Peter Willmott, *Family and Kinship in East London*, 1957.

2 H. S. Morris, *Report on a Melanau Sago-Producing Community in Sarawak*, H.M. Stationery Office (1953), p. 63.

3 R. K. Gordon, *Anglo-Saxon Poetry* (1954), p. 313.

4 Terms taken from J. Bosworth and T. N. Toller, *Anglo-Saxon Dictionary* (Oxford, 1882–98 and 1908–21).

5 C. D. Campbell, *The Names of Relationship in English* (Strassburg dissertation, 1905), p. 5.

6 G. S. Ghurye, *Family and Kin in Indo-European Culture* (1955), p. 27.

7 A. R. Radcliffe-Brown, *Structure and Function in Primitive Society* (1952), p. 64.

8 Parallel cousins are the sons or daughters of one's father's brother or of one's mother's sister; cross-cousins are sons or daughters of one's father's sister or of one's mother's brother. The distinction is in many primitive societies very important: especially it may be forbidden to marry a cross-cousin, or it may be obligatory to marry an available cross-cousin. EDITOR'S NOTE.

9 This does not mean that women held a markedly inferior status, in comparison with men, in Anglo-Saxon society. Quite the contrary is shown by Betty Bandel, "The English Chroniclers' Attitude towards Women", *Journal of the History of Ideas*, January, 1955.

10 Laws 3, 4, and 5.

11 Law 55.

12 In the Civil Law, the degree of relationship between collaterals is counted by the number of steps up from one of them to the common ancestor and thence down to the other; according to the Canon Law, by the number of steps from the common ancestor to the person more remote from him.

13 D. Whitelock, *The Beginnings of English Society* (1956), p. 150.

14 Compare VI Ethelred: "And it must never happen that a Christian man marries among his own kin within six degrees of relationship, that is, within the fourth generation . . ." A. J. Robertson, in *The Laws of the Kings of England from Edmund to Henry I* (1925), pp. 95, 332, reads this as referring to fourth cousins. There is no scholarly agreement on the interpretation of degrees of relationship for much material.

15 D. Whitelock, ed., *English Historical Documents, 500–1042* (1955), p. 746.

16 *Ibid.*, p. 810.

17 *Ibid.*, p. 813.

18 *Ibid.*, p. 858.

19 II Cnut 51, 51.1.

20 Whitelock, *op. cit.*, Law 6 1.1, p. 438.

21 *Ibid.*, p. 431.

22 *Ibid.*, p. 610; the biblical reference is to I Corinthians 1.

23 *Ibid.*, p. 226.

24 Whitelock, *The Beginnings of English Society*, p. 150.

25 Laws 75, 75.1, 76.

26 Whitelock, *English Historical Documents*, p. 431 (c. 975–1030).

27 *Ibid.*, p. 856.

28 See Anglo-Saxon Chronicle for year 1015.

29 Law 73.3.

30 A. R. Radcliffe-Brown, ed., *African Systems of Kinship and Marriage* (1950), p. 46; E. E. Evans-Pritchard, *Man*, vol. 34, article 194; I. Schapera, *A Handbook of Tswana Law and Customs* (1955), pp. 138–9.

31 Whitelock, *op. cit.*, p. 431.

32 *Ibid.*, p. 548.

33 *Ibid.*, p. 857.

34 Hlothere and Eadric, Kings of Kent (673–85), Law 6; Ine, King of the West Saxons (688–94), Laws 1a, 7.2.

35 VI Athelstan I.1; II Cnut 21.

36 Whitelock, *op. cit.*, p. 391.

37 Kent (c. 602–3), Law 31. The adulterous wife was to be replaced by a new one at the adulterer's expense.

38 Whitelock, *op. cit.*, pp. 753–4.

39 Law 42.7.

40 Bede, *Ecclesiastical History*, Book IV, chapter V.

41 *Ibid.*, Book IV, chapters XVII, XIX.

42 For criticism of this theory, advanced by a German scholar, see T. F. T. Plucknett, *A Concise History of the Common Law*, 5th ed., (1956), p. 712. For evidence of the later existence of different kinship and landholding systems see George C. Homans, "The Frisians in East Anglia", *Economic History Review*, December, 1957.

43 Laws 78–9.

44 The heriot, the customary payment due the lord, was usually the deceased's best animal. EDITOR'S NOTE.

45 The author refers us to Sir David Hughes Parry, *The Law of Succession Testate and Intestate*, 3rd. ed., 1953, for reasons for more properly referring to these Anglo-Saxon wills as "post obit gifts", or as a combination of these with "last words" specifying heirs and inheritance—the form known as *cwide*. The cases analyzed are taken from D. Whitelock, *Anglo-Saxon Wills*, Cambridge University Press, 1930. EDITOR'S NOTE.

46 The 39 wills all come from the years between the mid-tenth century and the end of the Anglo-Saxon period. Earlier wills do not mention heriot. [I have omitted the author's tabulation of dispositions of land. EDITOR'S NOTE.]

47 Whitelock, *op. cit.*, p. 54.

48 *Ibid.*, p. 71, case from early 11th century, probably before 1020.

49 Omitted here are examples of bequests to semi-kin (step-daughter), quasi-kin (foster-mother), and ritual kin (god-mother). EDITOR'S NOTE.

50 A. J. Robertson, *Anglo-Saxon Charters* (Cambridge University Press, 1939), charter LXXVIII.

51 *Ibid.*, charter XLI.

52 D. Whitelock, *English Historical Documents*, p. 431.

53 *Ibid.*, p. 562, for a charter of c. 957–67 recording a defense of status, and pp. 431 ff., for compilations on status specifying conditions of upward mobility.

54 See P. Grierson, "Election and Inheritance in Early Germanic Kinship", *Cambridge Historical Journal*, VII (1941).

55 Whitelock, *op. cit.*, p. 454.

56 Laws 53, 53.1.

57 III Ethelred 14.

58 II Cnut 72.

59 Throughout this section I have substituted for the technical term *Ego*, used by anthropologists in referring to kinship tables constructed around a "focal" individual, the word "one", likely to be clearer to ordinary readers. EDITOR'S NOTE.

60 A.J. Robertson, *op. cit.*, charter XLIV.

61 II Edmund I–I.3.

62 Law 30.

63 Law 11.

64 Whitelock, *op. cit.*, p. 548.

65 Law 23.1.

66 Alfred, Laws 30, 30.1, 31.

67 Ine, Kent, c. 602–03.

68 See discussion of *Eideshelfer* in F. Liebermann, *Die Gesetze der Angelsachsen* (Halle, 1912), vol. 2, part 2.

69 See Whitelock, *op. cit.*, p. 557.

70 B. Phillpotts, see above, p. 7.

71 VIII Ethelred 23; see also reference in n. 68, above.

72 VI Athelstan 8.2.

73 II Edmund.

74 Whitelock, *op. cit.*, p. 856.

75 *Ibid.*, p. 431.

3

Gilds

LUJO   BRENTANO

The family appears as . . . an archetype of the Gilds. Originally, its providing care satisfies all existing wants; and for other societies there is therefore no room. As soon however as wants arise which the family can no
longer satisfy—whether on account of their peculiar nature or in consequence of their increase, or because its own activity grows feeble—closer
artificial alliances immediately spring forth to provide for them, in so far
as the State does not do it. . . . In short, whatever and however diverse may
be their aims, the Gilds take over from the family the spirit which held it
together and guided it: they are its faithful image, though only for special
and definite objects.

* * * * *

The organization of the Gilds was thus in the ninth and tenth centuries . . .
probably already widely extended amongst the Anglo-Saxons. . . . At the
same time we see them forbidden and persecuted on the Continent by
ecclesiastical as well as by secular authorities. A series of Capitularies of
the Emperor Charlemagne and his successors interfered with all kinds of
combinations and unions, and especially with those which were confirmed
by mutual oaths.[1] Not only those which proposed directly unlawful objects
were threatened with scourging, nose-slitting, banishment, and such-like
punishments of their members, but even those whose object was protection
against robbery and other deeds of violence.[2] Unions were only to be tolerated for mutual assistance in fires, shipwrecks, and similar cases, and
even then without the members confirming their obligations by an oath.[3]
Under Louis the Pious, Gilds even among serfs are met with in Flanders
and other maritime districts, and their lords were called upon to suppress
them, under the threat of being punished themselves. . . . There is no

doubt that these *Gildoniae* of the Frankish Empire are the same as the Gilds of the Anglo-Saxons. . . .[4] The more developed character of the constitutions of these appears merely as a consequence of the later times from which the documents on them have been preserved for us. . . . But much earlier, though less detailed, information is afforded by the Capitularies of Archbishop Hincmar of Rheims, of the year 858.[5]

We find, already distinct, in these Capitularies, the two kinds which must be distinguished among the Religious Gilds. The one exists among laymen; and it alone is called *Geldonia.* It alone, too, bears already the complete character of the Religious Gilds as it existed during the whole of the Middle Ages. The other kind of Gild exists among the clergy.

In the Capitulary relating to the Gilds among laymen, Hincmar gives instructions to his clergy as to their allowed sphere of action, and as to the solemnities to be held at their meetings. He first tells them quite in general, that only that should be done which was required by dignity, utility, and reason; but he immediately defines this more precisely: "They shall unite for every exercise of religion, that is to say, they shall unite for offerings (especially of candles), for mutual assistance, for funeral services for the dead, for alms, and other deeds of piety." On the other hand, Hincmar forbids what other Capitularies term *diabolicum* (heathen), namely, feastings and drinking-bouts, because they led to drunkenness, gave occasion for unjust exactions, for sordid merriments, and inane railleries, and ended often even with quarrels, hatred, and manslaughter. If it was the priest of the Gild who acted against this prohibition, he was to be degraded, but if it was a layman or a woman, he or she was to be excluded until satisfaction was given. If it became necessary to call a meeting of the brothers, as, for instance, for the arrangement of differences which might have arisen among them, they were to assemble after divine service; and after the necessary admonitions, every one who liked was to obtain from the priest a piece of consecrated bread and a goblet of wine; and then he was to go home with the blessing of God.

These fraternities were spread in the Middle Ages, in great numbers, over all countries under the sway of the Roman Catholic religion, and they exist even now in such countries. . . .

As to the Gilds among the clergy, the capitularies of Hincmar contain ordinances against the extravagances of the priests at funeral meals, and at the feastings which used to follow their meetings, especially those of the priests of a deanery, on the first of each month. No priest was to get drunk at them, nor was he to empty goblets to the health of saints or of the soul of the deceased; nor was he to force others to drink, nor get drunk himself at the desire of others. The priests were not to burst out into indecent noise or roaring laughter; they were not to sing vain songs nor tell inane jokes; nor were they to allow scandalous performances of bears or female dancers to be made before them, nor delight in other mummeries, "because this was heathenish, and forbidden by Canon law." Nor were they on every occasion to provoke each other, or anybody else, to passion and quarrels, and still less to fighting and murder; nor was he who was provoked to assail at once his provoker. On the contrary, the priests were to breakfast with honesty and fear of God; holy stories and admonitions were to be read, and hymns sung, and everyone was to go home in good time. Exactly the same ordinances are contained in the Capitularies of Bishop Walter of Orleans, which likewise bear date in the year 858.

These passages do not, however, contain anything from which the existence of a Gild among these priests can be inferred; for the extravagances mentioned might be connected with any kind of meeting. In later times, however, the clergymen assembled on the first day of each month to deliberate on their interests, were united in special fraternities, which from their meeting-day on the Kalends of each month, were called "Gilds of the Kalenders". It is generally inferred from this, that probably even in Hincmar's time the priests bound each other by mutual agreement to pray for their salvation, and to observe certain rules with respect to their meetings; and these meetings are accordingly believed to have been Gild-meetings of the clergy. This is nothing but a mere conjecture, it is true. But it is also true that, in later times, the members of the Gilds of the Kalenders used to assemble on the Kalends of each month for divine service, for deliberation on their interests, and for common meals, like the priests in the time of Hincmar.

NOTES

1 *Monumenta Germaniae Historica, Legum,* vol. I, p. 37, cap. 16; p. 59, cap. 29; p. 68, cap. 10; p. 74, cap. 31; p. 133, cap. 10; p. 230, cap. 7; p. 232, cap. 4; p. 352; cap. 10; p. 553, cap. 14.

2 *Ibid.,* pp. 133, 232, 352.

3 *Ibid.,* p. 37.

4 *Ibid.,* p. 230.

5 *Labbei Concilia,* ed. Coleti, vol. X, p. 4.

The Church and Society

4

The Sociology of the Church in the Early Middle Ages

GABRIEL LE BRAS

Religious societies constitute, in the world, groups that are organized in order to establish relations with the powers that are hidden, and to safeguard, within the heart of nations, both their principles and their institutions. It follows that the sociology of religion has a threefold domain: the community of the faithful, the State of which they are subjects, and finally the Beyond. Its ultimate aim is to distinguish types of religious society, to explain these phenomena, to look for constants.

To attain these ends, sociology undertakes the study of all religious societies: it can base its conclusions only on methodological analysis of the structures and the life of each well-defined example. The first stage is purely descriptive work: to describe the localization, the membership, the morphology, of the religion studied; its internal activities, its dynamism, its relations with civil society and with other religions; its whole system of truths, rites, and discipline; the beliefs, practices, and behavior of its members. This detailed knowledge, which we term sociography, calls for understanding and explanation, and leads finally to attempts to construct typologies and to discern laws. For example, we try to distinguish the primary and secondary types of ascetic groups, these being the formal analogies behind communally organized monasticism (cenobitism) and anchoritism; we look to see whether similar or parallel patterns appear simultaneously.

When the Church proclaims that it is a perfect society, this is by no means to be understand as a value judgment, but rather as a way of declaring its autonomy, of saying that it possesses all the attributes of an organized, independent, and sovereign group. It lives among the nations and its

47

members are at the same time believers and citizens, to whom it dictates moral law; to its rights as a corporate group it adds those of moral teacher of the subjects of the secular power. Its official purpose, in a word, is to guide its people to heaven. It describes the heavenly beings and maintains, from this world, constant relations with them.

Thus the Church is an autonomous society intimately linked with two other societies, those of the World and the Beyond. The sociology of Catholicism accordingly operates in three sectors: it defines and explains the lines of internal organization within the Church, its external ties with the World, and its higher relations with the Beyond. Such is the program of a sociology of Catholicism.

This immense program has to draw on both sacred and profane branches of learning, and even on the most up-to-date techniques. You have heard me invoke all of these: theology, liturgy, canon law; geography, psychology, philosophy, with statistics and cartography as aids. The most urgent appeal is to history. Every society lives in time—a fact of which I never cease to remind untemporally-minded sociologists who too often ignore it. How are we to construct a typology of ascetic groups, or understand their etiology or the regularities they present, without bringing together all the information that is available about austere communities within Christianity, Hinduism, Buddhism, Islam and all other religions living and dead? How can we study Christianity without following the whole development of the institutions and actions of the baptized, from the Apostle Peter to the present Pope? Though resting on immovable foundations, Christian society has perpetually modified its forms: it split up into orders and tiny territorial divisions, only to merge these into larger groupings and provinces; the centers and the hierarchy of authority change, dogma and worship become richer. A sociology of Catholicism requires a series of investigations into all of the sources from each well-delimited period.

The Christian Church of the early middle ages provides one of these clear-cut periods. In the chronology that I have often proposed, the time between the accession of Pope Gelasius (492 A.D.) and that of Pope Zacharias (741 A.D.) constitutes the second age of the Ancient Law. I shall not conform to the custom of praising it as superior to other periods. We need only remember that it received the heritage of Antiquity and that through achieving a fusion of Roman and barbarian elements of culture, it enabled the Carolingian Renaissance to make the first affirmation of Christendom.

It is impossible in forty-five minutes to cover all aspects of this universal society. The most striking features will emerge, however, if we look in turn at its forms of organization, its points of contact with the world, and its internal life. It is split up, but coordinates itself into a whole, it Christianizes kingdoms which then tend to laicize its structure, it holds out to believers the means to personal salvation and also the opportunity for close fellowship. These are the three subjects on which we shall reflect.

I. Dispersion and Coordination

The Church of the early middle ages is a dismembered body striving to reunite itself. The most obvious change in Christian society at the end of the 5th century may be read from the political map: the break between East and West, the division of the Empire into nations. This political accident shatters the Church's organization. The wise distribution of dioceses by provinces, under a uniform law, is replaced by national divisions; the nations all differ in character, and the only principle they seem to share in common is that of opposition to the East.

I have many times stressed the fact that the Church exists inside political units, and the consequences of this for the hierarchical structure and for collective psychology. Italy, its unity dissolved, displays dramatic tension between the great sees of Rome, Milan, Aquilea, and Ravenna, while Gaul, partitioned among Franks and Bretons, Burgundians and Visigoths, is acephalous. Spain's unification under Visigothic rule, with the Church concentrated around the metropolitan of Toledo, is in sharp contrast with Ireland's fragmentation into clans, each with its monasteries. Each of these nations has its own character traits. How vastly different is the civilized, rational, juristically-minded Roman from the independent Celt with his fantastic imagination, and the unbending rigor of the Iberian from the fickleness of the Gauls!

These diversities are reflected in the development of Church law. Papal legislation fades out after Gregory the Great, there is no addition to the *Dionysiana* collection of papal decretals; in Gaul special collections of canons abound because of the frequency with which synods meet in the 6th century; the great series of national councils at Toledo gives rise to the *Hispana* collection; in the islands (Ireland, Britain) there is freedom for an over-rich growth of penitentials. We can comprehend all this better if we realize that we have different societies, producing law and building institutions independently.

Unity of faith is broken by the Arian heresy. In the time of Gelasius, when Alaric rules over the Visigoths, Gundobad over the Burgundians, Theodoric over Italy, all the Germanic peoples save the Franks profess Arianism (and the Lombards will soon give it new vigor). Nicean Catholicism survives, tolerated or persecuted, in its ancient areas. For a time, two theologies confront each other wherever Romans and Barbarians are neighbors.

An internal process of organization heightens the impression of a break-up: the diocese is gradually carved up through the creation of rural parishes; monasticism takes divergent paths through creating a multi-plicity of Rules. These two phenomena have been under study for half a century, yet our knowledge of them is still incomplete.

We identify the parish through certain definite features: a church, the center of worship in a district that has recognized bounds, with a rector and its own resources. The churches multiply, and though we cannot map parish boundaries, the institutions of the rectorate and the church patri-mony are clearly making headway.

As to monasticism, our conference has already noted the growing diversity of its forms: we find a dozen celebrated Rules; we cannot map their diffusion exactly, but it is clear that each is different in spirit.

Even in the Beyond, a new society emerges, innumerable saints receiv-ing popular recognition and veneration. My own country of Brittany dis-tributed saintly rank with its accustomed generosity. But haloes appear everywhere, and people even begin to assign the saints specialized func-tions. We ought not to dismiss this popular organization of the Beyond (doubtless instigated by the clergy) as a matter for mere idle curiosity. A religious sociology that failed to pay scrupulous attention to the way in which invisible worlds are represented would be false to its purpose, which is to study the *religio* between earthly society and supernatural society.

This process of break-up makes it essential to find means of coordination. Coordination will be realized, or attempted, through a fortunate loyalty to the Ancient Law both in the separate churches and in the Christian world as a whole, extending even to the conception of the Beyond.

The bishop consolidates ties within the diocese through synods and visits. He assembles his clergy to deliberate on local problems and to pub-lish their decisions: Auxerre, in 595, was the scene of the first assembly whose acts have survived. In Visigothic Spain the diocesan synod gives each parish priest a chance to report on how he carries out his duties, and is the occasion of informing the whole community of the decisions of provincial councils.

Again, the bishop personally tours his territory to inspect church buildings, supervise finances, enquire into faith and morals, hold confirma-tion services, preach, and punish. According to the Council of Tarragona (516 A.D.) this annual circuit was an "ancient custom". The second Council of Braga (572 A.D.) spelt out the program in detail, and the fourth Council of Toledo (633 A.D.), emphasizing the practical importance of carrying it out regularly, provided that a bishop who was too busy might delegate the duty to priests or to capable deacons.

The tradition of holding provincial councils seems to have been older. It was upheld with remarkable obstinacy long after the province had largely lost its original function, and when few such councils actually met. Reiteration of the rules requiring them that were drawn up at Nicaea, and at Antioch (341 A.D.) testifies to regret that they had lapsed, to a desire for greater regional cohesion.

This cohesion was achieved within a wider and quite new circumference, through the national councils which met, from the first quarter of the 6th century, among the Visigoths, the Franks, and the Burgundians. The context within which they will strike root is not that of the universal Church.

Christian unity is however restored by the collapse of Arianism. We know how the Visigoths abandoned Arianism, in France by 507 A.D. and in Spain at the Council of Toledo in 589; the Burgundians broke with it around 537, and the Vandals and the Ostrogoths at about the same time. Christological heresies disturbed only small circles. Symbols and guarantors of unity, the Empire and the Papacy strive to impose their leadership. Our conference here two years ago dealt with the ups and downs of these two sovereign powers, and with their periods of paralysis. Yet despite the long eclipse of universalism, we can observe two paradoxical movements of importance: the Celts, through the privileges obtained for the monastery of Bobbio, inaugurate the Papal power of exemption, and the divided peoples of Gaul are obscurely preparing the way for the return to unity. An order is being established in the representation of the invisible world, as hagiographers and chroniclers, poets and artists see it. They depict hosts of beings from the two Testaments, assigning them special functions and capabilities, in a décor and a hierarchical order borrowed from the royal courts of the age. This sociology of Heaven has a direct bearing on the sociology of the Church and of the profane world. The saints are agents of local, regional, and universal integration. They protect the city and the nation and watch over the bands of pilgrims that they attract. Through one of the saints, the Apostle Peter, the Pope is enabled to be present in many different places at the same time; this serves the cause of unity.

II. Christianization and Laicization

The work of the early middle ages was to bring a Christian society into being. In the Roman Empire, paganism ruled among the countryfolk and skepticism among the aristocrats. In the 6th century both the countryside and the towns will officially rally to Christ. But the religion, in the hands of its new followers, will be liable to change. Let us consider the effects of this twofold movement on the structure and the life of the Church.

The invasions, far from interrupting the preaching of the Gospel, made it even more necessary. We know the story of its advance, and the obstacles it encountered, fairly well, although the influence the latter had on the population of the Church, and on its forms, is still at some points a

matter for debate. Yet by the beginning of the 8th century, all of Western
Europe professes a common faith.

On the lands it keeps or conquers, the Church plants its buildings, its
institutions, and its law. We can plot the exact locations of monasteries on
the map, and can estimate the location of churches; and everywhere there
are little monuments—oratories, chapels, crosses—proclaiming the conquest of the land. Fields, woods, and villages—a considerable proportion
of them—are becoming ecclesiastical or monastic property. Now that spiritual hegemony has engendered earthly power, the dualism of ecclesiastical
society, already perceptible under the Christian Empire, becomes dramatic.
Rights of asylum create sacred space; royal immunities create autonomous
domains.

We meet peculiar difficulties in the problem of conversion. It is impossible to tell how many of those who were baptized became Christians. But
we have abundant evidence as to the beliefs, practices, and behavior of the
faithful. Such material belongs to the history of ideas and customs but is
of interest also for the sociology of the Church as revealing the life of
Christian society, its relations with supernatural society, and its position
in civil society.

The councils continually complain that belief is mixed with a great
deal of superstition, and the hagiographers themselves, who denounce
magicians and sorcerers, show a credulity far removed from pure doctrine.
Frustrated men taught elementary truths, in sermons, to a mass of illiter-
ates all steeped in ancient magic. This contaminated faith seldom mani-
fests any strength: rarely was there any resistance to adverse pressures or
any sign of desire for reform or improvement; the spirit of conquest fires
only a very few missionaries.

The Church was much less concerned to teach the ignorant than to
impose obligatory habits of worship on them. Thus institutional practice
develops a common rule for relationship with God. The criterion of belonging to a Christian society is three communions a year and the weekly
duty of hearing the entire mass on Sunday. Then the system of bargaining
with the Beyond is developed, through the oath, the vow, the acquisition
of merit though alms and sacrifices.

Moral precepts refer chiefly to life in civil society. They demand—of
people who were still uncivilized—purity, gentleness, justice, and charity.
Councils, pastors, and penitentials list the prevailing vices along with the
prescribed virtues. They show us what we might term the continuing coin
of evangelical teaching and patristic doctrine; they show us how far distant
the rules were from reality; we see how a society can be called Christian
without letting go of its pagan tradition.

The early medieval Church adds one original contribution to the
common rules of the Christian life: the detailed organization of the *status
vitae*, the estates. "There are three kinds of Christians", the classic doctors

will say. This trichotomy is generally accepted by the 5th century; its divisions and content are fully described between the 6th century and the 8th.

The status of the clergy was in essentials a legacy from Antiquity. From that time on, legislation aims at withdrawing them from the world, binding them more closely into diocesan groups, imposing on them a quasi-monastic austerity. They have to sever all ties with a profession or with a master. Not only are they forbidden to frequent public gatherings, but certain councils order them to live in groups, policing each other. The diocese forms an island; all of the clergy, up to those of the highest rank, must be recruited within its borders. These are guarded: no native may leave and no stranger enter, unless his credentials are in order. Relations with women are regulated by an ascetic protocol: cohabitation is restricted to the mother, sister, and other close relatives, and all conversation has to be in the presence of a witness.

In this manner the ideal constitution of an independent clergy is completed. But the clergy are not the whole Church. One of the legislator's concerns is to draw a clear distinction between the *ecclesia* and the body of clergy (*coetus clericorum*). The clergy have no absolute powers: personal privileges and the use of property are regulated by law. Numerous canons set out the basic laws that guarantee the integrity of the patrimony and publicly define the privileges attached to spiritual office and to temporal rights. The governing principle is to hold all positions and relationships within the hierarchy fixed, to keep the property of the bishopric and the parish intact, to maintain the existing condition of all who have taken the tonsure. Far from identifying itself with the clergy, the Church protected itself against them. It is a foundation, a divine foundation, not a corporation and still less a sacerdotal community.

The laity, too, are the Church. Their status too, like that of the clergy, reveals the sociology of the Church. For them, Christianization means belief in the Church, worship in the Church, conduct prescribed by the Church. They are the material of which Christian society is built. They are grouped in families whose form has been shaped by the canon law: repression of incest leads to very strict exogamy, prohibition of divorce and of free separation makes for domestic stability, refusal to recognize concubinage makes marriage the general rule.

Finally, the third kind of Christians, the monks, are the subject of a wealth of legislation. The authorities and the monastic founders fit monasticism into the structure and life of the Church, requiring community life, fixed residence, obedience. In place of hermits, wandering monks and little groups living as they please, we find well-organized groups within the Church, serving as centers of devotion within regions that intersect the diocesan units of Christendom. The bishops check the frenzied proliferation of Rules, trying to ensure that monasteries be established only with their permission and adhere firmly to an approved Rule.

We would do better to speak of a tripartite division than of a trichotomy, for there are no impassible barriers between the three estates. The clergy and the monks are recruited almost entirely from the laity. However, clergy do enter monasteries, and it is in our period that the number of monks who become ordained as priests increases. This practice had waned after the 4th century; its growth is due to the needs of the ministry and above all to the need for missionaries.

The spread of Christianization thus affects only the size of the Church, it in no way alters the principles on which it rests. It imposes a systematic structure of ordered relationships on each of the three estates. All of these organizational advances depend on the goodwill of the secular powers, who permit them to proceed. Will the barbarian world offer no resistance to such a radical transformation?

The advantages that the Church enjoyed through the favor of the secular rulers were offset by a perilous servitude. If the unity of national Churches is preserved, it is under the control of the kings. Christianity is a State religion, the Church is national. Let us examine the place of the King in ecclesiastical society and his influence on the structure and life of the Church.

It would be well to distinguish between different periods and places: there is some difference between the Frankish monarchies and the Visigothic dyarchy. But the essential features are the same and are quite obvious. Let us simply recall that the prince takes part in the selection of bishops by an assent which can amount to an order, that he convokes and sanctions national councils, that he regards himself as being in charge of ecclesiastical property.

The role of the great landed proprietors is also a commanding one. It is they who build the churches and oratories on their lands, and these form part of their private patrimony. They choose the priest, collect all the income, keep the buildings in repair and sell them at will. Ulrich Stutz made an illustrative study of this phenomenon, assigning it a Germanic origin. Thank Heaven, here we need only emphasize its place in the sociology of the Church. Along with a number of my teachers and colleagues, I believe that it originated with the conversion of the rural aristocracy, and developed during the 6th and 7th centuries.

The Church's encounter with the World dates back to the earliest Christian times. When the Empire was converted an alliance had been arranged; the barbarian Powers tended to lord it over the Church. The Church made it its business to maintain or restore the status it had acquired in public law under the Romans, a status which Pope Gelasius had defined in a famous letter.

The texts relating to the judicial, fiscal and local privileges that the emperors had granted have been interpreted in different ways. I believe that the struggle was sharper than some people admit. It had these two objects: to reduce, discreetly, the prince's interference and the subjection of the Church to the ordinary law of the State.

The Church owed the great landowners a certain gratitude for their cooperation, which was indispensable; but it steadily resisted encroachments on its discipline. The fourth council of Orleans (541 A.D.) requires that the founder of a church provide it with a suitable endowment and personnel and that he recognize the archdeacon's canonical authority over the clergy; the council of Chalon (about 650 A.D.) strengthened this stand. The Visigothic bishops were also persistently firm.

Could the Church hope to keep its independence in a society in which it existed only through the goodwill of the great? At least it clung to principles; these kept tradition alive and made the future possible. Meanwhile, in addition to the tension between the spiritual power and the temporal there was also, within the spiritual sphere, a deep-lying tension between individualism and fellowship.

III. Individualism and Fellowship

Unanimity of feeling reigned in the primitive Church, for people were all awaiting the triumphal return of Jesus. For a long time, common danger prolonged the solidarity made manifest in worship and the sacraments. In the barbarian world, this sense of solidarity seemed as it were to have crumbled; a sudden awareness of the self provoked an individualistic reaction.

The waning of public solidarity is evident in the very sphere formerly suffused by the sense of holiness. Baptism, penitence, the eucharist, without changing their nature, lose a part of their sociological character.

Instead of being conferred solemnly on fixed days, as in Antiquity, baptism is conferred on the infant as soon as possible. Private penance little by little replaces public penitence. Finally, in the 6th century, private masses are introduced. All these facts are well known, but we have perhaps not reflected enough on their sociological consequences.

The most obvious of these is the non-participation of the community. Formerly, the catechumen was led with his brothers among the brothers, there was a collective incorporation into the group: now, admission is automatic and unremarked. Formerly, penitence was a spectacle, a public humiliation preceding reintegration into the group. Now the custom of confession followed by a reparation that can be secret, is spreading; this is principally Celtic in origin. Formerly, the whole community attended mass, cooperating in collective prayer, offerings, fellowship: in the 7th century, mass is often celebrated for an individual, with no one else present.

Under this regime, the individual is less visibly bound to his group and more inclined to seek his own ways of assuring his salvation. He will confide his faults and his problems to a monk or to one of the clergy. To ensure his ultimate deliverance from Purgatory he will make a pious legacy, perhaps found a monastery. He will be inspired to turn to some saint, chosen for his specialized function or for his charm, to intercede for him.

This individualism is not to be confused with personal piety. The latter implies a real conversion in the whole of life, in beliefs, worship, and behavior, and can lead to asceticism or mysticism. The former shows not only a deepening of thought but is a symptom of disaggregation, of withdrawal from the group.

We cannot be certain that the early medieval Church was clearly conscious of this individualism. Yet it certainly made a sustained effort to revitalize the spiritual sense of community. An example of this is the insistence, at synods held in Gaul, on the clergy and the laity assembling together in the cathedral on the occasion of great festivals. To scatter among the oratories, as on ordinary Sundays, is on these days strictly forbidden. The bishop's intention is to affirm, through these periodic mass meetings, the unity of the diocese under his single crozier.

The Church tries to impose perfect unison on the people of different dioceses, in the matter of prayer. This unison depends in the first place on having a common calendar. We know how firmly Rome insisted on Ireland adopting its Easter date, and the Visigoths were no less intransigent. "For example, if we do not celebrate Pentecost in all churches on the same preordained day", it was said, "we shall not receive the gifts of the Holy Spirit". Councils in Gaul and Spain repeatedly prescribe uniformity in divine service.

No teaching better expressed the unity of the Church, of all the Churches—militant, suffering, triumphant, to use a still uncertain term—than the doctrine of the communion of saints. It gradually crept into the Creed.

Conclusion

Between the end of the 6th century and the beginning of the 8th, the Church had to adapt its forms to a new society. The partitioning of political power, the first thrust of seigneurial power, and the profusion of popular cults made both of the worlds with which it linked itself—the earthly and the celestial—extraordinarily complicated. In the seeming break-up of the Church, forces are born that work separately: the network of parishes and the apparatus of episcopal government take shape, monasticism and the exemption of monasteries from episcopal control prepare the way for domination by Rome. At the same time, protection by king and nobles introduces the dangers of royal domination and of lay patronage. The dramatic constituents of medieval society are already, in this obscure prologue, on the scene.

The Church underwent no sharp mutation in passing from the Empire to the monarchies and the lordships, from a brilliant civilization to one of semi-barbarism: for two and a half centuries it set itself to pour the ancient traditions into the new mold. It is the task of sociography to describe this operation in detail, while sociology will try to explain the changes that occurred, with particular attention to the interplay of the different societies—the religious, the civil, and even the supernatural—which were both the actors in, and the subjects of, change. It will offer a typology of religious institutions, of collective aspirations, of social ties.

Such analyses of actual conditions, followed by general propositions, contribute to a general sociology of the Church. They do so in defining the precise causes of integration, which in the dislocated society of the early middle ages are at the same time religious and social: uniformity of doctrine, assemblies for worship, moral taboos. They do so by describing in detail the types of authority that a Gregory the Great or a Caesarius of Arles represents, the points of correlation in the interplay of the Powers (that is, the similarities and the points at which they give each other mutual support), the comparative morphology of local churches and the ideals declared in the canonical sources.

I offer this little paper to the great seven-storey library which should be devoted to studies of the structure and whole life of every religion at every moment of its history.

5

Private Churches in Ancient France

IMBART DE LA TOUR

The general origin of patronage was in the foundation of a church on a private estate. If the church became a parish, the patronage then extended to the parish. These were normal and regular practices, accepted by actual canonical legislation. But they are not enough to explain the progressive numerical diminution of free churches. In the 7th century we already see the *vicus publicus,* the arch-priest's parish, falling into the hands of a magnate.

What causes or facts explain this conquest of the larger parishes by the landed aristocracy? It is difficult to discover them, the documents being either obscure or scanty. But a study of the documents conveys the impression that it came about through the need for protection which, in that troubled and anarchic society, was gradually building up lordship. In the disorder of the times, in an age when individual right was no guarantee, when men were willing to renounce freedom in order to go on living, social bonds were radically altered: as between the individual and the State they grew steadily looser; as between the rich and the poor, the powerful and the weak, they grew steadily tighter.

Now the Church had more need of protection than any individual, for it was vulnerable to every kind of covetousness and was powerless, alone, to defend itself. It was in special need of defenders both of its property and of its clergy. It had found its first defender in royalty. And from the 6th century, it was asking for royal charters of protection and immunity. Accordingly the kings, and later the mayor of the palace took bishoprics and abbeys under their protection and gave individual charters to bishops, abbots, and ordinary clergy who "commended" themselves

58

to their person. But was the king the only protector? And over the little group, the parish, would not his protection be too remote to be effective? Consequently, were there not similar contracts in local districts (*pagi*) between the parish and the locally powerful proprietor? Did the priests and clerks of the *vicus* not commend themselves to a lord? Did they not obtain charters for themselves personally or for their church?

For the feudal age, for the 10th and 11th centuries, we have a certain number of such contracts, assuring protection, or specifying commendation. We have none for the Merovingian period. There is no charter of this nature in the formularies of Marculf nor in any of the other collections of the 6th or 7th centuries, although there is one charter of protection from Charlemagne to a priest named Arnald. We must therefore search the documents for allusions to such customs, and to see whether certain historical facts do not presuppose their existence.

We find the first fact of the kind in the records of church councils. It is the fact of individual commendation on the part of rural clerks or priests seeking patronage (*patrocinium*). There is no doubt about the fact that these individual contracts resembled those which bound laymen to the king or to a great man and that they attest to a free and voluntary subjection. The clerk who commends himself becomes thereby the faithful man, the "man" of a *possessor;* he enters his clientele, perhaps gets some land from him, or at least his protection. Although the documents do not tell us, we may assume that this *possessor* is most likely to be the great proprietor who is a neighbor of the *vicus* or lives in the *villa*. The Church condemned these practices. By laws, by anathemas, it forbade patronage over ecclesiastics. But the very frequency of its decisions proves the futility of its efforts.

One can trace the progress of patronage in the 6th and 7th centuries through the canons of the councils. The Church at first thought of combatting it by prohibiting the ordination of slaves or of enfranchised men.[1] It always feared the influence of their master: the clerk who was a *colonus* or a serf always belonged more to the lord than to the Church. The Church further forbade priests and clerks who were of free status to commend themselves. The Council of Clermont, in 535, lets us see how common such individual acts were.[2] In 538 the Council of Orleans tells of priests who go looking for the protection of the rich promising to serve them, sacrificing the duties of the ministry to the demands of patronage. In 551 the Council of Éauze excommunicated both the clerk who seeks the protection of a layman and the layman who grants it against the will of the bishop.[3] In 614 the Council of Paris forbade ecclesiastics to go to the king or to leading men (*potentiores*) or to enter into their clientele. One can say that all through the 6th century, the hierarchy fought against the efforts of the rural clergy to obtain the protection of the great.

For patronage was not mere theoretical protection: it involved duties and services and in return it assured the independence of those who asked for it. It enabled clerks to defy their bishop, to brave his censures, to join together against him, and no doubt to hold on to ecclesiastical benefices that he had granted them but wished to take back again. One sees why the Church fought against it but in the course of time had to recognize it. It claimed, itself, the king's protection for bishoprics and monasteries; it could not deny the lower clergy that of the local lord. Around 665, the Council of Bordeaux authorized priests, deacons, and ordinary clerks to put themselves under private protection, the only condition being that they obtain the consent of their bishop.[4] This decision well proves the advance of patronage. It justifies us in thinking that a great many rural priests had by then already entered the clientele of the aristocracy.

One can see how disciplinary relations were weakened by these contracts and promises and also how the internal government of parishes was upset. Not every man who commended himself pledged only his services; more often, he "commended" his land. There can be no doubt that rural clerks had also to "commend" their private property. Did they do the same with the ecclesiastical property that they held in benefice? Was the parish property placed under the protection of a lord? Certain facts seem to give us a glimpse of this transformation.

In the Wissembourg collection there is a 7th-century charter which shows a church being put under the protection of a convent.[5] As the price of its protection, the convent received half of this church and some lands. In its capacity as protector, it also nominated the priest, but it was bound to acquit the bishop of all payments due from the church. We may conclude from this document that a church could be placed under protection (sub defensione) and that this patronage assured the protector of privileges similar to those enjoyed by anyone who founded a church on his estate.

It is probable that a great many contracts of this kind were drawn up between free parishes and lords. Only in this way can we explain the secularization of parishes that begins in the 6th century. Here is a council showing us laymen who have parish property in their custody and are usurping the management of it.[6] Other documents give us more detail on this subjection of the rural church to the aristocracy. In many dioceses, great proprietors take the title of priest. They are arch-priests, just as counts and lords, in the 9th century, will be abbots of monasteries. We find it difficult, today, to understand these customs, yet they are described for us in formal documents. As of 614, a council forbade secular men to be arch-priests, and the prohibition was renewed at three synods and another council.[7] The repetition of these measures reveals how strong the new customs were. Almost everywhere, the control of rural parishes passed into the hands of the aristocracy.

Assuredly, in taking the title, the magnates did not actually exercise the functions attached to it. They left spiritual government to members of the priesthood, for they could not perform mass, administer baptism or penance, nor instruct the faithful. But they retained part of the arch-priest's jurisdiction, the part consisting in supervision of the clergy and especially in the administration of property. Thus they were able to seize the revenue from the patrimony and to get their hands on the offerings of the faithful. They may indeed have had a share in the recruiting of the rural clergy, choosing those who would serve the chapels auxiliary to the church of the *vicus*. The complaints of councils about the venality of ec-clesiastical demands seem clearly to indicate that offices were not given to the most worthy and that laymen gave these rural functions to those who would pay the most for them.

It is therefore through the habit of patronage that parishes become secularized in the 7th century. One council of about the year 614 makes this quite clear. It shows us that in choosing lay arch-priests, the clergy and the people of a *vicus* were primarily seeking protectors. A magnate who was asked to protect a parish was entrusted with its control. If we set this document beside the ancient constitutions by which the Empire had for-bidden the patronage of the *vici,* the local administrative districts, we see that social habits have not changed. But in the 7th century the *possessor* has extended his protection both over the settlement and over the parish. Thus he has in his power the whole of the little social and religious group which later, in the feudal age, will almost always form the center of a *seigneurie.*

One sees, in this way, how ecclesiastical patronage grew out of the customs of private patronage. Both lead us to recognize the same phe-nomenon: the subjection of a church either to a community or to a man. . . .

In studying the origin of patronage, we have seen that the Church made room for it in its legislation. It allowed the founder and his heirs the right of presentation; it guaranteed the church a patrimony; it re-served control of the patrimony for the bishop. But by the 7th century an-other change occurs. The rural church becomes a piece of private property (*res privata*). It is owned in the same way as land. Whether it is a simple chapel or a church where baptism is performed, it can be given away, sold, or devised by will. Contrary to the principle of Roman law which made all sacred property public property, it thus becomes individual property; it has a master.

The oldest documents attesting to this right of property are charters of donations made to abbeys or to bishoprics. Here we read that such a one gives his land with the church or basilica that he has built on it. Look at this charter of Grimo the deacon in 636. He gives the church of Verdun the place called Domo and the castrum called Teulegia with the churches that he has founded in them. In 646 Dagobert II confirms a donation made by his daughter Irmina to a convent in Trier: the gift includes Loosa and

its basilica and Aneia with a chapel. Both church and chapel are described as allodial property. Here are some other charters of the Merovingian period. In 680, Nicet and Ermintrude give the convent of Moissac
a certain number of villages and estates. Some of the vills have churches;
among them is the church of St. Saturnin, which the donors had bought.
Another charter of the year 695 refers to a lawsuit before the king. Ebbo
has given a church to the monastery of St. Denis, but his son Bottharius
claims it. . . .

*   *   *   *

. . . in the 9th and 10th century the Church again tried to stop secularization. It sought by various means to have the property of private churches
transferred to bishoprics, chapters and monasteries. Already in Hincmar's
time laymen were complaining of bishops who took their churches away
from them and arbitrarily joined them to the episcopal patrimony.[8]
We have also a few examples, under Louis the Pious, Lothaire and Charles
the Bald, of the restitution of parishes given as benefices. But it was mainly
by gift, exchange, or purchase, that a great many churches or chapels became the property of bishoprics or of abbeys. Read the charters of the
great Carolingian monasteries—Beaulieu, Conques, Cluny, St. Bertin,
Savigny, St. Pons: many of them show the faithful ceding their vill or a
portion of it, with a church. Sometimes the church alone is ceded, with its
dependent churches. If one lists all these gifts there remains no doubt that
by the end of the 10th century a large number of private churches must
have been attached to a bishopric or to a convent. It was not that the right
of property altered in nature, but the property itself changed hands. The
rural church had always a master, but in these cases its master had now a
sacred character.

These measures did not bring the results that were expected. For
one thing, it was chimerical to look for the complete subjection of the
smaller churches to the church of the *vicus,* or for the maintenance of that
order and hierarchy among the clergy which were supposed to ensure
obedience everywhere. The episcopate could not arrest the fragmentation
that was dissolving religious and political society alike; it could not prevent the closer and closer union between parish and seigneury in a social
milieu where economic and political life rested on the land and were concentrated within the narrow limits of a local jurisdiction. Again, the gifts
of churches mainly benefited convents and made the power of the great
abbeys even more formidable for the episcopate. With their chapels, their
parishes, their properties, in each diocese they became an independent
organism which sought more and more to escape the episcopal jurisdiction. One can say that in the 11th century the religious unity of the diocese
no longer exists. Instead of one great community divided into smaller ones,
all administered by the bishop and his agents, we see in the ancient frame-

work of the diocese a swarm of little isolated, fragmented groups, with the bishop's religious power over them very often nominal, intermittent, or disputed.

Through new foundations by ecclesiastical or by lay lords, the number of these private churches kept on increasing. At the end of the 10th century in every diocese a very large number of parishes belonged to a monastery, to the count, to local lords. The convent of St. Hilary owned thirteen churches in the diocese of Poitiers; St. Cyprien's had more than thirty-three. Look now at the wills by which great men—counts, viscounts, etc.—made bequests. In 961 Count Raymond of Rouergue held at least sixty churches and chapels in various dioceses of the states he ruled; the viscount of Béziers at about the same period had around twenty; Garsinde, the countess of Toulouse, made a gift of seven churches and nine chapels to the convent of St. Pons; in 981 Count Roger of Carcassonne gave five churches to St. Hilary's.[9] Such liberal gifts give one some idea of the number of churches that were in the hands of lords.

At the same time there was a parallel change: in proportion as the number of free parishes shrank, the masters' power over the private churches grew.

The rules that the Carolingians had tried to apply to religious lordship little by little disappeared, for they were impotent to maintain them. In the Church as in the State, their work was a compromise. Charlemagne had reestablished public authority, the power of the laws, the rules of government. But he had also strengthened patronage, founding on its practices a whole system of obedience. He had applied these same ideas to religious society. He had given the Church a double head: the Pope and the Emperor. He had joined the religious body to the first by strict disciplinary bonds and to the second by the personal obligations of fidelity. Bishops and abbots commended themselves to the king as to their lord. Finally, he conceived of the parish as the image of the State. In the little center, the cell of religious and economic life, he established or favored the same practices. The priest was in turn bound to his lord just as he was to his bishop; he became the "man" of the first just as he was the representative of the second; he had simultaneously to obey a master and a chief.

The Carolingians had thought to establish order and unity in religious institutions in this way, just as in civil institutions, keeping the foundations of the State itself thereby in equilibrium. But the system worked only when there were powerful enough hands to maintain it. The moment the monarchy weakened, the balance between the power of government and the power of patronage was destroyed. Patronage became all-powerful and feudalism began.

We discover the same law in the parish. Just as in the large society of the State or the Church, it worked in the little one through the en-

feebling of the regular powers, of the natural organs of government both
of royalty and of the episcopate. Here it is the lord who gradually gets
hold of the church and of its patrimony. The rural priest, selected by him,
is his "man", often his serf or someone who had commended himself to
him. Thus the episcopal power slowly receded before seigneurial power.
Whoever he might be—a clerk, a layman, a cathedral chapter or a monastery—the lord is always the master. The abstract rules of law were an
inadequate counterpoise to his wishes. In the 10th century his property
right is admitted and extended; limitations on it are obliterated. The
ancient barriers set by legislation fall and the parish becomes part of the
seigneury....

*   *   *   *   *

It is, however, likely that the secularization of the public parishes, their
absorption into the seigneury, was less complete.

Founded on an estate, endowed with lands from the estate, the private
church remained more or less part of the estate. The proprietor who endowed it had first title to it; further, the officiating clerk, whom he nominated, was his clerk. But the public parish had a different origin: its patrimony consisted of a large number of separate gifts; its clergy, still
hierarchized under the control of a dean or of an arch-priest, formed a
little community. In most little towns it passed in the end under the lordship either of the count or of the royal viscount, or of the bishop. But
these masters were at a distance, and were for that reason less demanding
and sometimes less obeyed. One can therefore see why, even in its subjection, the public parish was much better able to preserve both the relative
independence of its clergy and the integrity of its property. The lordship
over it might demand no more than formal recognition through the payment of a tax. It might entail also some of the profitable rights which
weighed so heavily on private churches—a share of the revenues, the split-
ting up of the patrimony. We do not really know. But at least the proprietor inherited public power over it, as he did over most of the private
churches. He had the *vicaria* over the priest and the church, and over the
lands or the little town around the church.[10] This *vicaria* meant jurisdiction not only over misdemeanors committed in the parish—in the church
or at its entrance—but also over the priest, even in religious suits in which
he might find himself involved. One can hardly imagine a more complete
domination of the parish by lordship.

Whatever their origin or their condition, parishes in the 11th century,
like the bishopric, have a lord. For the most part, these lords are laymen.
Through secularization, through the transformation of the benefice or of
patronage, and through their own acts of foundation, the magnates have
in their possession the majority of parishes. Like the bishoprics and the
monasteries, they are masters of a swarm of rural churches.[11] If one thinks
of the consequences of this—the church a dependency of the castle and

often, like the castle, fortified, serving as an arms depot and a place of war; the ecclesiastical patrimony dismembered, the priest submissive to his lord, having become his vassal or remained his *colonus*—one can well understand the protests of the hierarchy against such developments and the angry desire for reform in their hearts.[12]

Caught in the bonds of feudalism, this rural clergy did not really know how to be free. In their turn, attached to their church as to a farmstead or a fief, they are secularized. Not content with bearing arms, and replacing service of the altar by service to their lord, they tend, like any holder of a fief or of a tenement, towards the principle of heredity. The rural priest marries and leaves his church to his son. In this way a petty ecclesiastical feudal class takes shape in the countrysides; it acquires a place in society and holds on to it by perpetuating itself.

In this feudal Church the ancient ideas of religious equality and of community became seriously weakened. The elective principle gradually disappeared, giving place to presentation, that is, the direct nomination of the parish rector by the bishop, the convent, or the lord. However, some vestiges of the *consensus* of the inhabitants in the choice of the rector persisted, for the forms of institutions to some extent outlived the spirit which had created them. But the inner life, the spirit of liberty, was gone from these little religious groups, enmeshed as they were in the feudal net and turned by the lords into mere capital to be exploited. It was not that men's faith was weakened, but it was debased. The practice of Christianity, the consciousness of its mysteries, the idea of its universality were to be found elsewhere, in the monasteries already given over to ideas of reform. Like the bishopric, the parish had too narrow an horizon to be illumined by thought or by religious activity.

Thus the whole life of the Church came to be concentrated in a few great abbeys, which were moral and economic powers because they were free. Already a radical change was seen to be necessary. The history of the parishes shows us, better than the history of the bishoprics or of the abbeys, the facts that made this inevitable: the obligation to reform the customary behavior, to free the altar, to break the ties which bound the mass of the clergy to the feudal body. Begun by Cluny, pursued by the Papacy, reform was soon to be spread, at the end of the 11th century, to all churches. It was above all to attack laicism, and one can see what it was to take over. To ban homage by clerks and their personal subjection, to restore to the parish the use of its revenues and its tithes and in so doing to reconstitute its patrimony, to deny the lord all property right and to return to the ancient rules governing patronage—in a word, to make the parish as a religious body free, as free as the bishopric, the convent, as the Papacy itself—these were the aims, and the result, of reform decrees. Reconstituted accordingly, the parish was to see a rebirth of social and religious life. Since there were interests on the same side as doctrine, favoring a reawakening of its spirit of independence, a political reaction against lordship was soon to follow the religious reaction. In the 12th century, it was in the framework of the parish that popular communities, the origin of our modern villages and communes, were established.

NOTES

[1] At the Council of Orleans (canon 6), in 549. The Church did not however venture to decide whether ordination of itself led to enfranchisement.

[2] Canon 4.

[3] Canon 4.

[4] In the canons referred to and in canon 10 of the Council of Mâcon (583).

[5] *Traditiones Wizemburgenses*, p. 43.

[6] *Concilium Cabilonense* (639–54), canon 5.

[7] *Monumenta Germaniae Historica, Concilia aevi merovingici*, pp. 200, 205, 209, 218. It seems that these canons did not contemplate a layman being made an arch-priest without prior conversion. Canon 5 of the Council of Chalon shows that laymen did indeed occupy these positions.

[8] Migne, *Patrologia Latinae*, vol. CXXVI, p. 274.

[9] *Histoire de Languedoc*, vol. V, documents no. 111, 150, 126, 134.

[10] See documents no. 50 and 26 in the Cartulary of Conques, also canon 17 of the Council of Narbonne.

[11] In abbey churches, seigneurial justice over the church arose through immunity; in churches possessed by laymen, it came from the *vicaria*.

[12] The consent of the inhabitants was still demanded in the 9th century, and charter no. 75 in the cartulary of Conques, from the 11th century, shows the lord asking for it.

6

Paganism to Christianity in Anglo-Saxon England

WILLIAM A. CHANEY

In Anglo-Saxon as in Christian history, many roads lead to Rome. This has been correctly noted and at times overemphasized in matters ranging from Augustine to Whitby, from numismatics to law, from banners to Bede. Indeed the Roman road has been so broad and so well marked with recorded *miliaria* that we may have missed the growth-ridden Germanic by-paths which were actually trod by the tribes in England. But surely the impact of culture on cult is as important in history as the reverse, and the terms in which the newly converted Anglo-Saxons interpreted the Christian religion were shaped by the tribal culture, impregnated, as it was, by the heathenism of the old religion. Gregory the Great's famous letter to the Abbot Mellitus,[1] advising that pagan temples in England be used for the worship of the Christian God that the people "ad loca quae consuevit, familiarius concurrat," and that the sacrificial animals of heathenism be now devoted to Christian festivals, agrees with the *responsa* of the same pope to Augustine concerning the choosing of local customs best suited to the conditions of the converted.[2] In a way, this study is a scandalous footnote to that wise anthropological advice, with the intention of setting forth some of the similarities of the old and new religion which allowed a syncretic merging. Thus many features of the Conversion period which have been interpreted *post eventum* as Christian were undoubtedly seen with other—and familiar—overtones by the Woden-sprung rulers and their people.

In the first place, although the Conversion of England transpired with little violence and few dramatic stands by organized heathenism, the opposition of tradition and embedded culture can be seen as the chief

bulwarks against the triumph of the Cross. It is not merely that the new
theology was translated into terms of northern life, with "the Chief of
princes, the Ruler of all peoples" giving *mund* to his *fyrd* from his high-
seat in the wine-hall of Heaven,[3] as Christ on earth had summoned his
thanes to him.[4] This often startling imagery has frequently been commented upon, and I have no desire to do so again.

But heathenism itself continued. In Kent King Eadbald, son of the
converted Aethelberht, returned to the older faith, leading his people
ad priorem vomitum.[5] There is no evidence that it was outlawed in Kent
until A.D. 640, when King Eorcenberht, Aethelberht's grandson, "was the
first of the kings of the English who ordered by his supreme authority
that the idols in his whole realm be abandoned and destroyed."[6] In the
last surviving Kentish law code, dating from the very end of the century,
it is still necessary for King Wihtred to forbid both freemen and slaves
to make offerings to devils.[7] In the realm of the East Saxons, the three sons
of King Sabert, all of whom had remained pagan, "gave free licence to
the peeople subject to them to worship idols" after their father's death,
and, Bede tells us, the people could not be recalled to faith in Christ even
after Sabert's sons had been killed in battle against the West Saxons.[8] The
apostasy of Redwald of East Anglia, the fourth of Bede's *bretwaldas*, is
perhaps too well known to cite, with his attempt to serve both Christ
and the old gods.[9] In Wessex, the earliest law code, that of King Ine, a
contemporary of Wihtred of Kent, does not legislate against heathenism,
but, as Miss Whitelock has recently reminded us,[10] this proves nothing
about the latter's survival, since we have these laws only in Alfred's edition
of them. Mercia, of course, remained staunchly heathen at least until
Penda's death in 654.[11]

Even before the reintroduction of paganism by the Viking invasions,
the synod of Clovesho in 747 and the legatine report to Pope Hadrian in
786 give evidence of the strength of a continuing paganism.[12] The numerous references to heathen practices in Anglo-Saxon laws after the invasions—under Alfred, Edward the Elder, Athelstan, Edmund, Aethelred
the Redeless, and Cnut—as well as in canonical collections [13] stem undoubtedly largely from their reintroduction in an age when, as Pope
Formosus wrote to the bishops of the English in the 890s, "the abominable
rites of the pagans have sprouted again in your parts."[14] However much
the merging of the two strands complicates the problem of survival,[15]
the latter is well attested—perhaps especially in the Anglo-Saxon charms [16]
—and the resulting syncretism at times makes for a virtual neo-polytheism.
"Woden wrought idols; the Lord wrought the spacious skies," says a
gnomic poem.[17] That the culture of the tribes and the old religion which
helped form it in their turn shaped Christianity, which was assimilated
to them, is in its principle surprising to no historian of the Conversion
period. As a result, the societal emphases in Anglo-Saxon Christianity may

themselves be a test of the vexed problem of Anglo-Saxon paganism's similarities to the religion of early Scandinavia, that "womb of nations," as Jordanes calls it. As a matter of fact, the Sutton Hoo finds have revealed hitherto unsuspected connections between at least the East Anglian royal house and the Uppland district of Sweden.[18]

Although no Anglo-Saxon work gives us full information on pre-Christian religion in England, almost no poem from before the Norman Conquest, no matter how Christian its theme, is not steeped in it,[18] and the evidences for pagan survivals and their integration into the new faith go beyond even the literary sources. Thus, as Lethbridge reminds us, "to say, 'this is a monument erected in Christian times and therefore the symbolism on it must be Christian,' is an unrealistic approach. The rites of the older faith, now regarded as superstition, are practised all over the country today. It did not mean that people were not Christian; but that they could see a lot of sense in the old beliefs also." [20] The rites of pre-Saxon gods in England, such as Helith at Cerne Abbas and Gourmaillon at Wandlebury, survived the coming of both the Anglo-Saxons and Christianity,[21] and the Germanic precursors of the Christian God seem to have been no less vigorous. We shall examine this continuity from paganism to Christianity primarily in two areas, theology and kingship, in relation to the heavenly and earthly leaders of the *folc*.

The importance of Woden for both is proverbial. The genealogies of the royal houses of Kent, Wessex, East Anglia, Mercia, Bernicia, Deira, and Lindsey all record the descent of their kings from Woden. The kings of Essex trace their lineage from Seaxneat, a god known among the Saxons of the Continent, identified both as a son of Woden and as the god Tiw (Tyr); only the Sussex royal genealogy is not known but there is little reason to believe that it too was not Woden-sprung.[22] Divine descent was a claim of Northern royalty, including that of the Angli, before the settlement of England,[23] and its continuation along with that of the Woden-cult is to be expected among a people which continued to identify itself by its ancestry. The importance of such divine descent for Germanic kings is testified to not only by the persistence with which it was clung to even after their conversion but by the results of its loss; "scarce one of the ancient royal kindreds survives," Alcuin writes, "and by as much as their lineage is uncertain, by so much is their power enfeebled." [24] The name of Woden continued in England in the "Nine Herbs Charm" and in place-names such as Wansdyke (Woden's Dyke), but of more importance to us is the assimilation of his cult to the new religion, since the culture of Woden-sprung kings and Woden-worship did not allow the name or cult to perish. Indeed, even his animals—the wolf and the raven—apparently continue in a sacral manner.[25]

As might be expected, he was, in the first place, equated with the Christian Devil. Wansdyke, the great pre-Saxon earthwork, for example, was also known after the introduction of Christianity as the Devil's Ditch, and local tradition maintained in time that it was built by the Devil on a Wednesday—which is, of course, Woden's day.[26] The burial-mound on the Wiltshire downs known in the Anglo-Saxon Chronicle [27] as Woden's Barrow became in time called Adam's Grave, although whether this Christianization took place in our period or later is now impossible to say. Certainly many pre-Christian barrows became associated with the Devil, showing a conversion of these sites from the gods of paganism. Post-Conquest though some of these may be, others date from Saxon times, as the *Scuccan hlaew* (the Devil's barrow) of Anglo-Saxon land-charters.[28] As the gods—Woden or others—were metamorphosed into giants, barrows were named for them, evidence for which dates from Saxon times,[29] but their association with Woden is at the most tenuous.

Much more significant is the equating of Woden with Christ. In the much discussed Anglo-Saxon "Nine Herbs Charm" the Christian emendator of an originally pagan charm against poison has added that the nine herbs, whose virtues are extolled in the charm, were invented by Christ while He hung on the Cross. "They were created by the wise Lord, holy in heaven as He hung (on the cross); He set and sent them to the seven worlds, to the wretched and the fortunate, as a help to all." Then the older god appears: "These nine have power against nine poisons. A worm came crawling, it killed nothing. For Woden took nine glory-twigs, he smote then the adder that it flew apart into nine parts." [30] Othinn, the Norse Woden, had gained knowledge of runes by sacrificing himself to himself, hanging and fasting on the World-tree, according to the Icelandic poem Havamal; [31] here, as Woden-Othinn masters the magic runes of wisdom by hanging on his Cosmic Tree, so Christ creates the magic herbs as He hung on His Tree, the Cross. Many relationships are focused here: Woden and Christ as the Hanging God; Yggdrasill the World-tree and the redeeming Cross; the sacrifice of Woden to himself, as the priest that offers and the victim that is offered, with the Sacrifice of Christ, the victim and the priest; the Germanic casting of lots with twigs marked by runes, reported by Tacitus (Germania, c. 10), and the casting of lots associated with the Crucifixion; the creative act in suffering and death displayed in Woden's mastery of the runes of knowledge and Christ's creation of the herbs. Although the problem of Christian influence on the Havamal is undoubtedly insoluble, the existence of Woden's association with runes in a partially Christianized charm still known among the Christian Anglo-Saxons will perhaps lead us to van Hamel's conclusion that "if a certain similarity should exist between the popular traditions of early christianity and pagan mythology, would it not be more natural to accept a fundamental affinity than a borrowing? . . . The christian God never supplanted the pagan deities. He only proved the stronger one. This is an evolution that leaves no room for the doctrine that a myth of Othinn should have been influenced by a christian legend." [32] There is at least good reason to believe that the traditions are independent; if so, this would lead a culture saturated with Woden-worship to take up with ease the cult of the new Hanging God when the old one—literally "the old one," *thone ealdan deofol, se ealda sceocca,* as Aelfric calls the Devil [33]—proves less potent.

Furthermore, the genealogies of the Woden-sprung kings have been assimilated to Christianity. In the familiar mythical lineage of King Aethelwulf of Wessex in the Anglo-Saxon Chronicle *sub anno* 855, Woden is sixteenth in descent from "Sceaf, who is the son of Noah and was born in Noah's Ark." [34] Appropriate as it is to have generated in the Ark one who in traditions recorded by Aethelweard and William of Malmesbury had drifted as a child in a boat to his future kingdom,[35] this "arcane" transition makes the West Saxon rulers collateral relatives, as Professor Magoun has pointed out, with our Lord.[36] If I may be permitted an *excursus* into wild Wales, this has its parallel in the court-pedigree of Hywel the Good, who traced his descent from "Amalech, who was the son of Beli the Great and his mother Anna, whom they say to be the sister of the Virgin Mary, the Mother of our Lord Jesus Christ"; [37] since Anna is probably Ana or Anu, a variant of Danu, the Earth Mother, and Beli Mawr may be, but less likely, the god Belenus, our Lord would be the nephew of the Mother of the gods, and the assimilation of a royal genealogy to the new religion would indeed be analogous to the Anglo-Saxon transition.

The absorption of the other gods into Christianity can be treated more summarily. In the case of Thunor or Thor the Thunderer, we may well ask if an Anglo-Saxon warrior would react as we do to a land grant of King Edward the Elder in A.D. 901 which opens, "In the name of the High Thunderer, Creator of the world," or a generation earlier (A.D. 872) to the phrase, "by the abundant grace of God and the gratuitous gift of him who thunders and rules." [38] As late as William of Malmesbury, Athelstan the Glorious is described as being "like a thunderbolt to rebels." [39] These, I believe, would be seen by northerners less in terms of *Jupiter Tonans* or of the "sons of thunder" of Mark's gospel and more in terms of northern religion. One of the panels of the Gosforth Cross in Cumberland has recently been interpreted as Thor's fight with the Midgard Serpent, a theme probably reintroduced during the later Norse settlement, as have three fragments of crosses in Durham Cathedral as his battle with Mökkurkalfi ("Cloud Calf").[40] Neither of these identifications can be accepted with certainty, however; he is, incidentally, never mentioned in the Anglo-Saxon charms,[41] but he appears perhaps more often than any other pagan deity in place-names in England.[42]

Perhaps the most puzzling parallelisms, with virtually insoluble problems, are those between the Devil and characters of northern paganism, especially Loki, to whom I shall confine myself. This, as R. E. Woolf has suggested, is partly because the Devil, like Loki, is the archetype of "motiveless malignity," partly because as the Devil is the evil-bringer, so Loki brings evil to the gods, and partly because, in more general terms, Satan as the "faithless retainer" and "eternal exile" would be understandable to Anglo-Saxon society.[43] But the analogy goes beyond this. The bound Satan of the Caedmon manuscripts has more relationship with the bound Loki and bound gods of the pagan North than with any Biblical source, in spite of the reference in Revelation (20, 2) to the bound Satan; Loki and the otter have been suggested as an interpretation of the Ramsey carving and, even more significantly, as the bound figure on the Gosforth Cross, both of the Viking Age.[44]

Two mutilated carved stones from Leeds also show a bound figure who has been suggested as Weland the Smith because of the presence of what seem to be smith's tools at its feet, although it does not fit the known versions of the Weland story. I should suggest the bound Loki, with the smith's tools as the symbols of that god; Loki, after all, is paraphrased by the later Snorri Sturluson as "Forger of Evil" and "the Bound God," [45] and the Anglo-Saxon Guthlac describes the devils as "smiths of woe." [46] This would help to explain the puzzling presence of smith's tools on the Halton Cross from Lancashire, which, even though here probably connected either with the Sigurd or the Weland story, would have further meaning because of its presence on a Christian cross, since smith's tools are found elsewhere on scenes of the Crucifixion. These have been suggested as symbols of the tortures of Christ,[47] but I believe they are more readily explained as the triumph of Christ over the "Forger of Evil," Loki, the fettered god, and, by projection, over the bound Satan.[48] The relations of these figures to the animal-headed or bird-headed figures on the Kirklevington Cross and similar figures at the foot of a Lancaster Cross, in place of the soldiers, with its probable relationship to a group on the Franks Casket and the figure between two beasts on the purse-mount from Sutton Hoo, serve to complicate the picture with possibilities of pre-Christian ritual,[49] but the possible translation of Satan and lesser devils of Christianity into these terms remains too strong to ignore. It may simply be noted here that a devil as human form with animal characteristics—familiar to us in his horns and tail—was known to Germanic peoples before the coming of Christianity and continues in part—for example, in Aelfric's homiletic descriptions of the Devil.[50]

May I now simply list other characteristics of Anglo-Saxon paganism which were so much a part of the tribal culture and outlook that the transition to Christianity was facilitated, even though they translated the new religion into sometimes wondrous forms? The Dream of the Rood, for example, important sections of which are carved on the pre-Viking Age Ruthwell Cross (c. A.D. 700) draws almost undoubtedly in its non-Biblical portrayal of the Crucifixion upon the death of the god Baldur; here "the young hero" mounts "the marvellous tree" and is wounded by darts: "the warriors left me standing laced with blood; I was wounded unto death with darts"—certainly an exaggeration of the spear at the Crucifixion but as Baldur was in the pagan myth, when the sport of throwing darts at him turned into the cosmic tragedy of the "bleeding god." [51] Furthermore, the same poem may relate not only Baldur to Christ but Frey as well to the Christian Lord. "Frey," which has become identified with "Lord," is used for "*the* Lord": "geseah ic tha Frean mancynnes . . ." ("I saw there the Frey of mankind"); this is found in a more general sense in Beowulf, where "frea" is used seventeen times for "lord," [52] even though the goddess Freyja and her maidens nowhere appear to be "converted" into the Virgin Mary and three (or nine) Marys, as they are in the Scandinavian North.[53] The possibility of an early pagan trinity of gods in the North, based on the later evidence of Odin, Tyr, and Thor as a trinity, Odin, Thor, and Frey in Uppsala, and other trinities of Odin, Hönir, and Lodur (Loki), Odin, Wili, and We, and Har, Jafnhar, and Thrithi [54] would aid the assimilation of the Christian Trinity.

However, in the Anglo-Saxon world-view, the Son tends to be merged with the Father and appears often as the Creator. "When Christ, the God of heavenly hosts, the Father almighty, the radiant Creator, shall sit on his throne," states the poem Christ, ". . . then on the right hand of Christ Himself the pure people shall be gathered . . . and there the evil-doers shall be assigned to the left hand in the Creator's presence." Or again, in Christ and Satan, "Lo!," Eve says, "Thou, Lord wert born into the world by my daughter to aid men. Now it is manifest that Thou are God Himself, the eternal Author of all creatures." And in the Andreas, reference is made to "the immortal Son of God ye call man, Him who with hands wrought land and sea, heaven and earth, and the raging waves." But examples are numerous; [55] theological confusion reigns even more completely when the Three Persons are merged, as in the Christ: "The third leap, the bound of the heavenly King, was when He, the Father, the Comforter, was raised on the cross." [56] This is not Roman or Mediterranean in origin, but Germanic. To a people accustomed to conceiving of god or the gods as immanent in nature, this refusal to distinguish a transcendent Father from an immanent Son is perhaps not surprising. Its influence continues, as in a letter from Boniface to King Ethelbald of Mercia [57] and the dooms of Alfred the Great; [58] indeed, I should have suspected Anglo-Saxon determination in this matter in the Norman Anonymous, had not the President of the American Society of Church History removed him firmly from York to the archepiscopal palace of Rouen; [59] the Scandinavian home of the Normans, however, was also full of the creating Christ.

Parallels of Heaven and Valhöll, and of Hell and the Germanic regions of Niflhel, abound in poems as the Anglo-Saxon Judith; [60] *wyrd*, fate, becomes Christianized among the Anglo-Saxons; [61] heavenly Grace appears in Beowulf as Christianized *mana*; [62] the monsters of paganism

become absorbed into the new faith also, as Grendel turns into the seed of
Cain; [63] the possibility of a Flood story in the North independent of the
Christian importation of Noah's Flood appears,[64] as does the possible use
of the word *husel* (related to the Gothic *hunsl,* a sacrifice) before the Conversion for a sacrificial victim and after Anglo-Saxon Christianization for
the sacrifice of the Mass; [65] but perhaps the point is now clear. A violent
conversion to the new religion was unnecessary when the old provided so
many parallelisms that the tribal culture could absorb the conquering God
without disrupting many of its basic preconceptions; only in time were
these to give way before an ecclesiastical conquest.

Not only in concepts of theology but in those of rulership as well was
a syncretism between pagan culture and Christian cult possible, and it is
to this that I turn in conclusion. At the beginning it may be well to emphasize an important point; in northern paganism, not only was Woden or
Odin the god of the ruler,[66] but the ruler was the leader of the tribal cult.[67]
The king's god was the people's god, and the king as *heilerfüllt* stood between his tribe and the tribal gods, sacrificing for victory and plenty,
"making" the year. Tied into temporal and cosmic history by divine
descent, he represented and indeed *was* the "luck" of his people. It is in
this Germanic tradition that the Anglo-Saxon ruler is to be seen; "just
within the shadow at which the records of English history fail," as Jolliffe
says, "stands the sacrificial king." [68]

Consequently the conversion of the *folc* stemmed from the conversion
of the king to the more powerful deity, since it was the king's relationship
with the gods which "saved" his people as much as did the gods themselves; this royal function, when translated into Christian eschatology, was
to be part of medieval rulership throughout the Middle Ages. It is this
factor also that dominates the character of the Germanic conversion;
inasmuch as English kings were converted without violent incident, by
so much is tribal conversion without great external drama; when politico-
cultural opposition is greater, as often occurred in Scandinavia, as under
Olaf Tryggvason and Olaf the Holy, by so much is religious opposition
greater.[69] Thus, the new Christian God—"the Almighty, the Lord of great
kings," as the Anglo-Saxon Christ calls him [70]—was seen in these terms of
the god of the king, and the latter continued to "make the year." "In the
king's righteousness," wrote Alcuin to King Aethelred in A.D. 793, "is the
common weal, victory in war, mildness of the seasons, abundance of crops,
freedom from pestilence. It is for the king to atone with God for his whole
people." [71] In these Christian translations the earlier pagan "luck" of the
Anglo-Saxon king is heard in not too transposed a key. The fate of the *folc*
is related to the fate of its prince; "let us all in common urge the afore-
mentioned king to reform himself with his people," wrote Boniface to
the priest Herefrith concerning Aethelbald of Mercia, "that the whole
nation, with its prince, may not perish here and in the future life, but that,

by amending and reforming his own life, he may by his example guide his own people back to the way of salvation." [72] If the leaders do not serve God, Aelfric preaches in one of his homilies, "God will manifest to them their contempt of him either by famine or by pestilence." [73] Further, "peace and joy among the people, fruitful years, and victory over their foes" were given "by the aid of God" to King Ecgfrith and Queen Aethelthryth, rulers of Deira and Bernicia, as long as they were obedient to Bishop Wilfrid, but when the king was no longer at one with the bishop, his "luck" left him.[74] Here, of course, unlike the old religion in which there was no powerful priesthood to be equated with the Divine Will and the *principes* themselves performed priestly functions,[75] the possibility of division between two functions of the pagan Anglo-Saxon royal *persona mixta* appears, which in time will transform the Folklore Kingship of the post-Conversion period into the Liturgical Kingship of a later period. But that is another story. Suffice it here to add that apostasy from the Christian faith was regarded as bringing about the loss of kingdom and on occasion the deletion from the line of Woden-sprung monarchs who had made the proper sacrifices, in this case to the God who had conquered Woden. Thus, when Cenwealh succeeded his father, Cynegils of the West Saxons, Bede reports that he "refused to accept the faith and sacraments of the heavenly kingdom and not long after lost even the power over his earthly kingdom." When he was converted in East Anglia, however, he was restored to his realm.[76] And both Bede and the Anglo-Saxon Chronicle assign an extra year to King Oswald of Northumbria "on account of the heathen practices which had been performed by those who had reigned the one year between him and Edwin," i.e., Osric of the Deirans and Eanfrid of the Bernicians.[77] However, when Eadbald of Kent apostacized after the death of his father Aethelberht, he was not removed from the king-lists, even though his subjects followed him,[78] nor was Sighere of the East Saxons when he returned "with his part of the people" to his ancestral gods during the great plague of A.D. 664–665.[79] In both cases, however, they returned to the faith; this cannot be said, though, of Redwald of East Anglia, whose temple to the old gods, whom he worshipped along with Christ, was still remembered in Bede's day,[80] and who was still listed as a *bretwalda*. Thus, while the tribal culture was still strong enough after the Conversion to bring royal apostacy, both the old and the new religions related the fate of the kingdom to the cult of the king.

It is, consequently, not surprising that the old concept of the king as bringer of victory also continues. The Christian God, "king of victories," gave triumph to the earthly rulers who served him, as Edwin, for example, "in omen of his receiving the faith and the heavenly kingdom, received increased power also in his earthly dominion." [81] Aelfric cites Alfred, Athelstan, and Edgar as three kings victorious through the help of God,[82] and many battles are won by Christian kings "Christ aiding." [83] On the other hand, in a British source, Nennius reports that the pagan Penda of Mercia "was victorious (at Maserfelth) by diabolical agency." [84] So much is the royal person associated with victory in battle and royal devotion to God or the gods a part of maintaining the kingdom's "luck" that Sigbert, King of the East Angles, who had retired to a monastery, was forced to come forth to lead the *fyrd* into battle against Penda; however, "ipse professionis suae non immemor," he—like the priests of Anglo-Saxon paganism—refused to carry a weapon but, with only a little rod in his hand, went into battle and was slain. [85]

The frequent examples of sainthood bestowed upon kings who die violent deaths may well be regarded as a Christian substitute for the ritual king-slaying of paganism. Not only were northern kings sacrificed to get good crops, as the Ynglingar Domaldi and Olaf Tretelgia of Sweden, [86] but kings were worshipped after their death. [87] So in England kings such as Edwin and Egfrid of Northumbria and Edmund of East Anglia, who fell in battle against the heathen, Oswini of Deira, who was murdered by King Oswiu, Aethelberht of East Anglia, beheaded by Offa of Mercia, and others who died unjust and violent deaths became popular saints. [88] On the other hand, these early English king-saints were not represented in the early dedication of churches, which were predominantly Roman in character, except for a church of St. Cuthbert and St. Oswald near the spot where King Elfwald of Northumbria was murdered. [89] I suggest that the Church regarded it as dangerous to strengthen royal cults by official dedications of churches, in spite of its apparent blessing of these saints and the popular cult, since their localization might lead analogously to the local "high places" and sanctuaries of heathenism. In spite of the general adoption of Pope Gregory's advice, the ecclesiastical organization, wary of royal saints, preferred Roman dedications. The continuation of earlier attitudes toward ritual king-slaying is further evidenced, however, in the commemoration in an early eighth century Anglo-Saxon calendar of the very Osric of Deira who was excised from the king-lists of Northumbria for returning to the old gods; [90] his violent slaying by Cadwallon placed him, heathen though he was, among the commemorations of Christianized royal sacrificial victims, the saints. Here indeed we see the enshrinement in the new religion of kings "sacrificed" by violence, as we see the royal nature of mediatorship with God in the fact that most Anglo-Saxon saints belong to royal families. [91]

As pagan priest-kings staved off tribal calamity by offering *blot*—even themselves—to the gods, so Anglo-Saxon kings of the new dispensation ordered religious duties to be fulfilled by the *folc* for the same reason; King Edgar was the first to do so in his fourth code (A.D. 962–963), which was issued as a result of a pestilence which the king related to sin and the non-payment of tithes. [92] Church dues were a subject of royal *dooms* previously, although never as an equivalent for *blot* to end the anger of the Deity.

The dating of these ecclesiastical requirements is interesting. When the fourth *doom* of Ine of Wessex states that "Church dues shall be rendered at Martinmas," [93] it should be noted that St. Martin's Day was (and is) November 11th, the great feast day closest to the old Winter's Day festival of November 7th, on which the king sacrificed for a good year, and that November in pagan England was *blotmonath,* the month of sacrifice.[94] The popularity of the feast of St. John the Baptist (June 24th) is undoubtedly a continuation of the Midsummer observance of paganism.[95] Reflecting the mixed character of this dating, tithes in the second code of King Edgar are due at Pentecost, the equinox, and Martinmas.[96]

Nor do the festivals of the two religions alone relate the king to the transition from paganism to Christianity. The sacredness of the king continues in a persistent tradition of royal "divine" names, in the *character mixtus* of the English ruler, and in sanctuary connected with the king's person. Of the first, the prefix "Os-," probably signifying "divine," occurs in the names of twelve Northumbrian kings. Margaret Murray finds comfort for her theory of the Divine King in England in the fact that all but two of these died violent deaths and so are, to her, royal sacrificial victims.[97] We need not go this far, since in seventh and eighth century Northumbria, it was difficult *not* to become a royal sacrificial victim; nonetheless, the names are not without significance for the penetration of the *heilerfüllt* king of paganism into Christian times. The "Os-" prefix has also been suggested as a reminiscence of the Aesir, spirits of the North and a word applied in Icelandic to all the gods but who appear only once in Anglo-Saxon, in a charm against rheumatism, in which they are combined with elves and hags.[98] But harking back to an age when elves were larger, one may well conjecture that the syllable "Os-" rang bells in an Anglo-Saxon head that it does not in ours.

Secondly, a culture imbued with priest-kings would receive its new cult in those terms, so that the "mixed character" of the ruler would continue. It is in that light that we may see the Anglo-Saxon king speaking as a homilist, as he does in the laws, attending assemblies primarily lay, primarily clerical, and intermediate, and signing a charter at the head of the bishops and at the head of the princes.[99] The problem of the *Eigenkirche,* with the king as lay lord of monasteries, lay abbot, and perhaps even bishop (if Henry of Huntingdon is correct in describing the ninth century King Aethelwulf as Bishop of Winchester),[100] is too complicated to enter into here, but it may be regarded, I believe, as influenced by pagan background, as Stenton suggests in discussing the ownership of heathen shrines.[101]

Thirdly, the question of asylum is intimately linked with the transition from the old to the new religion in the light of tribal culture; the "peace" of certain places and the right of asylum, so common in Anglo-Saxon law, stem here not from constitutional but from sacral realms.[102] We

know from Bede's story of Coifi defiling the pagan temple that priests of
the Angli were forbidden to carry arms and that weapons were banned
from their temples, as they were in Scandinavia.[103] This priestly peace is
continued in Christian times in the same area of the North in the Law of
the Northumbrian Priests: "If a priest comes with weapons into the church,
he is to compensate for it." [104] Icelandic saga informs us that an outlaw was
not permitted by the god Frey even in the vicinity of his temple; [105] this
and the early northern notion that the area surrounding the king was
mikill grithastathr ("a place of great peace") [106] are undoubtedly based on
the premise that one who enters a sacred area becomes himself *heilerfüllt*.[107] This continues in Anglo-Saxon law, where we read in IV Aethelstan 6 that "if (a thief) seek the king, or the archbishop, or a holy church of
God, he shall have respite for nine days," [108] a royal asylum granted also in
the eleventh century laws *Be Grithe and be munde*.[109] In the latter, however, this right, which is granted also to an archbishop or a prince, can be
extended beyond the nine days—or rather nine nights here—by the king.
In yet another law, the king's peace is said to extend from his *burh*-gate
"III mila and III furlang and III aecera braede and IX fota and IX
scaeftamunda and IX berecorna." [110] Here the pagan North breaks through
even more; the length of a grain of barley as one of the measures of the
king's *grith* combines with the number nine, found also in the other two
laws of royal asylum, which is the magic number of the north, related to
fertility, magic, and royal cult.[111] And with these overtones of sacred number, fertility cults, barley and sacrifices for good crops, sanctuary and the
king's person, we must draw this to a not very Christian close.

If I plead that the break between pagan and Christian England has
been overemphasized, this thesis has, of course, been put forward in extreme form by Margaret Murray in The Divine King in England; I do not
myself detect covens of witches everywhere nor regard Charles I as a royal
sacrificial victim of the old religion. One need not go so far, however, to
see more heathenism lurking behind the manuscripts and artifacts than is
visible to the twentieth-century eye. To become an Anglo-Saxon, pagan or
Christian, is impossible, but we divorce too much, I think, Anglo-Saxon
Christianity from the culture, shaped by paganism, which formed and even
warped it. Our view of both politics and religion is consequently influenced. I do not think, for example, that one can understand King Oswald,
"the most holy and very victorious king of Northumberland," as Bede calls
him, without considering the relation of the Cross which he erected at
Rowley Water and northern pillar cult, the hand and knee as sacral objects, Germanic tree cult and its connections with Heimdall and Christ,
pillars of light above Anglo-Saxon royal saints, royal protection against
pestilence, division of the king's body after the battle of Maserfelth with
dismemberment of kings to protect their realm, the hanging of sacrifices
to Woden, King Oswald as a Bavarian and Tyrolean lord of the weather,

and the raven of Woden and Oswald as a sacral bird. If only some of these make sense, a dimension is given to the wars of Northumbria and Mercia. And if, to move from example to thesis, culture and cult are related, a dimension is added in the past-enmeshed Conversion story in the transition from paganism to Christianity in Anglo-Saxon England.

NOTES

1 Ven. Bede, *Historia Ecclesiastica*, I, 30.

2 *Ibid.*, I, 27; on the genuineness of the *responsa*, cf. Wilhelm Levison, *England and the Continent in the Eighth Century* (Oxford, 1946), p. 17, n. 1; W. J. Moore, *The Saxon Pilgrims to Rome and the Schola Saxonum* (Fribourg, Switzerland, 1937), p. 9, n. 3. M. Deanesly and P. Grosjean, "The Canterbury Edition of the Answers of Pope Gregory I to St. Augustine," *The Journal of Ecclesiastical History*, X (1959), pp. 1–49, have recently examined the arguments against the authenticity and have concluded that, within limited distinctions not touching the *responsa* cited above, "the *libellus* may be held to be Gregorian."

3 See, e.g., Christ, 514; Christ and Satan, 93, 219, 309; The Lord's Prayer II, 47–48. Line references to Anglo-Saxon poems throughout this paper are, unless otherwise stated, from *The Anglo-Saxon Records* (ed. Krapp and Dobbie; New York, 1931–1953). Cf. Jean I. Young, "Glaed waes ic gliwum——Ungloomy Aspects of Anglo-Saxon Poetry," *The Early Cultures of North-West Europe* (H. M. Chadwick Memorial Studies, ed. by Sir Cyril Fox and Bruce Dickins; Cambridge, 1950), p. 276.

4 "The mighty Lord, / The Prince of splendour, summoned His thanes, / The well-loved band, to Bethany": Christ, transl. in C. W. Kennedy, *Early English Christian Poetry* (New York, 1952), p. 98. Christ, 456–458.

5 Bede, *Hist. Eccl.*, II, 5.

6 *Ibid.*, III, 8.

7 Wihtred c. 12, 13: F. L. Attenborough, *The Laws of the Earliest English Kings* (Cambridge, 1922), p. 26; cf. p. 3 for dating of code.

8 Bede, *Hist. Eccl.*, II, 5.

9 *Ibid.*, II, 15.

10 Dorothy Whitelock, ed., *English Historical Documents* c. 500–1042 (London, 1955), p. 331. This volume has been used for many sources in this paper because of its convenience to most readers.

11 This is true even though one may hesitate to accept T. C. Lethbridge's explanation that this was probably the kingdom in which "the race of Angles remained relatively free from a large admixture of British blood"; T. C. Lethbridge, *Merlin's Island* (London, 1948), p. 129.

12 Whitelock, *op. cit.*, pp. 75, 772.

13 References are collected in F. Grendon, "The Anglo-Saxon Charms," *Journal of American Folk-Lore*, XXII (1909), pp. 140–142.

14 Whitelock, *op. cit.*, p. 820.

15 In Wulfstan's "Sermon to the English," probably preached in 1014, for example, in discussing the presence of "wizards and sorceresses" in England, he uses the word "valkyries" for the latter but apparently not in the customary Scandinavian sense of the term; *ibid.*, p. 859 and n. 1.

16 F. Grendon, *op. cit.*, pp. 123, 134; G. Storms, *Anglo-Saxon Magic* (The Hague, 1948), esp. pp. 27–48, 114–115, and, for the Christianization of the charms, pp. 115–117. Cf. the recorded forfeiture of an estate in the late tenth century because of the practice of witchcraft: Whitelock, *op. cit.*, p. 519.

17 Maxims II, 132–133.

18 F. P. Magoun, Jr., "Beowulf and King Hygelac in the Netherlands," *English*

Studies XXXV (1954), pp. 203–204; for an extensive bibliography of Swedish-East Anglian connections, cf. Prof. Magoun's review of D. Whitelock's *The Beginnings of English Society* in *Speculum*, XXVIII (1953), p. 220.

19 Cf., e.g., Friedrich Brincker, *Germanische Altertümer in dem angelsächsischen Gedichte "Judith"* (Hamburg, 1898), p. 5, where this point is insisted upon, and *passim*.

20 Lethbridge, *Gogmagog. The Buried Gods* (London, 1957), p. 136.

21 *Ibid.*, esp. pp. 23, 81–82, 159 (in which the imaginative author tells of a May 1st night spent looking in vain for still surviving rites at the head of the fertile Cerne Giant); cf. also Lethbridge, "The Anglo-Saxon Settlement in Eastern England. A Reassessment," *Dark Age Britain. Studies Presented to E. T. Leeds* (D. B. Harden, ed.; London, 1956), p. 119.

22 Whitelock, *op. cit.*, pp. 12–13, with collected references on p. 12, n. 11; for recent and useful discussions, cf. Gordon Copley, *The Conquest of Wessex in the Sixth Century* (London, 1954), pp. 38–39, 40 (references in Bede), 134 (Woden in the West Saxon king-lists); E. Philippson, *Die Genealogie der Götter in Germanischer Religion, Mythologie, und Theologie* (Urbana, Ill., 1953), pp. 34 (Seaxneat), 88, n. 152 (bibliography); K. Sisam, "Anglo-Saxon Royal Genealogies," *Proceedings of the British Academy*, XXXIX (1953), pp. 288, 293, 309–314, 323.

23 H. Munro Chadwick, *The Origin of the English Nation* (Cambridge, 1924), pp. 300–303.

24 Letter to Eanbald of York; cf. Bishop Daniel's letter to Boniface, 719–722 A.D. J. E. A. Jolliffe, *The Constitutional History of Medieval England* (New York, 1947), p. 44.

25 Brincker, *op. cit.*, p. 6; Ladislaus Mittner, *Wurd. Das Sakrale in der Altgermanischen Epik* (Bern, 1955), p. 59.

26 L. V. Grinsell, *The Ancient Burial-Mounds of England* (2nd edition; London, 1953), pp. 72, 79. For other place-names containing forms of Woden's name, cf. Bruce Dickins, "English Names and Old English Heathenism," *Essays and Studies*, XIX (1934), pp. 154–155.

27 *Sub annis* 592 and 715. In the new edition by G. N. Garmonsway, *The Anglo-Saxon Chronicle* (Everyman's Library; London, 1953), the "Christianized" form of Adam's Grave is, unfortunately, used; it is not in the Anglo-Saxon text.

28 Grinsell, *op. cit.*, p. 79, with examples of long and round barrows associated by tradition with the Devil.

29 *Ibid.*, p. 78; the twelfth-century "translation" of skeletons from barrows to monasteries and into saints' relics is well recorded: *ibid.*, pp. 80, 110.

30 Storms, *op. cit.*, p. 189, with Anglo-Saxon text on p. 188 and discussion of these lines on p. 195. For the parallel of Woden and the Latin Mercurius, who also created letters, cf. B. Dickins, *op. cit.*, p. 154.

31 Havamal 138 ff.; cf. Storms, *op. cit.*, p. 195; A. G. van Hamel, "Othinn Hanging On the Tree," *Acta Philologica Scandinavica*, VII (1932), pp. 261–262.

32 *Ibid.*, p. 262.

33 Nelius O. Halvorson, *Doctrinal Terms in Aelfric's Homilies* (Iowa City, Iowa, 1932), p. 29.

34 Thus in MSS. B and C; the Parker Chronicle omits three generations and has Hrathra born in the Ark; cf. Cisam, *op. cit.*, p. 315, on Bedwig as the ancestor in the Ark.

35 Chadwick, *op. cit.*, pp. 256–267, in which the Scyld-Sceaf traditions are analyzed, and 272–276.

36 F. P. Magoun, Jr., "King Aethelwulf's Biblical Ancestors," *Modern Language Review*, XLVI (1951), pp. 249–250. Luke iii, 36–38, is the suggested source for the Biblical names.

37 A. W. Wade-Evans, *Nennius's "History of the Britons"* (London, 1938), p. 102; N. Chadwick, ed., *Studies in Early British History* (Cambridge, 1954), pp. 132, 196.

38 Whitelock, *op. cit.*, pp. 499, 490; cf. p. 522, a grant of 977: "inspired with speech of the Thunderer." For non-Anglo-Saxon parallels of God as "the Thunderer," cf. Hibernicus exul. MGH., *Poet.*, I, p. 395, v. 10 ff., and Godeschalk, *ibid.*, p. 94, no. 7 (in which the appellation refers to Christ); H. Fichtenau, *The Carolingian Empire* (transl., P. Munz; Oxford, 1957), pp. 47–48.

39 *Ibid.*, p. 280.

40 Brian Branston, *The Lost Gods of England* (London, 1957), pp. 116–117, 120–121. However, cf. Christabel F. Fiske, "Old English Modification of Teutonic Racial Conceptions," *Studies in Language and Literature in Celebration of the 70th Birthday of James Morgan Hart* (New York, 1910), pp. 282–285, on identification of Thor with the Devil. Also, Peter Paulsen, *Axt und Kreuz bei den Nordgermanen* (Berlin, 1939), pp. 187–233, on relation of St. Olaf cult and Thor cult in the North.

41 Storms, *op. cit.*, p. 148.

42 Branston, *op. cit.*, p. 105; Dickins, *op. cit.*, pp. 155–156. For the identification of eleven of his shrines in southern and eastern England, cf. Sir Frank Stenton, "The Historical Bearing of Place-Name Studies," *Transactions of the Royal Historical Society*, XXIII (1940), pp. 1–24 and map.

43 R. E. Woolf, "The Devil in Old English Poetry," *Review of English Studies*, IV, N.S. (1953), pp. 2–4, 6.

44 H. R. Ellis Davidson, "Gods and Heroes in Stone," *The Early Cultures . . .*, pp. 132–133; this important article, pp. 123–139, has been used as the basis for the following, even though the relationships of Christian Devil, Loki, and smith have not been fully developed in it. For the Gosforth Cross, cf. Knut Berg, "The Gosforth Cross," *Journal of the Warburg and Courtauld Institutes*, XXI (1958), pp. 27–43, in which the Cross panels are interpreted as scenes of Ragnarok, the twilight of the pagan gods on three sides and the Christian rebirth and victory of the Cross on the east side; the bottom scene on the west side is interpreted as the bound Loki (p. 35).

45 Skaldskaparmal, c. 16; A. G. Brodeur, transl., *The Prose Edda by Snorri Sturluson* (New York, 1916), pp. 114–115.

46 Guthlac, 205; cf. Jean I. Young, *op. cit.*, p. 285.

47 Davidson, *op. cit.*, p. 135.

48 For the later Norse similarities between Loki and Satan, cf. E. A. Philippson, *op. cit.*, esp. pp. 48, 56, 71, 73.

49 Davidson, *op. cit.*, pp. 127–129, 136–138, where these works are discussed.

50 Halvorson, *op. cit.*, p. 30.

51 Branston, *op. cit.*, pp. 157–162; the use of *baldor*, "prince," in *Judith* relates this god to ruler-cult: Brincker, *op. cit.*, pp. 12–13.

52 Branston, *op. cit.*, p. 137. Cf. Chadwick, *Origin . . .*, pp. 243–267, on relation of Frey, Freyja, Gefion, and the possible continuation of the cult in England.

53 Birger Pering, *Heimdall* (Lund, 1941), p. 173.

54 Philippson, *op. cit.*, pp. 14–15, 19, 36, 42–52, 67–68, 73, 76.

55 Christ, 1216–1227, Christ and Satan, 439–440, Andreas, 746–750. In the convenient ed. by R. K. Gordon, *Anglo-Saxon Poetry* (Everyman's Library; London, 1926), pp. 171, 146, 214, respectively; other examples on pp. 144 (Christ and Satan, 201–204), 160 (Christ, 659–660), 206, 213, 215 (all from Andreas, 324–328, 700–703, 786–787). In the Gnomic Verses of the Cottonian MS., we find "God alone knows it, our Father the Savior": A. S. Cook and C. B. Tinker, *Select Translations From Old English Poetry* (revised edition; Boston, 1926), p. 68; cf. pp. 80, 82–83, 87, 99, 123. A. S. Cook, "King Oswy and Caedmon's Hymn," *Speculum*, II (1927), p. 71, n. 2, on reference in 7th–8th century Voyage of Bran to Christ as Creator.

56 Gordon, ed., *op. cit.*, p. 161; Christ, 726–728.

57 E. Emerton, tr., *The Letters of St. Boniface* (New York, 1940), p. 126.

58 F. Liebermann, ed., *Die Gesetze der Angelsachsen* (Halle, 1903), I, pp. 26 ff.

59 George H. Williams, *The Norman Anonymous of 1100 A.D.*, Harvard Theological Studies, XVIII (Cambridge, Mass., 1951), p. 130.

60 Brincker, *op. cit.*, pp. 10–11.

61 Mittner, *op. cit.*, esp. pp. 85–95, 99; cf. Brincker, *op. cit.*, p. 8.

62 Francis P. Magoun, Jr., "On Some Survivals of Pagan Belief in Anglo-Saxon England," *Harvard Theological Review*, XL (1947), pp. 33–46.

63 Beowulf, 102–108.

64 Branston, *op. cit.*, pp. 32, 35–37.

65 Halvorson, *op. cit.*, pp. 61–62.

66 Cf., e.g., Axel Olrik, *Nordisches Geistesleben in Heidnischer und Frühchristlicher Zeit* (Heidelberg, 1908), pp. 41, 96; Pering, *op. cit.*, pp. 116–119.

67 Hans Naumann, "Die Magische Seite des Altgermanischen Königtums und Ihr

Fortwirken in Christlicher Zeit," *Wirtschaft und Kultur. Festschrift zum 70. Geburtstag von Alfons Dopsch* (Baden bei Wien, 1938), pp. 1–12, esp. pp. 2–3. For the role of kings in the migration period and the pre-invasion development of the Anglo-Saxon kingship, cf. H. M. Chadwick, *op. cit.*, pp. 146–148, 284, 289–292, 295–303.

68 Jolliffe, *op. cit.*, p. 42.

69 Helmut de Boor, "Germanische und Christliche Religiosität," *Mitteilungen der Schlesischen Gesellschaft für Volkskunde*, XXXIII (1933), pp. 26–51; F. W. Buckler, "Barbarian and Greek—and Church History," *Church History*, XI (1942), p. 22.

70 Christ, 941–942; Gordon, ed., *op. cit.*, p. 166. God is often described as a king; cf. p. 316: "Then the Ruler of heaven radiant as the sun shall sit on the high throne glorified with his crown" (from Doomsday).

71 Quoted in Jolliffe, *op. cit.*, p. 43.

72 Whitelock, *op. cit.*, p. 757.

73 *Ibid.*, p. 853; cf. pp. 783 (letter of Alcuin to Offa of Mercia), 784 (letter of Alcuin to Eardwulf of Northumbria).

74 Eddius Stephanus, *Life of Bishop Wilfrid*, c. 19 in *ibid.*, p. 694.

75 Naumann, *op. cit.*, pp. 7–9.

76 Bede, *Hist. Eccl.*, III, 7. Later also, when his kingdom lacked a bishop, "he understood that a province forsaken by its prelate was rightfully forsaken also by divine help."

77 Anglo-Saxon Chronicle *sub anno* 634 (MS. E); Bede, *Hist. Eccl.*, III, 1, which adds that the British King Cadwallon slew them both without delay *iusta ultione*. Peter Hunter Blair, "The Moore Memoranda on Northumbrian History," *The Early Cultures . . .*, pp. 248–249, discusses this and suggests Anglo-Saxon familiarity with the Roman custom of *damnatio memoriae*.

78 Bede, *Hist. Eccl.*, II, 5; A.-S. Chronicle *sub anno* 616.

79 Bede, *Hist. Eccl.*, III, 30.

80 *Ibid.*, II, 15.

81 *Ibid.*, II, 9.

82 From *Judges*; Whitelock, *op. cit.*, p. 854.

83 E.g., A.-S. Chronicle *sub anno* 937 at Brunanburh; at Ashdown in 871 A.D. Aethelred remained praying at Mass—occupying himself with *blot*—and refusing to leave for the battle until worship was concluded, and "the faith of the Christian king availed him much with God": Florence of Worcester, *Chronicon ex Chronicis* (Rolls Series), I, p. 83.

84 Wade-Evans, *op. cit.*, p. 83.

85 Bede, *Hist. Eccl.* III, 18.

86 Ynglingasaga, c. 18 and 47; H. M. Chadwick, *op. cit.*, pp. 236, 301–302; Andrew Rugg-Gunn, *Osiris and Odin. The Origin of Kingship* (London, 1940), pp. 116–117; Vigfusson and Powell, eds., *Corpus Poeticum Boreale* (Oxford, 1883), I, pp. 409–410.

87 Vigfusson and Powell, *op. cit.*, I, pp. 414–415; H. M. Chadwick, *op. cit.*, p. 301.

88 A.-S. Chronicle *sub anno* 633; Bede, *Hist. Eccl.*, IV, 26; A.-S. Chronicle *sub annis* 870, 650–651, and 792 (794), respectively. H. A. Wilson, ed., *The Calendar of St. Willibrord from MS. Paris. Lat. 10837* (Henry Bradshaw Society, LV; London, 1918), dating from the first quarter of the eighth century, commemorates Edwin, Egfrid, and Oswini, besides Oswald; cf. introd., p. xxii. Another early eighth century calendar, in P. Romuald Bauerreiss, "Ein angelsächsisches Kalendarfragment des bayrischen Hauptstaatsarchivs in München," *Studien und Mitteilungen zur Geschichte des Benediktinerordens und Seiner Zweige*, LI (1933), p. 179, commemorates Egfrid and King Osric of Deira, the latter remarkable in view of his excision from the king-lists as an apostate, slain by Cadwallon. Whitelock, *op. cit.*, p. 31, believes the early cult of St. Edmund of East Anglia "is understandable only on the assumption that something other than his death in battle took place"; in the light of the evidence concerning Egfrid, Osric, *et al.*, and the entire concept of the "sacrificed" king, I see no difficulty in this cult.

89 Levison, *op. cit.*, p. 36.

90 See above, n. 88.

91 F. Liebermann, *Die Heiligen Englands* (Hanover, 1889), *passim*.

92 A. J. Robertson, *The Laws of the Kings of England from Edmund to Henry I* (Cambridge, 1925), p. 29.

93 Attenborough, *op. cit.*, p. 37; in the Welsh laws of Hywel Dda, "every freeman between the feast of All Saints and the feast of St. Martin"—i.e., between November 1st

and November 11th—"is to pay the lord what he is bound to pay": Melville Richards, *The Laws of Hywel Dda* (Liverpool, 1954), pp. 84, 136.

94 On the three annual great festivals of Scandinavia, cf. H. M. Chadwick, *op. cit.*, pp. 227–228, 248, and on November as sacrificial month in England, p. 228; Joliffe, *op. cit.*, p. 42: "The three high feasts of English heathendom were Winter's Day (November 7), Midwinter's Day (December 25), and Summer's Day (May 7). . . . These, in the pagan North, were the great ceremonial feasts when the king sacrificed for the people, on Winter's Day for a good year, at Midwinter for good crops, and on Summer's Day for victory in battle." Cf. Vigfusson and Powell, *op. cit.*, I, pp. 404–405, 414. Cf. Storms, *op. cit.*, pp. 9, 90, on the blessing of herbs in Anglo-Saxon England at three Masses on Midwinter's Day.

95 Storms, *op. cit.*, p. 9; one only wishes one could know whether the former custom of visiting Silbury Hill Wilshire, the largest artificial mound in Europe, on Palm Sunday and feasting there extended back into Saxon times, if in other forms; Grinsell, *op. cit.*, p. 81.

96 Robertson, *op. cit.*, p. 21.

97 Margaret Murray, *The Divine King in England* (London, 1954), pp. 45–46, 218.

98 Storms, *op. cit.*, pp. 50, 142–143, 147; the northern smith also makes his appearance in this charm: pp. 140–141, 146–147 (in which he is related to Weland the Smith). K. Helm, *Altgermanische Religionsgeschichte* (Heidelberg, 1913), p. 217.

99 F. Liebermann, *The National Assembly in the Anglo-Saxon Period* (Halle, 1913), p. 17; the charter is Birch 201 B.

100 T. Arnold, ed., *History of the English*, by Henry, Archdeacon of Huntington (Rolls Series, LXXIV), p. 141; Corvoc was king and bishop of Ireland: J. W. Ab Ithel, ed., *Brut Y Tywysogion* (Rolls Series, XVII), p. 19.

101 F. M. Stenton, *Anglo-Saxon England* (2nd edition; Oxford, 1947), pp. 101–102, 538–539; H. Boehmer, "Das Eigenkirchentum in England," *Texte und Forschungen zur Englischen Kulturgeschichte* (Halle, 1921), esp. pp. 338–339; Whitelock, *op. cit.*, pp. 77, 83, 543, 719, 741–743, 764–765, 839, 852, and on Eadberht Praen, a priest who was made king in Kent, pp. 27, 794; cf. p. 246, on King Osred tonsured at York and deposed.

102 Ortwin Henssler, *Formen des Asylrechts und ihre Verbreitung bei den Germanen* (Frankfurt-am-Main, 1954), pp. 54–55.

103 Bede, *Hist. Eccl.*, II, 13; cf. H. M. Chadwick, *op. cit.*, pp. 302–303; Henssler, *op. cit.*, p. 74; Vigfusson and Powell, *op. cit.*, I, p. 407.

104 Whitelock, *op. cit.*, p. 437.

105 Bertha Phillpotts, "Germanic Heathenism," *Cambridge Mediaeval History* (New York, 1913), II, p. 493.

106 H. M. Chadwick, *op. cit.*, pp. 302–303.

107 Henssler, *op. cit.*, pp. 71–73.

108 Attenborough, *op. cit.*, p. 149.

109 Liebermann, *Die Gesetze* . . . , I, p. 470.

110 From Pax, dating c. 910–c. 1060 A.D., in Liebermann, *Dei Gesetze* . . . , I, p. 390 (with Latin text of Quadripartitus, p. 391). For *scaeftamunda*, the origin of which is unclear but which was apparently a measure of about six inches, cf. J. Bosworth and T. Toller, *An Anglo-Saxon Dictionary* (Oxford, 1898), p. 821.

111 This complicated problem, which is related both to the "Nine Herbs Charm," above, and more largely to the whole problem of the "king's number," is treated in my "Aethelberht's Code and the King's Number," *American Journal of Legal History*, VI (1962), pp. 151–177. For the ecclesiastical "mile" of asylum at Ripon and Beverley, connected with King Aethelstan, cf. Whitelock, *op. cit.*, p. 42. Edward the Confessor's shrine granted asylum to a thief even before the king was canonized, but then the Confessor was *heilerfüllt* almost at birth, since he was presented on the altar at Ely by his parents while still in his cradle; cf. F. E. Harmer, *Anglo-Saxon Writs* (Manchester, 1952), pp. 13, n. 2, 222. Indeed, the holiness of throne and altar is reflected in the word "gifstol," which is also related to asylum; cf. my "Grendel and the *Gifstol*: A Legal View of Monsters," *PMLA*, LXXVII (1962), pp. 513–520.

Social Gradations and
Social Mobility

7

On Social Mobility in Medieval Society: Service, Freedom, and Freedom of Movement as Means of Social Ascent

KARL BOSL

I

In spite of the habit of contrasting medieval society with modern by labelling it static, the fact remains that a static society—one in which although conditions alter, ways of thought stay always the same—is an illusion. We shall be nearer the truth if we assume a certain amount of change to be normal, even though in some periods there may not be adequate written record of the movement of thought. Archeology and ethnology now offer a wealth of objective historical evidence that change occurs in the outlook of primitive societies. One has only to recall the orientation of graves, in the 8th century A.D., and the cessation of offerings to the dead in them. If we see how the doctrine of a spirit of the age can distort and over-simplify history, if our concern as historians is not just with ideal types of mankind but takes account of anthropology and of sociological interpretation, then we find it perfectly natural that there should be socially mobile men in the early middle ages and that medieval man and his groupings should be shifting, socially speaking, both horizontally and vertically.

It is not just a matter of migration from one place to another, from one region or lordship or people to another. This in itself does not alter social status; it shows only that traditional groups tolerated some differences in thought and behavior. But besides this there is upward and downward mobility between groups and classes within the same society. A consequence of this is skepticism and doubt as to the received view of the world, a state of mind which finds its most forceful expression during the 11th and 12th centuries in the transition from mythological-symbolical thought to dualism—in scholastic philosophy, in politics, in the whole style of life. For in societies without much vertical mobility the members of different groups—peasants, artisans, long-distance traders, nobles and clergy—experience the world very differently. But in any society, social circulation tends to dissolve closed castes and classes or at least to make their bounds fluctuate.

Romantic historical thought, which saw the past as the Paradise it longed for, a confirmation of its ideologies, and sought thereby a kind of self-understanding, was able to represent the middle ages with its doctrine of orders as the ideally stable society, the division into upper and lower classes being grounded in authority and in the social prestige of upper-class activities. A certain school of intellectual history, too, took a similar view, by accepting treatises that give the ideas of an organized group of intellectuals as statements of historical reality or as authentic clues to it. Research is still too backward for us to be able to say exactly when, in the process of democratization, the existence and activities and thought of the lower classes, or agitation among them, came to be considered important enough to have any influence on the policies and behavior of the ruling classes. A phenomenon like the mass influence of preachers such as Berthold of Regensburg or David of Augsburg, in the 13th century, has not yet been studied from this point of view. Raising sociological questions, our essay tries to find historical answers based on the sources and backed by examples, and thus to clear the way for more detailed knowledge.

Social ascent can be planned and controlled from above, implementing the desires and designs of those in power. In all ages, service to the State and to men of power has raised some individuals and enabled them to share in the social prestige that attaches to power. A strongly organized group that is determined to achieve power, prestige, and a higher position, may also plan its own ascent. But the leaders of the upward movement will then have to be distinguished from the rank and file. The former will forge ahead of their fellows and may even join the ruling class; the rank and file will acquire only such influence and regard as accrues to them collectively. Ascent from below through the initiative or leadership of individuals occurs only in a society where there is already strong vertical and horizontal mobility; we find it increasing from the late middle ages, and examples can be found in the earlier centuries. However, in a slow-moving agrarian world where social life is localized, the initiative in movements of ascent comes from above; it operates in such a way that service leads always to freedom. Freedom will then become hereditary though perhaps only as freedom of movement or only as a privilege. Freedom of movement may lead to the formation of a special hereditary group; this will not, however, be an elite but will be differentiated from other groups only as a broad class. Trends in early and high medieval society will be treated here from this point of view. There will be an attempt also to show why medieval society, in which favor and grace come by fulfillment of service, nevertheless displays such unexpected boldness in the challenging of law, of lordship, and of power. The themes of our enquiry into the social mobility of the middle ages are service, freedom, and freedom of movement.

II

Service, especially military service and high administrative service involving responsibility for carrying out far-reaching policies, and in the employ of a great and powerful ruler, elevates not only individuals but all who are connected with them. It binds them into a social group; they not only achieve special importance, it is ascribed to them. This seems to me to be a characteristic not only of Germanic history but in some form or other of all societies and cultures. But since we find service creating groups in the early middle ages in three ways: (1) among service nobility in the form of high vassalage, (2) among the king's freemen and other free, (3) among retainers and administrative servants, this group developing in the high middle ages as the *ministeriales,* we clearly have every right to suspect that the various Germanic peoples held service in unusually high regard. If philology is a guide, we can go on to say that this is a trait deeply embedded in Celtic-Germanic tradition.

H. Kuhn has in my opinion produced good reasons for not defining the nature and significance of *Gefolgschaft* (followership, best known as the institution of military companion-followers) in terms of the conditions of one age alone. I agree with W. Schlesinger that this was a prime social institution of the Germans, and that it evolved and was flexible: there must have been mixed types in which there were some features of vassalage. The idealized literary picture we have in Tacitus fails to reveal this. I agree also with Kuhn that in addition to *Gefolgschaft* the Germans have *Gesinde*—other followers including administrative and court officials, army soldiers and nobles in the royal service; these have a status very close to that of members of the *Gefolgschaft*. Some of the *Gesinde* stand out as being on daily duty as retainers at court, the center of lordship. These are recruited from men who owe service either as serfs or as settlers on the lord's land or as unfree vassals, yet their duties are honorable and are highly regarded. Army soldiers include groups that were summoned for particular enterprises and groups that assembled of their own accord; from the 9th century on, the latter was probably the method by which most of the Viking fleets and armies were raised. Army soldiers and other *Gesinde* may rise either into the *Gefolgschaft* or into the position of court retainer. Nobles in the royal service have a high position of their own. Already in the earliest historical times we find the beginnings of a hierarchy of service.

The position of the *Gesinde* is based, in the widest sense of the term, on obedience: menial servants, for example, have no freedom. In contrast, *Gefolgschaft* rests primarily on freedom, and on fidelity. Seemingly the latter does not require an oath; the oath may have come into general use only through Christianity. Nor need the companions in *Gefolgschaft* be of the same tribe as their leader. This is clear from the work that R. Wenskus has done on tribal origins, and as the general result of replacing romantic racial ideology by sober and critical scrutiny of the problem through the magnifying glass of research. The unilateral oath that comes to be associated with the exercise of freedom could in my opinion only have arisen in the context of a strong and enduring relationship of service. In the long run, peace and fixed residence were not a favorable soil for free *Gefolgschaft,* for the leader's position was always endangered by peace. The free companion never wants peace; quick to take offense, he will turn peace into an occasion for seeking vengeance. Consequently in time of peace the lord relies on retainers and vassals, whose duties are clearly defined. Since Christianity won over the lords' courts first, before it reached the huts of the peasants, it sought first to reinforce the ethics of service and fidelity through its conception of every man as a servant of God.

Among the Lombards and the Franks the *gasindus* or *gasindius* is a vassal or a man in a similar position, both being on the road to a nobility of service. They are in the service of the king or of some other lord, though not residing at his court; and they themselves have men of their own as vassals. The Frankish *gasindi* and the royal *antrustiones* are alike to be regarded as magnates; so is the English thane, who through being a vassal, an administrative officer or a warrior rose from lowly status to the royal court and became noble.

From the Carolingian age on there was a greater stress, in vassalage and feudal ties, on fidelity; no one denies this. The accepted doctrine, which I myself long held, saw the vassal's fidelity as an extension and heightening of the loyalty inherent in the Germanic *Gefolgschaft*. But Kuhn now rejects the idea that *Gefolgschaft* made any contribution to this ethical strengthening of vassalage. He sees the heart of vassalage as resting—again, this is not contested—in the idea of service, in the formal act of submission through commendation, homage, *hominium* (the act of becoming a lord's man). This was a surrender of personal freedom, redefining a man's position in society. The point to be emphasized now is the obligation to swear fidelity: one who commends himself becomes his lord's man, which means that he belongs to him almost as a serf does.

The free companion's oath could serve the purpose in the case of powerful men only if it were somehow interpreted as conceding a merely symbolic submission, which would be tolerable for them. In that case, despite earlier views, we must conclude that two kinds of motivation, two forms, came together in medieval vassalage: service with full obedience as the Celts and Germans knew it, and the mentality of the *Gefolgschaft*. The latter was effectively adapted only through a strong religious oath which bound the follower not to raise his hand against the power and authority of his closest lord. Commendation is fundamentally incompatible with the spirit of the free Germanic follower's oath.

There is also serious ground for believing that both kinds of oath become so rigidly formal in the 8th century as to make it inconceivable that they could have inspired a free and elevated relationship. I confess that it seems more to the point to derive them both from a common Celtic-Germanic origin, identifying the oldest form of vassalage with service and obedience. All that remains is to acknowledge the profound influence of Christian conceptions of fidelity and service. This seems relevant enough, for it was the kingship that raised vassalage to aristocratic dignity, that same kingship which from the time of the alliance between Pepin and the Roman Church so greatly heightened its own status and capacity for leadership through Christian teaching on office, on God's grace, and on related ideas. Besides, it was Isidore of Seville, himself half a Goth, who first gave the Germanic world a clear-cut formulation of Christian thought on office, service, and lordship. It was he, too, according to H. Beumann, who first gave written expression to German thinking on nationality. In my view, however, it is W. Ebel who has made the most vital contribution to the issue, in demonstrating that German and feudal ideas on inheritance and property are in basic opposition: from this he infers the entry of Christian ideas into feudal thought.

Kuhn does not deny that vassalage had a Germanic root. He sees this, however, not in *Gefolgschaft* but in the older groups of vassals who in earlier times performed most of the military and higher-status service for men of middle and upper rank, for the magnates, and above all for the kings. He identifies the Germanic precursors of the later vassals with the retainers whose duties lay originally in the household and on the landed estate. W. Schlesinger's research has shown how important these were for future development: we are here at the origins of all lordship and all society. The service of princes has always ennobled even menial servants, only customary servile labor being not so honored. Even Christianity, in the middle ages, fails to raise regard for this, for Christianity has to accept the feudal order with its ranking of laborers and peasants as unfree and half-free. The economic support of noble households must have required that great numbers remain at these levels, and archeological finds of the 7th century suggest that their number was increasing. From this point of view we can see that the free peasant, the man who is legally, socially, and economically free, working his own farm independently, is the great enigma of early medieval social history. To put the matter plainly, we can't find him; we can't fit him into an age whose character seems to render him superfluous.

The word "man", which comes to be applied both to noble vassals and to retainers, and later also to peasant holders of land, and which in the modern term "man-power" signifies the economic unit with which the sovereign state has to deal, goes back to the late Latin concept, *homo*. Among the Anglo-Saxons around 700 A.D. *mann* referred to slaves, around 900 to free vassals or to men in the service of a lord. Except in the vassal's commendation, the ceremonial placing of the hands in the lord's hands is a sign of submission, or surrender of armed resistance, and leads to servitude. The Anglo-Saxon term "thane" corresponds to the late-Latin and early medieval *puer* (boy), especially to the Merovingian *puer regis* (king's boy); it rises in status as high administrative functions pass from the king's hands to the group of high service nobility. The word *baro*, perhaps of Celtic origin, undergoes a similar promotion: originally it must have signified a rustic boor, but already in the Merovingian *sakebaro* it refers to high royal officials. I confess to finding the history of these words, revealing as it does the ascent of "the man" through socially elevating royal service, most impressive: philological findings as to changes of meaning prove the progress of upgrading through service. Although H. Dannenbauer disagrees, I hope to show that this is true of the majority of medieval nobles, for vassalage and feudal ties in general. In that way we shall explain *one* element of feudal society. In its heyday, when it combined service with rights to lordship over land and people and with participation in political life and in the decisions of the supreme royal power, naturally it shows a very different face. So we may coin a paradox, that lordship created freedom, and not only for the group that rose to noble status.

However, when we look at the early medieval nobility as a whole, there still remains a problem. Who are the Merovingian nobility of blood? How did this group arise? What was the basis of its power? It cannot have been created through *Gefolgschaft*, for a noble status derived from blood would have preceded the contractual arrangement through which nobility was bestowed on entering the band. There are two possible explanations. Nobility of blood could have arisen, especially among tribes on the move, from military kingship, smaller kings becoming partially subordinate to greater ones; there would also have been groups and lineages of leaders. On the other hand, among people who had long led a sedentary life, we may think of nobility of blood as stemming from what G. Necker styles the great peasantry of early times, the *Odalbauern*. If I interpret H. Jankuhn correctly, archeological evidence of these is to be seen in the graves found along the shores of the North Sea and along the northern reaches of the Elbe; the problem cannot be carried any further here. If this original nobility refrained from service, as indeed Tacitus indicates in chapters 13 and 14 of the *Germania,* then service must have been the determining factor in the rise of the Frankish nobility and of the majority of the nobles we meet in the sources, with the exception of Saxons. And it must have been service of the kinds we can identify, for retainers, in the clearer light of the sources of the 10th and 11th centuries.

It is in keeping with the archaic bent of medieval German social history that a new formation of service nobility should occur at the start of the high middle ages, that is, in the wave of crises in the 11th century. New social forces are then at work, new styles of life and thought prevail. That trend towards rationality, which Max Weber took to be the underlying characteristic of European history and development, seen as a whole, then becomes visible.

* * * * *

The fact that there is a probability of Celtic influence on the *Gefolgschaft* in southern Germany, and a possibility also of some Roman influence, calls for a reversal of commonly accepted opinion. Kuhn views the Celtic organization of retainers and vassals (*devoti* and *solduri*) in the first centuries before and after Christ as providing the initial impulse for, and as prefiguring, the central forms of political and social life so long believed to be distinctively German. He recognizes, the Czech medievalist Frantisek Graus agrees, and I myself, that the distinctive German contribution to *Gefolgschaft* is not fidelity but freedom. At this point I confess that it was never clear to me why vassalage and feudalism should have played no part in the formation of the German state while in England and France they were assimilated into the law of the state and helped to create the national monarchies.

* * * * *

If freedom, rather than fidelity, is recognized as the German contribution to vassalage, then we have a ready historical explanation for the divergence of social development in Germany and France from the 10th century. Wherever fidelity is associated primarily with the oath of service and the idea of service is not only Christian but already an ancient Celtic idea, then when the duty of obedience takes on new life through primary allegiance to the liege lord, as it does on Frankish soil from the 10th century, there, in spite of social anarchy, it will become the back-bone of feudalism. In Germany, on the other hand, the old German idea of service, which is so close to freedom and has had centuries of expression among the aristocracy and in independent lordship under the shelter of the monarchy, experiences a revival, in the swell of the high middle ages, in the new administrative class of the *ministeriales.* In the end this leads again to freedom and to lordship, much as the antrustionate had, and noble vassalage.

My last remark on this area of our social development is related to the retention, in Germany, of so many separate legal statuses for different ranks of people. My explanation is simply that France—the old Celtic and Gallo-Roman Gaul—through social mobility and the evolution of social ideas developed constructive institutions which set it a full century ahead of Germany, which remained heavily static. The process extended even to the lower classes. France begins to assimilate groups that were anciently separate into a general peasant class, by the 10th century. The old group of the king's free were retained no later than that; they became known as the people of God's house. In Germany, however, these differentiations at the lower levels live on to a much greater extent, hindering the formation of a broad peasant lower class with a common social and legal character. Here, too, Germany remains at an archaic stage.

I am not implying that Germany was backward: no serious historian would make such an assertion. Politically, Germany is the leading power of the 10th century, but it throws its whole strength into political tasks that are European in scope. In my opinion, Germany's greatest contribution to the universal history and culture of Europe perhaps lies in the hegemonial Ottonian kingship and its role in the shaping and stabilizing of Europe. Behind the mighty German shield, France safely survives social and political anarchy under its feeble monarchy, generating and maturing new and progressive social and spiritual ideas.

It seems also that a different conception of service was responsible for the diversity of development in the two countries. In France, besides the greater social mobility, it may have been the more profound and mature grasp of Christian ideas of service, office, and the oath, that led to the revitalizing of vassalage through liege homage; this enabled the duty of obedience to emerge again, in the interests of all. In Germany, however, the new formation of the *ministeriales* is only a duplication of a precedent which had been revived there time and again over a thousand years, whenever conditions favored the peaceful civil functions of what today we call the state. Here we are perhaps touching on a very ancient artery of German life, a phenomenon at the very root of Teutonic social and political evolution and of the people's psychology.

A thousand years after the Germanic migrations, the Anglo-Saxon *Gefolgschaft* evoked, in the region of England known as the Danelaw, a Norse imitation which flourished in the Viking world from 1015 to 1066. In the western part of the continent vassals had been accepted as followers since about 500 A.D.; in France, as also among Anglo-Saxons coming from the northern mainland, their status derives from Celtic vassalage. The dominating position of these vassals at court in peace and in war cradled a new nobility, which attained its highest functions in the leadership group that G. Tellenbach calls the imperial aristocracy. The empire of conquest that was newly strengthened in the 8th century and was to be enlarged by further expansion, offered political opportunity for such ascent. The mode of life of these vassals made for social integration among people with similar duties and functions. Out of this there grew an image of the ideal man of the time which was still binding on its later heirs, the *ministeriales*. These vassals had forerunners in the retainers and servants who were in an analogous position before 500 A.D.; the position was openly modelled on the older Celtic pattern of the time, for Celts were still independent. The final Celtic form of our loan-word, *Eid* (oath), which derives from the Celtic *oitos,* must come from this period. Of course this does not exclude the possibility of a genuinely German retainership. It is certain that the retainership that preceded *Gefolgschaft* was tightly contained within the society and community of the household (*hiwisk*), and certain also that it involved only slight social divisions. But in *Gefolgschaft,* which according to Kuhn was at its height in the first five centuries A.D., army and warriors become distinct from the *Gesinde;* graded groupings are differentiated. The free *Gefolgschaft* was therefore a transitional form between patriarchal society and late ancient and medieval forms of society.

Since F. Genzmer's devastating attack on the clan (*Sippe*), that showpiece of German legal and social history, there has been a skeptical reaction against racial explanations. In this mood H. Kuhn has naturally sought to detach *Gefolgschaft* from Germanic hinges. In pointing to Germanic-Celtic vassals, in the older sense of that term, and to retainers, he is obviously right.

In the Frankish period before 800 we can observe three stages of vassalage, from that of simple poor freemen (as shown in the Tours formulary, number 48) to that of the poorer free *vassi* in the palace, to the higher vassalage of the powerful *vassi* as they appear in the Lorsch annals in 802. This evolution also enables us to view the context in which *Gefolgschaft,* too, may have arisen. For alongside the various social grades of *vassi* are people who had quite recently come to be called by a new name, "the king's free". They are bound to the soil but being allowed to occupy a farm they are better able to perform military service than humbler groups. But they cannot rise to the nobility nor become *ministeriales,* as Dannenbauer thinks. Among the East and West Franks they must have been very numerous. It is a fair inference that Merovingian times saw not only vassalage, but some development of forms prefiguring the retainership of the high middle ages: indeed, the research that led up to my work on the imperial *ministeriales* under the Salian and Hohenstaufen dynasties proved this to be the case. All this seems to me to indicate that the *Gesinde*—retainers, household officials, and army groups—played a significant role not only alongside the *Gefolgschaft* but before this arose and after its decay. The highest level to which any of the *Gesinde* attained seems to have been that of nobility in the royal service.

If the early history of the oath can be restudied in relation to religious history, we shall be better able to judge whether the oath of fidelity arose with *Gefolgschaft* or with the more ancient retainership, and to tell how far it is Christian. Kuhn's notion that the guiding principle of *Gefolgschaft* is freedom, is new; if it is correct, then *Gefolgschaft* did not in any way alter the structure of the nobility as a ruling class, for leader and followers were equal, by birth. Again, *Gefolgschaft* depleted the ranks of the nobility through warfare, just as the service of nobles did, and the exercise of lordship, Genealogical research has taken too little note of this. It is however safe to say that the ministerial service of the high middle ages, the importance of which is crucial to this first part of our argument, stands in a social, ethical, and spiritual perspective, associated throughout with state-like centers of power, which runs back into the Celtic-Germanic pre-Christian era.

* * * * *

III

Turning now to the theme of freedom, let us look at the people who are known as the king's free. Why are they singled out as free? What does the term mean, in the middle ages?

* * * * *

As to the ancient nobility of blood, despite R. Sprandel's work we still know very little about it. We cannot say definitely whether it arose from a free or from an unfree status. Its freedom is however different from that of the free companions in *Gefolgschaft*. Among the settled peoples no one was really free in early historical times except the great peasantry, whose power resembled that of nobles. . . .

In South German sources of the 8th century we meet lists of people who had given land to churches, and of witnesses to such gifts. Among the donors there are many counts, who in the 8th century are occasionally described as *nobiles* and in 9th-century sources are usually so described. The Bavarian law, which was compiled in the 8th century, speaks of powerful men (*potentes*) who resist the count's authority, the duke then intervening with military force. The capitulary of the *missi* in 802 and the annals of Lorsch tell us that Charlemagne replaced the small vassals whom he had sent out as *missi* by great vassals because the small men had been bribed and intimidated by powerful men. Who were these? They were not the leading aristocracy of the realm. Either they were an ancient nobility of blood, or, as can be proved for the royal provinces in the central Frankish lands in the 8th century, they were an anciently rooted provincial nobility of Frankish origin. According to the capitulary of the *missi,* when they are judges the powerful men oppress "the poor free men who owe army service". They also oppose the king's interest and his whole lordship.

The Bavarian law does not recognize any special noble status at this time. But it gives the genealogies of five families standing close to the duke. These families are believed to be those of petty kings or chiefs of Bavarian administrative districts (*gau*). They might also be described as service nobility of the Frankish empire, especially since the Agilolfing dukes were not Bavarians. . . .

J. Sturm has shown from the Freisinger traditions that from about 450 there was a circle of fairly large landholders whose names (or those of their ancestors) appear in place-names ending in *-ing*. A great many counts, bishops and abbots came from these families. These same people are listed among groups of freemen named in the Bavarian law. In the earlier sources the landowners who make gifts never seem to be named as freemen (*liberi*).

Again, the freemen named in the Bavarian law are apparently in a status very close to that of serfs and freedmen (*mancipia*). When the law fixes a penalty for the freeman or the serf who does servile work on Sunday, the freeman in question is not the landed man who gives his name to a settlement, who is one of a group of relatives wearing the dignity of count, who builds churches, has his own priest, and is able to give away large amounts of property. A man of this kind cuts no hay on Sunday, because he does no servile work on any day. It is not he who is liable to the shameful punishment of two strokes on the back or to forfeiture of a third of his possessions or, in case of repeated offence, to forfeiture of his "liberty". It is inconceivable for men who rank with counts to be named in the same phrase as serfs, who are liable to penal amputation of the right hand.

When we read that the penalty for murdering a freeman is 160 shillings, to be paid, in the event that the victim has no relatives, either to the duke or to that person to whom the freeman had given himself, we naturally think not of a noble but of a duke's freeman who has put himself under a lord, probably a church. The Bavarian duke's free is the brother, as it were, of the Frankish king's free, with the same status in law. If he were one of those "ancient free" whom Th. Mayers equates with nobility of blood, it would not be necessary for the law to provide that "a free person can freely give his allod to the Church", for the nobility of birth always have free disposition of their property. Nor is it credible that anciently free nobles can be the same as the freemen "who require just laws", who have to be guaranteed free possession of their inheritance. The provision that a poor freeman can surrender either his liberty or his inheritance and freely commend himself, can hardly apply to landed proprietors who have mismanaged their affairs, but only to freemen who were not really free, to the duke's free. In the Salic law and in other Frankish sources there is mention both of the duke's free and of the king's free. These "freemen" need special protection by the duke and the king lest they fall into bondage to a man of power.

That freedom was originally connected with peace and friendship, as G. Neckel contended over twenty-five years ago, has never been regarded as proven. Yet the American Germanist Mezger (in the 1956 *Festschrift* for Th. Frings) has lately supported this view on philological grounds. . . .

Some of the sources represent the *liberi* as an inferior kind of free, already under a lord and paying him tribute, but still clinging to free status. The free who in 832 give themselves to the monastery of Kempten are tribute-payers (*tributales*). So are the people on farms at Rednitz and Obermain in the 8th century, who belong to the church of Würzburg, a missionary church for the Slavs. These Bavarian people live as settlers (*coloni*) on land that belongs to nobles and are given to the church with this land, just as king's free are given with their farms to the great monasteries and episcopal churches. They do "free service", and they personally cede themselves to the church, no doubt by order of the duke. This step was not really necessary, for this church was under the protection and lordship of the ruling duke. Those "poor freemen who owe army service" must have been in the same kind of position. In Bavaria, however, they are also known as *barscalci,* which signifies that they were Roman as well as free. . . .

In Bavaria these free (historians used to call them the "ordinary free") are no doubt a numerous class. They are a kind of appendage to the Frankish king's free who are given special protection both in the Bavarian law and in royal ordinances, and are not very different from serfs and freedmen. But in Bavaria a superior group emerges among them in the 8th century, described as witnesses (*testes, tradentes, comites*). From 817 there are more of these, and by 837 they are beginning to be called *nobiles.* We understand these superior free to be armed settlers who are bringing new land under cultivation. The king and the duke establish them at strategic military points and at centers of political importance and allow them free possession of a farm. They pay rent for their land, also a head tax, and a tax in lieu of army service when they do not turn out for it or are no longer capable of doing so.

Now head-tax, and taxes on marriage and at death were not originally marks of slavery and bondage (the debate between Verriest and Marc Bloch clarified this important point) but of a kind of partial unfreedom or dependency. If this was not indeed a heritage from the late Roman colonate, which though bound to the soil had something of Roman citizenship's public liberty and retained the obligation to pay taxes long after the citizen's military responsibility was a thing of the past, it was a condition that at least permitted of aspirations for real freedom. In the Frankish realm these free were both taxpayers and the unique source of the king's soldiers. It should be noted that the king had no such authority over the various grades of the unfree who belonged to the Church or to nobles and never acquired any authority over them, except in matters of public order, throughout the whole of medieval history. This is why the king and the duke protect their free. For as the realm is enlarged through conquest, in regions where the king's arm cannot reach they are likely to be helpless against oppression; to escape this, or to avoid the burden of military service, they will then voluntarily put themselves under the protection of some man of power.

The freedom of these lowly helpers and supporters of the conquest-state, their legal status and their chances of rising, are essentially grounded in such protection and shelter as the king cares to give this special brand of subjects. But the king can in a moment lose interest in them. As the technique of war switches over to cavalry, their military importance wanes. Their legal status is eroded by the development of feudal ties, especially under Charlemagne. As the Church, more firmly organized, intensifies its administrative service, they are less needed in this sphere. In short, they cease to be of any political or social value. In France they sank through being given to the Church and became wholly assimilated to the soil-bound serfs. In Germany, in spite of being given to the Church, they manage to retain their legal status intact into the 12th century because the Church equips them as the mounted vassals it has to send to the royal army. Thus in archaic and conservative Germany royal protection and military duty combine to isolate them as a special group longer than elsewhere, and this in spite of their having to pay head tax and death dues....

IV

We come now to our enquiry into freedom of movement as a means to social ascent.... There was a large group of personally unfree people who were not bound to the soil, who indeed had no holdings from which fixed services were due. Instead, they are dependent on the lord for housing and are wholly at his disposal, performing whatever service he chooses to assign them in his household, court, or fortress, or on monastic or episcopal properties. It is their special characteristic that they can be set to different duties over a wide territory, that they are not tied to a particular peasant holding, to support themselves and pay rent and dues from the produce.

We call this group, as distinct from the *liberi* or king's free who are bound to the soil and from the hutted serfs, the free-moving, in the literal sense of the term. It comprises the numerous servants who carry on a great variety of activities, from special attendants at the lord's court to day laborers, messengers, artisans and mercantile servants to the higher servants—the marshall, the butler, the steward, the chamberlain, the master cook and the trusted retainers, from all of which, at the greater courts, the class of *ministeriales* arose. At Fulda in the 8th and 9th centuries they are freedmen, and unlike peasants on the land, when given away they are listed by their names.

* * * * *

Among the above there belong also the servants and laborers on the permanent staff of the lord's demesne farm, who are either given a food allowance or paid a wage, and are bound only to their lord and to his court. It is those who have freedom of movement who also, from the 10th century, populate the growing non-agrarian settlements which become the nucleus of new urban development. . . .

The common distinguishing mark of all these servants is that they are under their lord's immediate jurisdiction, not under the jurisdiction of the territorial judge, the *Vogt*. This is significant: the *ministeriales* started out in the same way. The law that governed the *ministeriales* and their service was a cross between feudal law grounded on their oath of service (not on homage), and a superior kind of territorial law guaranteed by the lords who had powers of jurisdiction over them as a group.

* * * * *

Freedom of movement is an obvious prerequisite for attendance on the lord on his travels and for participation in his military expeditions and also for transport service, which often required long journeys. We must also regard much early medieval mercantile enterprise as a form of service to lords. For since we find few late Roman groups of townsmen surviving the dark ages it is rare to find a fully free merchant class: one such regional group may have persisted in the Rhone valley, as far north as Lyons. W. Schlesinger has been able to show that 10th-century merchant custom does not eliminate the power of lords over merchants. This is not to say that merchants had no freedom at all. As has been seen, they come from the circle of personal servants who are responsible for seeing that adequate supplies reach the daily and weekly markets in the non-agrarian settlements on the lord's lands. Documents from the regions of the lower Main and the middle Rhineland show them transporting goods and acting as traders.

So long as self-sufficiency is the ruling principle, in a much-divided world, there is no place for large-scale merchant enterprise. But as the needs of lord's residences and of ecclesiastical centers grow and become more varied, as tastes differentiate, and as men begin to travel more widely, enterprising servants are sent out further afield to buy luxury goods and arms. It is likely that they would do this from the beginning at their own risk, that is, with their own capital. In this way groups of long-distance traders arise, who are able to make money faster than anyone else. They are not homeless vagabonds, as was once supposed, but have a home base in a settlement belonging to the lord. Indeed, it is from this that they derive their status and their cohesiveness as a group, especially when the settlement is an important regional or political center attracting population. The lord permits the growth of a customary law peculiar to the merchants because he can insist on getting a share of tolls and market dues. The lords' right to these is recognized by the king, but they are often simply usurped. Freedom of movement is essential here and is indeed claimed from the lords; it is the take-off point for social ascent for this particular group; it is the cradle of citizenship (though not of town law, which is more often withheld than granted). . . .

Thus the nature of their occupation elevates merchants above their former class associates, the lower serving-men. This is especially true of those who become rich through long-distance trade; they enjoy protection throughout the realm and are called "merchants of the empire". In turn the artisans also rise, as increasing division of labor enables them to produce for export. The two groups nevertheless unite in sworn associations, and by their solidarity win emancipation from such oppressive restrictions as control over their marriages, and from the inability to testify in courts of justice. In short, they break away from the lord's jurisdiction, gaining a measure of jurisdictional autonomy and self-government. But the new burgher community, for self-protection, as W. Ebel has shown, imposes very strong legal and ethical controls over its members. The individual makes a free decision to join, but we should guard against thinking that the new town associations allowed much scope for individual freedom of action.

The environment in which the *ministeriales* served also brought social elevation. In the halls of the high nobility they often won noblewomen as wives, and sat with them at the knightly table. As a result they finally climb into the lower nobility.

To sum up: throughout the complex and many-sided process of the rebuilding of society and culture between the beginning of the middle ages and the 11th and 12th centuries, I discern certain driving forces. These can be a guide to the organization of historical research, for they were actually operative in medieval society; I did not arrive at them arbitrarily. It is as operative principles that I have tried to describe service, freedom, and freedom of movement, and thereby also to analyze the problem of social mobility in medieval society. This leads us to the important insight that freedom, which we regard as the real heart of our history, came less by design than as the reward of hard service, and to grow strong needed princely protection.

SELECT BIBLIOGRAPHY

Karl Bosl, *Frühformen der Gesellschaft im mittelalterlichen Europa,* 1964.
—— *Franken um 800. Strukturanalyse einer fränkischen Konigsprovinz,* 1959.
H. Beumann, "Zur Entwicklung transpersonaler Staatsvorstellungen", in *Das Königtum. Seine geistigen und rechtlichen Grundlagen,* 1956.
O. Brunner, *Land und Herrschaft,* 1959.
H. Dannenbauer, "Adel, Burg und Herrschaft bei den Germanen", *Historisches Jahrbuch,* vol. 61 (1941).
—— *Grundlagen der mittelalterlichen Welt,* 1958.
W. Ebel, *Der Burgereid als Geltungsgrund und Gestaltungsprinzip des deutschen mittelalterlichen Stadtrechts,* 1958.
V. Ernst, *Die Entstehung des niederen Adels,* 1916.
—— *Die Mittelfreie,* 1920.
—— *Die Entstehung des deutschen Grundeigentums,* 1926.
F. Genzmer, "Die germanische Sippe als Rechtsgebilde", *Zeitschrift für Rechtsgeschichte, Germanische Abteilung,* vol. 67 (1947).
F. Graus "Ueber die sogenannte germanische Treue", *Historica,* vol. I (1959).
H. Kuhn "Die Grenzen der germanischen Gefolgschaft", *Zeitschrift für Rechtsgeschichte, Germanische Abteilung,* vol. 73 (1956).
Th. Mayer "Die Königsfreien und der Staat des frühen Mittelalters", in *Das Problem der Freiheit in der deutschen und schweizerischen Geschichte,* 1955.
H. Mitteis, "Formen der Adelsherrschaft im Mittelalter", in *Festschrift für F. Schulz,* 1951.
W. Schlesinger, "Herrschaft und Gefolgschaft in der germanischen-deutschen Verfassungsgeschichte", *Historische Zeitschrift,* vol. 176 (1953).
R. Sprandel, *Der merowingische Adel und die Gebiete östlich des Rheins,* 1957.
J. Sturm, *Die Anfänge des Hauses Preysing,* 1931.
G. Tellenbach, *Studien und Vorarbeiten zur Geschichte des grossfränkischen und frühdeutschen Adels,* 1957.
M. Verriest, *Collections des documents anciens relatif au Hainaut. Institutions médiévales,* 1946.

8

A Family of the Barcelona Countryside and Its Economic Activities Around the Year 1000

PIERRE BONNASSIE

It is not very often that one comes across family archives going back to the year 1000. Yet the Archives of the Crown of Aragon contain, scattered through the series of *Pergaminos condales,* a quite exceptional collection of documents of this type, detailing the activities of a single family—the Vivas family of Provençals—over the last years of the 10th century and the greater part of the 11th. The collection is unusual in its spread, for it covers about a hundred years, from 986 to 1084.[1] Again, it is unusually rich: I have counted 91 parchments (all, it seems, originals!) . . . Finally, it is remarkable because it refers to a family which, at least at the start, was relatively humble, and played no notable part in the public life of the time. . . . Let me first introduce the family: [2]

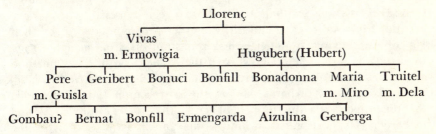

The ancestor Llorenç, who was dead by 987, perhaps even before 985, is known to us only indirectly, through later documents. He lived in Provençals, a coastal hamlet to the east of Barcelona, almost at the gates

of the town.[3] There, he must have owned several houses—two, certainly—,
no doubt modest dwellings of stone, flanked by a barn-yard and a few sheds
for the animals. Around the family home lay quite a large free holding
divided into a number of gardens, vineyards and fields. If the air is unhealthy because of the proximity of swamps, the alluvial soil is easy to
cultivate and gives good crops. At the division of the paternal goods in
December, 987 (six months after harvest, three months after the grape-
picking), Llorenç's sons are able to share out about 55 bushels of grain,
probably barley rather than wheat, and some 24 hectolitres of wine.
Llorenç also had some livestock: two pairs of cattle, including a cow, for
work, and a flock of 70 sheep feeding on the field stubble and along the
swamp edges. His personal property seems not worth mentioning except
for a garment of wool and a hauberk. Here, then, is a man who is com-
fortably off. To be sure, a great deal more is needed to raise oneself to the
level of the aristocracy—besides, we know that Llorenç works his land
and plants his vines himself—but this is enough to mark him off sharply
from the general run of rustics. Llorenç can stand as typical of a peasant
elite which is enterprising, free (all his property is allodial), and capable
of self-defence when necessary (witness his possession of a hauberk).

He apparently leaves two sons, Vivas and Hubert (who by 987 is
described as a deacon). The two immediately quarrel: they inherited the
paternal property undivided, but this communal arrangement pleases
neither of them. Vivas, the more ambitious and active, appropriates the
better part, and Hubert, embittered by his brother's action in seizing what
was a common patrimony, sues him. A tribunal made up of friends and
neighbors and presided over by the Bishop and the Archdeacon of Barcelona has to arbitrate this dispute: it simply orders an equal division between the two heirs. This judgement of Solomon is far from meeting the
desires of Vivas, who proceeds to try to buy out his brother. What justice
has taken from him, he will recover by gold: the year 993 sees the first of a
long series of transactions, sixteen in all, between the two brothers. Bit by
bit, Vivas buys back the family patrimony; now a vineyard, now a field,
then a garden, and abruptly, in January and March of 1004, the final
piece: Hubert's house, with its yard and two pigeon-houses.

But Vivas wants more and turns to other people besides his brother.
He keeps on buying: from neighbors, from strangers, from men and from
women, from laymen and clergy, from the Archdeacon of Barcelona and
even from Count Borrell. Everything looks good to him—arable land,
vineyards, gardens, orchards, houses, sheds, irrigation canals—provided
that the property is within his field of action, the district of Provençals and
its borders. His horizon is still limited, that of a peasant on the rise: the
pieces of property he acquires are usually small and almost always adjoin
his own on one, two, or three sides, or sometimes are enclaves within his
own. He further acquires, for two shillings, a shed on the market-place

in the faubourg of Barcelona: an isolated purchase, but a presage for the future. However that may be, at home in Provençals his power grows. It is symbolic of his new standing that he is able, in September 1008, shortly before his death, to buy a fourth part of the local fortress, the White Tower. So, quietly and almost furtively, as it were, Vivas moved a considerable way along the road towards the honors and powers of a position of command. Fruits of a truly ant-like labor, these honors and powers will come to his children.

By his wife Ermovigia he had four sons and at least three daughters. We are short of information on the latter, in two cases having only the name. The third, Truitel, is better known, through the will she signed shortly before her death in 1040. Married to a wealthy freeholder of Saint Boi of Llobregat in Dela, she seems to have had an important landed fortune, derived from her inherited share in Vivas's property and from the dower that her husband set up for her. Furthermore, bequests of alms in money (to the extent of three mancuses), of a dress and a silk girdle, of sheets and towels, of cattle, pigs, sheep, a pack-mare and above all—a new feature—of a horse, permit us to assign her quite a high place in the social scale. As to the sons, our first information comes from 1022, when two of them, Geribert and Bonfill, decide to go on pilgrimage to St. James of Compostella and in consequence make their wills. The two travellers have a horse and a mule, and Geribert has the full equipment of a knight: hauberk, shield, lance, and sword. Their lands are not described, but they leave behind them, in February, ample stocks of wine, barley and peas, and some farm animals.

After 1022 we lose sight of Geribert, who perhaps died on the pilgrimage or soon after. But we can still follow, through the documents, the career of Bonfill, which from 1029 is bound up with that of his brother Bonuci. On through 1046 Bonuci and Bonfill continue their father's policy of systematic purchases. By the same means—the mancus—and with the same end—the rounding out of the family domain. Again we have a long litany of acts of acquisition: little Provençals houses with trellised walls, yards and pigeon-houses, gardens on the edge of the village, fields and vineyards in the neighborhood one by one fall into the hands of the Vivas family. A fine sign of continuity, another portion of the White Tower, this time a fifth, is bought in 1029. But Bonuci and Bonfill now venture beyond their native district, buying two houses in the Barcelona suburb of the Archs and even, picturesquely, two arches of the Roman aqueduct after which the quarter is named; and further afield, lands at Banyols and Pedralbes to the west and northwest of Barcelona; and still further away, vineyards and gardens in the castellany of Piera, west of Llobregat. Thus, patiently and methodically, the fortune of the Vivas family is built.

There remains the case of Pere. Being the eldest son, he inherited the ancestral house and the enclosed land around it. He inherited also in special measure his father's ambition and spirit of enterprise. His marriage is a great success. True, he does not marry a virgin: his wife, Guisla, had two daughters by a previous marriage. But she is the niece of Pons, master of the Barcelona school; this is a large compensation, for Pere now moves into the entourage of the cathedral chapter and of the bishop. He will use this new support on two fronts: to push himself into the aristocratic milieu, on the one hand, and to crown the work of his father and brothers, on the other.

The first part of the program is the more arduous by far. Pere carries it out by championing his step-daughters. Taking the place of their deceased father, he undertakes the defence of their patrimony and in 1019 sues one of the magnates of Vallés, Vital, over an involved question of their right to pieces of land on the banks of the Ripoll. No matter that he loses the case: the fine flower of the lay and clerical aristocracy assembled to judge it. Seniofred d'Avinyonet, Seniofred Flavi, Ramon de Montbuy, Llob Sans assuredly stood by Vital, but Ramon the Archdeacon of Barcelona and his brother William, with their *milites,* Pons the schoolmaster and many others, including the Gombau and the Adalbert families, had to back Pere. . . . The activities of Pere Vivas, his influence and his fortune now break through the narrow limits of the Barcelona district, reaching into Vallés. He is not only a notable of Provençals, he is a county notable. A pilgrimage to the Holy Land made at some date unknown, cannot help but heighten his prestige, and it seems entirely fitting to find him in 1040 among the *proceres* who meet on the porch of the church of St. Just of Barcelona to arbitrate a dispute between the bishop, Gilbert, and Elliardis, a magnate's widow who held the castellany of Cervelló. This was an important affair, both as a clash between two powerful figures of the day, and in drawing in the Viscount of Gerona to preside over the tribunal. Sitting beside him, with a status equal to that of other dignitaries, Pere Vivas is henceforth one of the group of leading men. Truly a fine promotion for the grandson of the working peasant Llorenç.

But Pere did not climb so high without making sure of his foundations. His dealings in Provençals and neighboring districts extend those of his brothers. There are no deeds recording them, but the results are plain in his will of 1053: a property bought from Guitard, a house and land from Guimaran, another from the estate of the deceased Hendalic, a field from Oliba Isarn, another from some Jews, a third from Els the fisherman, a fourth from Amalric, etc. The list may be incomplete, but even so is impressive. There were other purchases at Palou, in the Haut-Vallés, including a mill. Rich in lands, Pere is rich also in gold; he counts his gold not by the mancus, as his father did, but by the ounce, giving his daughters sumptuous dowries and making princely gifts as alms to Santa Maria del Mar and in other works of piety.

Finally, wealth brings power over men. His neighbors come seeking share-cropping leases, a reversal of the situation in which his grandfather Llorenç had sought these from men wealthier than he. He has his own precarial tenants and like his brothers Bonuci and Bonfill, finds himself surrounded by personal dependents who are his men (*homines*). But his authority rests mainly on his power over the Provençals church, St. Martin's; this is mentioned for the first time in his will. Belonging half to Pere and half to Bonuci and Bonfill, had it been built by the brothers Vivas? Or was it one of their numerous purchases? This is more probable, for the patronage of St. Martin suggests that it was a very ancient church. However this may be, the revenue that it yields—even though divided with the mother church of Santa Maria del Mar—are far from negligible: tithes, offerings from the sick who come to implore the saint for a miraculous cure, and revenues in salt. Further, ownership of the church is a means of domination over the congregation. Need we add that Pere, the new "lord" of Provençals, has long since abandoned Llorenç's humble dwelling and built himself a pleasant two-storeyed house of stone whose strong walls and large tiled roof must surely both excite the envy of his neighbors and command their respect?

With the death of Pere, early in 1054, the Vivas history is near its end. One of his sons, Bernat, abroad to see the world, never returns; the other, Bonfill, died in his prime, leaving no direct heir. We know little of Pere's daughters save that they take tender care of their old uncle Bonuci; he lives on, the last surviving member of the family, to die around 1090.

The history of the Vivas family is manifestly one of social ascent. Great land-collectors, Llorenç, Vivas, Bonuci, and Bonfill, and finally Pere, were able at the same time as they built up a growing fortune, to climb, one by one, the rungs of the social hierarchy. Such a phenomenon is unusual enough at this period to warrant a fuller analysis.[4] The first problem is that of the means of ascent—the economic means. The next is that of the social milieu that watched and permitted the ascent. Finally, it will be well to enquire into the family structure itself, to discover how far it could favor this advance and how far it was a hindrance.

The Economic Climate

What is most striking is the frequency of transactions. Vivas alone, in less than 23 years . . . makes 45 purchases . . . up to five in a year (992–993) or even six (989). Further, the deals often refer to several pieces, sometimes to an entire domain (1007). Lands even change hands very rapidly, being no sooner bought than they are resold. . . . The turnover of land is thus revealed as particularly lively, which is astonishing in such a period. Two types of explanation of this phenomenon are possible, according as one looks at the state of supply or at that of demand.

What is offered for sale is land, or more precisely, immovables. Now what is the situation when Vivas begins his operations, around 986? Al Mansour's invasion has just ravaged the Barcelona "Pla": the town was burned, the countryside pillaged, the monasteries destroyed, and thousands of men and women were taken off to Cordova as captives.[5] The economic repercussions of the catastrophe are easy to imagine: the burning of crops induces a sudden rise in food prices, while the ransom of captives entails an unprecedented flight of money. Most of the survivors are therefore in urgent need of cash, yet on the other hand all ranks of the population are sadly burdened, in consequence of the invasion, by having more land than they can cultivate. Hardly any families were spared: few individuals have not inherited a garden, a vineyard or a whole estate, from some brother or cousin. There is a plethora of land being offered for sale: the monastery of Sant Pere itself sells its Provençals lands. And like every epoch in trouble, this one has its profiteers, among whom we can count Vivas. . . .

But the invasion does not explain everything. There are still numerous sales even after 990, even after 1000. We must look for lasting causes for their frequency, and these will perhaps be disclosed through looking into the structure of agriculture. What slows down land sales almost everywhere else in the West, is the extreme fragmentation of property rights; a sale requires the consent of a large number of people. Nothing of the sort is necessary here: all the lands of the Vivas family—except a few that Llorenç had worked under co-planting tenure—are allodial. One can even affirm that they are free allodial property, free in the sense that they are exempt from any public tax. Indeed, the Barcelona territory, like the Vallés and the Penedés, enjoys special privileges that date far back.[6] These privileges, solemnly confirmed by Count Béranger-Raimond I and the Countess Sancia in January 1025, forbid anyone to impose rent or services on the inhabitants of "free places", and guarantee the latter the right to dispose freely of all their property. In these conditions, the property system is almost that of *proprietas integra,* a system perfectly adapted to the habits of a region deeply imbued with Roman law. Thus land can be put up for sale at any moment, a situation quite unknown at this period in most Western countries.

But this very special status of landed property is still not enough to explain the economic climate. Land is far from being the only merchandise offered for sale: one can see this by looking at the Vivas family wills. For example, Geribert and Bonfill order that in the event they come to grief on the way to Compostella, their horse and mule, and Geribert's armour and saddle, be sold; Bonfill provides also for sale of all his barley and pea crops, his livestock and farm equipment. . . . It is inconceivable that provisions of this kind would be made unless there was a fairly lively market, and this in turn implies that means of payment were relatively abundant.

What monetary resources, then, did Vivas and his compatriots command? A study of the payments made between 986 and 1040 will perhaps throw some light on this problem:

Dates of land purchases by Vivas	Payments made in kind	Payments made in local money	Payments made in gold	Total
986–990	0	11	1	12
991–1000	2	5	19	26
1000–1009	0	1	12	13
Dates of land purchases by his sons				
1029–1046	3	1	18	22
Totals	5	18	50	73

One is immediately struck by the rarity of payments in kind—only five out of 73, and these occur in rather special circumstances: two were transactions between brothers, a third was a matter of an exchange rather than a true sale (a piece of land was traded for a vineyard and four sacks of barley), and the two latest cases relate to purchases in the castellany of Piera, an inland district less open to the circulation of money. Actually, payments in kind play usually no more than a supplementary role; most of a payment will be in money, with some small balance being settled in grain.[7]

Normally, then, payments are in money. Before 990 this is generally local pennies, after that date gold mancuses. . . .[8] It may well be that the influx of Arab dinars provoked a rise in prices, which from the year 1000 was appreciable.[9] In any case, Muslim gold, from the last decade of the 10th century, becomes essential to the economic life of the Barcelona region.

But how do Vivas and his sons get gold? Where does it come from? The mancuses that Vivas uses are Cordova dinars (struck in the time of Chafar, master of the mint under Al Hakam II); those that his sons use are sometimes Cordovan and sometimes Barcelona imitations (struck by Bonhom the Jew, moneyer to Count Bérenger-Raymond I).[10] Does their possession of all this gold mean that they are in direct touch with the markets of Muslim Spain? To put it another way, is the Vivas family one of those families of large-scale international traders for whom historians of the early middle ages hunt so eagerly?

A few points, admittedly, favor this hypothesis. In the first place, the location of Provençals, at the gates of Barcelona, on the *Via Marina* and close to the *Via Francisca,* is convenient for long-distance trade.[11] Next, we find some Jews there, and we know the part that Jewish communities played in large-scale trade. Finally, the Vivas men are money-lenders them-

selves, and lending at interest is already a speculative business. The departure of Pere's son, Bernat, for distant lands may refer to a business voyage.

But these points are too feeble to be convincing. The *Via Marina*
serves only a few little agricultural market settlements, of no great interest
to merchants; the *Via Francisca* goes not to the Muslim Eldorado but to
impoverished regions of the Frankish world. The few Jews whose names
appear in Provençals deeds are known to us only as allodial proprietors,
and their activities—like that of other men of their religion at this period
—must have been limited to working their vineyards and gardens.[12]
Finally, the practice of money-lending is so widespread around the year
1000 that one cannot regard it as distinctive of a special social group: besides, the main object of lending may have been to get hold of the land
that was pledged for the term of the loan. As to Bernat's journey, there is
no reason to suppose it was not a pilgrimage, like those his father and his
uncles had undertaken earlier.

To these objections one can add a further argument, perhaps more
decisive. Looking at the series of purchases that Vivas made, one sees that
the mancus was by no means the necessary and sufficient explanation. In
particular, almost all of the early purchases were made in local pennies. . . .
Vivas's land deals were therefore not due to the influx of Arab dinars;
they in fact preceded it.[13]

Rather than yield to the seduction of hypotheses, it is better to leave
the Vivas men in the context of their rural horizon and to seek the origin
of their fortune there, in their agricultural activities. Was the Provençals
land rich enough to make such an explanation possible? The first observation that can be made is that it was new land, still at the end of antiquity
undersea. True, this circumstance is not wholly favorable: the shoreline is
not yet firm by the year 1000 and there are brackish pools and swampy
areas overgrown with reeds; the region is not free from malaria and has the
reputation of being unhealthy.[14] But these inconveniences are largely offset by man's ability to turn the situation to his advantage: the alluvial soil
is light and fertile, perfectly suited to the techniques of cultivation of the
time. Being dead level, it lends itself readily to irrigation. For there is
abundance of fresh water: these low lands are the natural receptacle of
flood waters, especially from the Hortá and Besós rivers. And the men of
the year 1000 dug canals, such as the *aquaductum* and the *gutta* that Vivas
buys in 1006, the *regarium* that his sons buy in 1031. . . . Again, the sub-
surface water table is high, and innumerable wells permit frequent water-
ing.

In these conditions, the period sees a great development of horti-
culture. The Barcelona "Pla", from the faubourg of the Archs to Besos, is
essentially a zone of gardens. Cut into countless little enclosures under
constant cultivation and well irrigated, these lands must have yielded
ample produce for the market, assuring the inhabitants of the city a wel-

come supplement to the eternal cereal diet—in the form of legumes and possibly water-melons. Trees are cultivated, too: at Provençals, and to some extent all through Catalonia at this period, the tree is king; there are few deeds describing property that do not list some fruit trees. Apple-trees, pomegranate trees, fig-trees? In the Vivas deeds only the last are specified, but several times: figs, eaten fresh or more often dried, must certainly have been an important element in Mediterranean diet at this time. Still another activity is viticulture. It is spreading everywhere. Llorenç was planting vines in the 970's and his grandsons in the 1050's; vines cover the isles of Besos and between there and Barcelona they run down to the sea. Co-planting contracts, which benefited the lessee by giving him full possession of half the land planted at the end of seven years, must have encouraged this expansion. Wills show wine to be the prime source of wealth, the first thing that people decide to produce commercially. For a large proportion of all this agricultural produce is sold in Barcelona (one has only to consult the wills to be convinced of this); there, in the faubourg of the Archs, no doubt in those sheds that Vivas and his sons bought beside the market, it is traded for pennies or for mancuses.

The Vivas fortune is thus not to be explained by the hypothetical dealing with distant countries, something that was very exceptional. It is the direct result of the progress in agriculture—especially the progress in irrigation—that was achieved in the Barcelona region around the year 1000, perhaps a little earlier. To be sure, Muslim gold flowed in to quicken the economy, but it cannot be regarded as the sole cause of its development. Wealth is born of men's labor. It was by selling the fruits of their labor—or that of their dependents—that the Vivas men were able to grow rich and to advance themselves. . . .

The Social Milieu

* * * * *

When Vivas, around 986–990, begins his long series of land deals, we notice the very frequent recurrence in the lists of witnesses to his deeds and those of his neighbors, of a certain number of names . . . of inhabitants of Provençals. How are we to find out anything about these people's manner of life? At best the deeds give only some dry information as to the property that they own. . . . But interestingly enough, one can see that many of the names are signatures: if they could not read (but how can we tell this?) the allodial proprietors of Provençals at least knew how to write their names.

But one name recurs at the foot of almost all the deeds, more often than any other, a name followed—God be thanked—by a specification of his trade: *Paulus faber*. And along with the name is a sign, always exactly the same, traced by clumsy fingers more used to handling a hammer than a pen; three vertical strokes barred by two that run horizontally. How can we fail to recognize this crude grill as the artisan's trade-mark? Or to recognize Pau the smith as Vivas's closest friend, his indispensable adviser in most of his transactions? We can see him as the man in whom the community of Provençals has confidence, the man who makes or repairs the plough-shares, the most precious things of all in this peasant world, and perhaps also the swords and armor that everyone keeps by him against days of danger; he impresses them by his technical skill (perhaps secret?); naturally, they look to him to arbitrate a dispute or guarantee the execution of a contract.

The importance of the village smith's role in early medieval society has already been stressed; the case of Pau the smith should now be added to the dossier.[15]

There is certainly also a priest in this village circle. Of all the clerical names which abound in our documentation, we note especially that of Langovard. Possessing allodial lands in several parts of Provençals, active in several deals, Langovard can probably be identified as the incumbent of Sant Marti. No doubt a humble person with apparently little education (he is never entrusted with the drawing up of the documents) he is nonetheless a party to them as a pledge or as an arbitrator in village affairs. For a genuine community is grouped around these two men, the priest and the smith. Small, consisting of only seven or eight families (probably the richest in the village or at least those owning allodial lands), it is characterized by a fundamental identity of ambitions and mentality and joins together in many collective measures.

These men and women—one feels it despite the laconic nature of the deeds—love the soil. Apart from God—to whom they nevertheless sacrifice some of it as alms—it is the only thing they value. Gold is only a means: acquired through the land, it is immediately turned into land. As soon as mancuses are won, they are reinvested in land which in turn procures more mancuses for new purchases....

The identity of aims and concerns enforces a certain solidarity, which finds expression in a variety of places and occasions. The group assembles on a field that is up for sale, deliberates over the price, is present when the deal is settled, and finally each man accompanies the buyer to the home of the scribe and has his name placed at the foot of the deed: thus the conclusion of a contract is as much a village affair as a family affair. The group assembles around the death-bed of the head of a household, prays for his soul and prepares to carry out his last wishes: when Bonhom dies, in 1004, Vivas is executor and Pau buys the house whose price the dying man has allocated to charity. At a judicial dispute the group forms a commission to arbitrate it under the presidency of some high dignitary (the bishop or the count); it tries to resolve all quarrels within the community. ... All these men are at some point promoted to the rank of *boni homines* and charged, in accordance with Visigothic law and under the direction of a judge, with customary judicial liquidations: for example, to order the seizure of goods pledged as security for loans not repaid, to value them and decide on their sale. ... Free men, they affirm their freedom publicly by helping—if only at a very humble level—to apply the law justly. And the best guarantee of that freedom lies in solidarity.

But it would be wrong to overestimate the importance of these collective actions. If it is correct, since there are attitudes making for mutual aid and some degree of cooperation, to speak of a community, this has nothing like the force of the village collectivities of Northern Europe. It is more a group of individuals or rather, of families, than a cohesive entity. The first rule is always: every man for himself. Land and even water are objects of individual appropriation, and if transactions occur between members of the group it is through contracts drawn up in proper form. In these conditions, the spirit of cooperation is not the result of applying rules, of communal pressure, but of free decision on the part of the various family heads. It depends on what each man wants to do. It has therefore no firm basis, and in the course of the 11th century the community will be powerless to oppose the rising tide of individualism.

Besides, it is not a closed community. The proximity of the town prevents any kind of autarchy: if the Provençals men often go into town, the citizens often take part in village affairs. In the file of deeds one can see a constant coming and going, which shows that besides economic ties between the town and the country around there are close personal relationships. These spring up the more readily because many Barcelona people own property in Provençals: their lands adjoin those of the villagers, and their relations with them are those of neighbors.

Here are men of the faubourg, half-urban, half-rural: artisans and fishermen, they buy and sell with Provençals people, visit their houses and frequent the market-booths some have acquired beside their dwellings; they belong to the same parish, Santa Maria de la Mar. But the men of the faubourg are of too low status, their mode of life is too much like that of the villagers, for contacts here to explain the social ascent of the Vivas family. To understand this, we must turn to other circles.

First, to the ecclesiastical milieu. A number of priests frequented the Vivas household, drawing up contracts and rendering other services. Around the year 1000 a priest named Elias was retained as the family's official scribe. His handwriting and his style show him to be unusually well educated. If, as is possible, he was one of the cathedral clerks, he may well have acted as an intermediary between Vivas and his peers on the one hand, and the episcopal milieu on the other.

Still more suggestive are the relations that the Provençals men form with a much more highly-placed familiar of the bishop's palace, the archdeacon, Sunifred Llobet. Like so many other citizens, he buys and sells land in Provençals; in fact he becomes one of the largest allodial landowners there. Moreover, he seems often to have acted as a protector of the community. May it not have been he who arranged for Hubert's admission as a deacon of the cathedral and perhaps for Pere's marriage with the schoolmaster's niece? Admittedly this is a speculation, but the Vivas ascent could not have occurred without the protection of a patron.

With Pere's marriage to the schoolmaster's niece we enter still another milieu that could help to explain the Vivas history, that of the cathedral school and the men whom it undoubtedly trained: the judges. There are still many problems to be solved regarding the existence in early medieval Catalonia of professional specialists in law; we shall touch on the question here only from the social point of view. Usually priests or deacons, and familiars of both the bishop's palace and the count's, they mix with the local aristocracy, but seem to be a group apart. They regulate many of the affairs of communities of free peasants. They are rich—rich in land and above all in gold—and having quasi-discretionary authority over lending at interest and no doubt over business in general, they seem to be disposed to go into business themselves. The judge Auruci, whom we meet a number of times in Provençals as a witness, a landowner, etc., seems to be a case in point. Taken prisoner to Cordova by Al Mansour in 985 but freed soon after, he took over the direction of ransoming prisoners and may have retained permanent contacts with the capital of the caliphate. His activities may have been one of the channels through which Cordovan dinars came into the hands of our peasant family, to be invested in land around Provençals.[16]

But the judges are intermediaries in another fashion. Familiars of the count they are also, to use a term that is necessarily anachronistic, his business agents. Advising him on the management of his revenues, they help him to buy land, and when he needs money, to sell land: each of three contracts of sale between Vivas and Count Borell, in 989, is signed by a judge. First the gates of the bishop's palace, and then the gates of the count's palace, are thus opened to the men of Provençals. Other profitable connections, with monasteries and with nobles, may have been opened to them in the same way.

It is by taking account of all these webs of relationships running through the whole society from top to bottom, networks of friendships,

patronage, and of relations with neighbors, that we can perhaps best understand the means by which the Vivas family rose, and best understand the
social climate of the city of Barcelona and its environs, around the year
1000.

It is a society that seems at first sight to be made up of groups, of
microcosms, each with its own type of life, its own customs, its own tonality:
the Provençals landowners, the cathedral circle, that of the chapter and the
school, and the count's entourage. But just as there is no real separation
between the town and the country around, everyone being more or less a
townsman and more or less a countryman, so there is no barrier between
these different worlds. On the contrary, they interpenetrate: numerous
intermediaries (judges, priests, scribes, etc.) offer their services; a protocol
that is still patriarchal softens differences of rank; above all, complementary needs are felt, and thus there are incessant currents of communication.

For example, the link between Provençals and the ecclesiastical circles,
one that the documents reveal most clearly, arises from the fact that the
latter have to rely on the market-gardeners of Provençals for produce.
True, the cathedral has its own estates, but these are too far away to supply
the perishable delicacies—fresh fruit, vegetables and fish—that are needed
for the dignitaries' tables. Barley and wine, too, are bought and paid for in
gold. Such traffic brings clients and purveyors into perhaps daily contact;
they know each other well, and the latter can rely on the goodwill of the
former to protect them in their careers.

When we see the scene as a whole, then, it is clear that the existence
of separate interests does not destroy the homogeneity of the social milieu
of Barcelona, where one can pass gradually, without any sharp break, from
the condition of a peasant to that of an aristocrat. It remains, and this is
the real problem, to explain this astonishing homogeneity. The explanation can be summed up in one word—privilege. All these people, whoever
they may be, are privileged. They are privileged, in the strict sense of the
term, in that they have enjoyed, for generations, charters of freedom guar-
anteeing them personal liberty and property rights. But they are also privileged economically, for all of them, down to Pau the smith and Llorenç the
working peasant, have not only enough to eat but can dispose of a surplus.
This is due to particularly favorable agricultural conditions, to a precocious progress. While elsewhere, even in Catalonia, the line of cleavage
between the "greater people" and the "lesser people", between notables
and rustics, between free and serf, is located much higher up the social lad-
edr (just below the status of the castellan), here it is relatively low down, at
the level of the small and middling allodial owners. Beneath this line, we
may imagine a plebeian mass of laborers, dependants and poor people; we
have to use our imagination, for the documents say not a word about them.

But the equilibrium established in the world of the "upper" class could not be a stable one. Economic progress brings social transformations and these will stamp the 11th century. The accumulation of profits, the development of luxury, the multiplication of wants will unceasingly whet the appetite of the more fortunate, and the ascent of some will have for its corollary the fall of others. This phenomenon was surely already in evidence before the year 1000, when Vivas begins buying up his neighbors' lands. Those who sell out are in danger of sinking into the lower ranks. We need point only to the case of Bellit and his wife Adalez, who in 1006–07 find themselves obliged to sell most of their property and to mortgage the remainder.

Thus a period of relative equilibrium in Provençals is followed by one of tension. The wealth of the Vivas family excites jealousy and deep rancor among the children of those who had succumbed to the lure of the mancuses offered for their land. We have many examples of these hatreds, which henceforth poison the atmosphere of the village; they are evident in so-called pacts "of evacuation and security". By 1044 the heirs of a certain Gerbert Bonuci are engaged in a struggle with Bonfill and Bonuci Vivas, accusing them of usurpation; to end it, the latter have to buy peace at the price of four mancuses. Then a new war breaks out. . . .

It is therefore evident that the village community is breaking up. The pretensions of the Vivas men, who after this brook no opposition, make the situation worse in other ways. Masters of the church, they appropriate the village road. . . .

In the end this concentration of power in the hands of a few usually means that the majority of the others are obliged to become dependents. One sees clienteles forming around Bonfill Aruci, around the new archdeacon Ramon, and above all, around the brothers Vivas. We do not know the names of their *homines;* but might they not be those of sons of some of old Viva's friends and neighbors? The very franchises, which for generations had protected small and medium-size property, come to be impaired: by the 12th century, perhaps even before this, certain "evil customs" (rents, etc.) are being imposed on the inhabitants of the free territory.[17]

Thus in the space of some fifty to a hundred years, economic changes profoundly altered the face of society. The surpluses created by agricultural progress and by the development of the market have been confiscated, through conflicts involving violence, by a few people, among whom we can count the Vivas brothers. The social conditions inherited from the early middle ages, on the whole kindly, relatively undifferentiated as to status, still patriarchal in type, and surviving up to around the year 1000, have been shattered: the 11th century has accepted inequalities, wiped out resistance, heightened the power of the strong. Can this process of change in the society as a whole be detected also in the narrower sphere of the family?

The Family Group

Is this an extended family of patriarchal type or a small nuclear family? [18] We can safely say it was the latter. The three Vivas wills are explicit on the point: the family horizon is virtually limited to the group of parents and children. Hardly any legacies go out of this group. Except for a few barrels of wine to a nephew, those of Geribert and Bonfill are to their brothers; those of Truitel, except for a dress left to a woman cousin, are to her husband and brothers; those of Pere go all to his children. Collateral kin therefore count for very little and except for a cousin who stands as coexecutor in the will of Geribert and Bonfill, play no role in family affairs.

Even so, high fertility makes the group large. And all legitimate children, even those born to a spouse by a previous marriage, inherit equally, daughters equally with sons. The law is clear on this point, and at this period it is applied strictly.[19] Obviously, therefore, there is a danger: that of a rapid break-up of the family patrimony, automatically annulling all the persistent efforts spent on building it up. The inheritance system, passed on from another age, is here totally at odds with the new situation which makes for the concentration of wealth. Again, a second danger ensues from the first: that of a break-up, an atomization, of the family group itself, which becomes incapable of maintaining its cohesion when the patrimony is divided. The men of this age were well aware of these dangers that dogged them, and sought remedies.

In the first place, through a conscious policy of restricting marriages, they sought, so far as possible, to limit the number of children.[20] This plan is clearly illustrated in the case of the Vivas family: in each generation only one of the sons marries; celibacy is the lot of the others, backed on occasion by entry into orders.[21] In this way, the number of grandchildren is unlikely to exceed the number of children.

The second plan currently followed is that of joint possession. The father leaves all or a major part of his property to several sons in common. Vivas and Hubert so shared before 987, then Geribert and Bonuci, then Bonfill and Bonuci; this procedure is perpetuated into the third generation, for Pere leaves the heart of his Provençals domains to his sons Bernat and Bonfill in joint possession. When it works well, the plan is a success and even allows of expansion: witness the many purchases that Bonfill and Bonuci made in common between 1029 and 1046.

Lastly, there is some recourse to the practice known as *inmelioratio*. On his deathbed the father decides on systematic preference of one of his sons (perhaps the eldest?) at the expense of the others. Such a departure from the ordinary law is based on a very free interpretation of Visigothic law,[22] and calls for a special procedure, consisting of public declaration of the father's wishes, the drawing up of a will and the upholding of the will in a judicial court. Presumably (we have to guess, since we do not have Vivas's will) it was by this means that Pere was favored with the most important part of the paternal heritage: the ancestral home, the domain around it, and the fourth part of the White Tower. The son whose share has been "ameliorated" thus receives the most valuable part of the patrimony but regards himself also as invested with the duty of assuring the continuance of the family (it is he who marries), and of raising its prestige still higher. He may have been prepared for this task (did not Vivas arrange Pere's advantageous marriage?), and in principle he should be able to rely on the family's support. This system of *inmelioratio* is a distant and imperfect anticipation of primogeniture. Could it not, by preserving the core of acquisitions made through the generations by families of modest origin, have been the means of engendering veritable dynasties, and thus of preparing for the birth of that new aristocracy which in the 11th or 12th centuries took the place of the old lineages of the early middle ages? [23]

These two practices—joint possession and *inmelioratio*—seem at first sight to be contradictory, but if we read the documents carefully we see that this is not so; they actually complement each other, in two different ways. In the first, in the case of Vivas's children, joint possession affects only the property left the sons who remain celibate, *inmelioratio* favoring the son who marries. The heritage is then divided into two parts, one for the guardian of the patrimony and his numerous offspring, the other as compensation to the celibate brothers. In a second case, that of Pere's children, the situation is inverted: *inmelioratio* and joint possession work together to benefit the two sons, Bernat and Bonfill, who receive a major share in common, their three sisters dividing the remainder.

The successions thus reveal a real "family system" at work, designed to assure the continuance of the group and its wealth. This system, very strong, may even be crowned by a practice illustrated in a deed of 1040: that of repurchase of the dowries of married daughters. In that year Bonfill buys back from his brother-in-law Dela a share of Provençals lands and vineyards which his sister Truitel had inherited and had at her death bequeathed to her husband: it would not do for an enclave in the family domain to pass out of the family hands, even to the husband of one of its daughters! Nothing seems to have been left to chance. The rules which the Vivas family set for itself in matters of succession should have held the patrimony together forever. But were these rules applied correctly?

In the first place, we must not forget God's share. Alms remain one of the imponderables in the system: nothing fixes the amount that any member of the family may leave to works of piety. To be sure—and this is the most favorable case—charitable legacies may refer only to the deceased's movable goods, that is, to livestock, equipment, reserves of wine and grain; they may nevertheless be very considerable. What is more serious is that they most often cut into the landed patrimony; already in 1040 Truitel

left her best vineyards to the Barcelona chapter, and in 1053 Pere sur-
renders not only his military equipment but a very large quantity of landed
property to the church. So anxiety for personal salvation regularly works
against the collective aspirations of the group.

And this individualism, though especially apparent at the hour of
death, finds many other occasions of displaying itself. Despite the precautions taken, the number of heirs is always large enough to give rise to
rivalry and conflict. In particular, the practice of *inmelioratio* can defeat
the end in view; instead of subordinating the family to the authority of a
head, designated and given preferential advantages as such, it runs the risk
of stirring up bitter jealousies. Joint possession is a very hazardous practice,
liable through incompatibility of temperaments and interests, as in the
case of Vivas and Hubert, to terminate disgracefully in open quarrelling
and scandal.

Far from subsiding with the passage of time, these conflicts could not
fail to be exacerbated in the new economic climate. Increasing production
opened possibilities of increased wealth, and it was everyone's ambition to
profit from these. The development of the market brought golden opportunities for personal enrichment. Land, once a sacred value cementing the
family group, to many people became just merchandise, instantly con-
vertible into money. From then on, there are some people, like Hubert,
crazy for mancuses and impatient to improve their position, who think
only of getting rid of their land as fast as possible; others, like Vivas, on the
contrary think only of buying, of getting personal control of what was
formerly the patrimony of the group. In consequence relations between
brothers often became mere business relationships! And not only relations
between brothers: a neighbor of Vivas buys from his mother, by written
contract and for half a *pensa* of money, a vineyard she had received from
her husband. From the end of the 10th century purchases and sales multiply within families, creating inequalities there as elsewhere.

The economic changes which weakened the village community therefore undoubtedly also undermined the structure of the family community.
The chances of escaping the collective rules and of leaving the group become more numerous, and correspondingly the will to leave it grows. Are
the pilgrimages undertaken by men of the Vivas family not a response to
the call of adventure as well as of faith? And a temporary journey may often
lead to permanent removal. Such escapes are a serious matter, for they
make all the measures taken to ensure the survival of the family and its
patrimony futile. Procreation having been limited as much as possible, by
restricting marriage, if the son chosen to continue the family line disappears, the line is doomed. It is in this way that the Vivas line is extinguished
at the death of Pere: two of his sons have died young, Bernat has gone away,
and there is no collateral line able to supply a substitute heir.

Striking a balance, we see that the forces making for the break-up of family structures are at least as strong as those tending to consolidate them. One could even judge the former to be stronger, but for the part played by women in maintaining the cohesion of the group. The high place that women held in southern European societies of the 10th or 11th centuries has already been shown through broader research; [24] in a much narrower context, let us now stress the primordial role that devolved on the Catalan woman.

As a wife, she is protected by the setting up of a dower—a *decimum,* as our documents say. Admittedly, the purpose of this is to protect her against the risk of repudiation, but in reality its function in the social and family life of the time is much more important. It only exceptionally gives rise to a written contract; better still, it is not as a rule exactly defined; the *decimum* is actually the wife's right to receive a tenth of all her husband's property. She therefore has the right to withhold consent, in *all* transactions he makes. And more than just a right: the documents show that she enjoys a real power of decision, on an equality with her husband. In no case do the documents indicate any degree of difference in the juridical status of husband and wife. And it is remarkable—this shows how well the condition of women was protected—that the constitution of dowers applies even to concubines.

The wife shares in the management of her husband's personal property, but the converse does not always hold. Catalan women seem perfectly prepared to defend their own patrimony against husbands who try to exceed their rights, and on occasion they show a fine fighting spirit. A case in point is that of Maria, Vivas's daughter. Having agreed with her husband Miró to sell a field she had inherited, for the needs of the household, she insists on compensation. None being offered, she succeeds in dragging her husband to the scribe to have a contract duly drawn up assigning her a piece of land from Miró's personal patrimony. The unfortunate husband is obliged to concur, as the deed says, "pro pax meritum", which can be translated only as "for the sake of peace". Either through the dower or through being hot-tempered, the Catalan wife knew how to win herself, within the context of the family, a privileged economic position.[25]

In the final case of widowhood, the woman's authority is augmented further by the right of usufruct that she obtains in her husband's property and by the guardianship she exercises over her children. For example, Guisla, Pere's wife and executor of his will, is invested with discretionary power in the management of the lands he leaves at death.

Taking an active part in maintaining the family patrimony as well as in extending it, the wife receives a return for her services—this is well understood—in the shape of ornaments, cloth, even of furniture. As a rule it is very difficult to determine what proportion of the fortunes of the period is represented by these things, for no records of their purchase survives. In the case of the Vivas family, we are lucky; thanks to Pere's will

(1053) we know the value of the wedding presents he had given his two daughters. In addition to their shares of the inheritance, received in advance, Ermengarda was given movables estimated to be worth 25 ounces of gold, and Aizulina had the equivalent of 40 ounces of gold, in clothing and other goods. Now 40 ounces of gold in that period would buy four war-horses, or an important fortress; it was probably more than Vivas had spent in his whole career! Gold, silk and brocade come from the ends of the world to adorn the shoulders of the Barcelona girls. The growth of luxury, and especially of feminine luxury, is in the last analysis the most visible result of the economic progress realized over long decades, and the wealth born of unprecedented Catalan effort is perhaps finally assembled on the bodies of women.[26]

Through the fate of one family—which can neither be called very typical nor very exceptional—we thus see in profile the whole history of Barcelona society: can we draw any lesson from it? To many the story will appear too unrepresentative, and certainly one cannot deny the unusual nature of this world where money plays a leading role in the year 1000, where the grandsons of peasants hold audience with bishops, where woman finds herself surrounded with the greatest possible consideration. Some, faithful to the schemes of the social life of this period that studies focussed on more northerly regions have bequeathed us, will perhaps be inclined to discard the picture offered here as a special case of no significance. Is it permissible to generalize from it? Certainly, the geographical and economic environment and even the political environment, at first sight seem very special: the rapid market development was favored by a relatively abundant supply of money, in turn linked to the proximity of the Muslim world; the advance of agricultural production was made possible by exceptionally favorable climatic conditions as well as by the opportunities for irrigation; the existence of a free and enterprising peasant class is due to the charters granted in the atmosphere of the reconquest, which was *sui generis*. Gold, water, liberty: indeed an astonishing conjuncture. But is it not the same conjuncture that under different forms, half a century or a century or two centuries later, will sustain the prodigious urban development of Western Europe; the multiplication of means of payment, the exploitation of rich lands around the towns, the benefit of communal charters? Viewed in this light, the history of the Vivas family and of the social milieu of Barcelona, which it reveals, will not appear as a phenomenon isolated in time and space, but as the herald of another, vaster, more complex history: that of the rebirth of the towns of the West.[27] The petty conflicts that rend Provençals seem presages of the bitter struggles far ahead in which "the fat" and "the thin" people of so many Mediterranean cities will be involved. Finally, does not the high position of woman in the civilization of the troubadours stem from the high status which the Catalan woman enjoys by the 11th century? It is only a few decades after the death of Pere Vivas's daughters that the so polished Court of Alphonse I, the king-poet, will be glittering in all its brilliance, in this same Barcelona.

NOTES

1 If earlier documents existed, they may have been destroyed in 985, when Al-Mansour burnt Barcelona. It is remarkable that the bulk of the documents date from before 1010. The latest (1084) comes from a little before the death of the last representative of the family. [This article has been slightly abridged in translation; readers wishing to see the archival references which support the author's statements should consult the full documentation of the original article. The author notes that a few of the documents were printed in F. Udina Martorell, *El Archivo Condal de Barcelona en los siglos IX–X. Estudio critico de sus fondos* (Barcelona, 1951), and in F. de Bofarull y Sans, "Origenes del pueblo de San Martin de Provensals", in *Memorias de la Real Academia de Buenas Letras de Barcelona*, t. V (1893), pp. 199–253, but that neither of these authors noted the family character of the series. EDITOR'S NOTE.]

2 Since surnames were not in use at this period, the application of *Vivas* as a surname is purely arbitrary, a matter of convenience. The greatest care has been taken in identifying members of the family as such by two criteria: (1) documentary statements of relationship, so far as these exist, and (2) indication of domicile.

3 Provençals is about two kilometres from the cathedral. Today the site is covered with factories, making any study of the terrain impossible. On the history and geography of the village see F. Carreras y Candi, *Geografia general de Catalunya*, t. I, *La ciutat de Barcelona* (Barcelona, 1916), pp. 313–315.

4 For example, there is nothing of the kind in the Mâconnais. See G. Duby, *La société aux XIe et XIIe siècles dans la région mâconnaise* (Paris, 1953), pp. 36–38.

5 On the havoc wrought by Al Mansour's army, see for example, R. d'Abadal i de Vinyals, *Els primers contes catalans* (Barcelona, 1958), pp. 328–332.

6 Very certainly, from the Carolingian reconquest. On the problem of these franchises see J. A. Font Rius, *Franquicias urbanas de la Cataluña vieja*, Barcelona, 1960.

7 The situation is very different in Castile, where payment in grain is much more common and from 1040 even preponderates. See R. Pastor de Togneri, "Ganaderia y precios. Consideraciones sobre la economia de Leon y Castilla en los siglos XI–XIII", in *Cuadernos de Historia de Espana* (Buenos Aires, 1962), pp. 37–55. On the other hand, in southern France, conditions are much the same, money continuing to be the chief means of exchange in the 10th and 11th centuries. See M. Castaing-Sicard, "Monnaies féodales et circulation monétaire en Languedoc—Xe–XIIIe siècles", in *Cahiers de l'Association Marc Bloch de Toulouse*, no. 4 (Toulouse, 1961), pp. 5–6.

8 On the problem of the influx of Muslim gold, opposite opinions are held. M. Lombard argued that it was due to a favorable balance of trade. See "L'or musulman du VIIe au XIe siècle", in *Annales. Economies, Sociétés, Civilisations* (1947), pp. 249–298. But many Catalan historians believe it represented the wages of Catalan mercenaries fighting under Muslim princes. See S. Sobreques Vidal, *Els grans comtes de Barcelona* (Barcelona, 1961), p. 22.

9 The marked rise in prices in Christian Spain from the end of the 10th century to the beginning of the 11th has been described by Cl. Sanchez Albornoz, "El precio de la vida en el reino astur-leonas, hace mil años", in *Logos*, t. III (Buenos Aires, 1944), pp. 225 ff., for Leon and Castile by R. Pastor de Togneri, *loc. cit.*, pp. 37 ff., and for Galicia by E. Sáez, "Nuevos datos sobre el costo de la vida en Galicia durante la Edad Media", in *Anuario de Historia del Derecho Español*, t. XVII (1946), pp. 865 ff. It was perhaps still more marked in Catalonia.

10 On the nomenclature of the gold pieces circulating in Catalonia at this time see J. Botet i Sisó, *Les monedes catalanes*, t. I (Barcelona, 1908), pp. 37–45, 72–82, 230.

11 These routes are described by F. Carreras y Candi, *op. cit.*, pp. 14–15.

12 On the condition of the Jews in the Mâconnais, for example, see G. Duby, *op. cit.*, p. 30.

13 Statistical study of a greater number of deeds would show the massive influx of Arab dinars to have occurred between 990 and 1020, whereas Vivas's greatest activity occurred between 986 and 990, when he averaged three transactions a year.

14 Documents of the 13th century refer to the unhealthy climate of the district. See F. Bofarull y Sans, *op. cit.*, p. 217.

15 On the role of the villagesmith see G. Duby, *L'économie rurale et la vie des campagnes dans l'Occident médiéval* (Paris, 1962), t. I, pp. 78–79. Pau seems to have been fairly prosperous, as was his son after him.

16 There are some references to the career of the judge Auruci (or Orús) in R. d'Abadal i de Vinyals, *op. cit.*, p. 331, and in F. Carreras i Candi, *op. cit.*, pp. 211, 218.

17 See F. Carreras i Candi, *op. cit.*, p. 293.

18 It was chiefly Marc Bloch, in *Feudal Society* (tr. by L. A. Manyon, Chicago and London, 1961), pp. 137–41, who raised this question. Very different views have been held.

19 *Lex wisigothorum*, IV, 2, 1, in *Monumenta Germaniae Historica, Leges*, t. I, p. 174.

20 This phenomenon of restricting marriage has been noted by G. Duby both in the Mâconnais, in *La société aux Xie et XIIe siècles dans la région mâconnaise*, pp. 8–9, and in northwestern France, in "Les *Jeunes* clans la société aristocratique", in *Annales. Economies, Sociétés, Civilisations*, t. XIX (1964), p. 842.

21 Neither step insured chastity. The deacon, Hubert, had at least two concubines. The restriction of marriage resulted in the proliferation of bastards, but this did not affect the family since they could not inherit.

22 There is a *melioratio* in the Visigothic law but it refers to quite different circumstances. See *Lex Wisig.*, IV, 5, 1.

23 L. Génicot, who has studied the rise of this new aristocracy in the Namur region, sees its origin in the *ministeriales* (*L'économie rurale namuroise au Bas Moyen âge*, t. II, *Les hommes, la noblesse*, Louvain, 1960). G. Duby sees it as composed of men "enriched through administration, business or even through patient peasant thrift": "Une enquete à poursuivre: la noblesse dans la France médiévale", in *Revue Historique*, t. CCXXVI (1961), p. 3. It is the latter position which is illustrated here.

24 See D. Herlihy, "Land, Family and Women in Continental Europe, 701 to 100", in *Traditio*, t. XVIII (1962), pp. 89–120.

25 We cannot explore this problem here in depth. For D. Herlihy (*loc cit.*, pp. 110–111), it is to be explained both by the survival of Visigothic tradition, which gave women power to choose, and by the precocious development, in these southern countries, of the ideal of chivalry. Can we not also see the high position of women as being a consequence of the general improvement in living standards?

26 The clothing is not actually described in our documents, except for one mention of silk. There may of course have been other types of luxury expenditure; the passion that men of this period had for thorough-bred horses, for example, merits attention. One is still however impressed by the importance accorded women's adornment. Let us not forget that the political life of the county of Barcelona in the mid-11th century is dominated by two women: the countesses Ermessend and Almodis.

27 The precocious revival of towns in the Midi of Gaul has been studied by G. Duby, who notes, from the end of the 10th century, the burgeoning of concentric faubourgs around such cities as Marseilles, Narbonne, Nimes, Carcassonne and Orange. See "Les villes du Sud-Ouest de la Gaule du VIIIs au XIe siècle", in *Settimane di studio sull' alto medio evo*, t. VI (Spoleto, 1959), pp. 231–58. It is not surprising that the first signs of this revival should be more marked at Barcelona, which has a better geographical location.

9

A Serf in Anjou at the End of the 11th Century

JACQUES BOUSSARD

Constant le Roux, one of the serfs of the lord of Chantoceaux, had been bought by Countess Hildegarde of Anjou and given by her to the abbey of Ronceray.[1] The nuns put him in charge of the wine-cellar, which was near the church of St. Evroult, in Angers, and of the vineyards of the Doutre. The countess made him a gift of a cellar for storing wine of his own, abutting the town wall at the Chanzé gate, on the condition that at his death this cellar would go to the abbey.

A widow named Ermentrus had a house outside the walls near the Chanzé gate, with a bakery and a small vineyard about three quarters of an acre in size. She had an only daughter, whom she had married to a certain Hubert Sauvage, giving her half of her property. One day, in a fit of rage, Hubert threw a stone at his wife and killed her. The mother came to the countess in tears to tell of her daughter's sad end, and asked that in revenge she be permitted to give all the deceased woman's property to Ronceray, and also, at her own death, her own property, that is to say, the house, the bakery, and the vineyard. In return she asked that the nuns bury her. All this was accordingly done. The nuns then gave Constant le Roux a life-term lease of the legacy, to encourage him to take good care of their property. They further put him in charge of the property with which the office of the chamberlain was endowed: the land of Espau, the land, meadows and pastures of Femart, which were held in common by the abbey and by Dominique of Evière, and the land of Aunay. Constant managed all of this property, submitting accounts to the chamberlain.

He married, but had no children. Then he took over the lands of Espau and Femart, expelled the tenants and began to work the property himself on a share-cropping basis, keeping half the crops. After a time, driven by insatiable greed, he went to the nuns and, lying atrociously, complained that the returns under this share-cropping were too meagre, both for him and for them. He demanded that they give him a lease of the lands, for a rent, for any term they pleased. The nuns agreed to this.

But his covetousness did not stop here. The wife of Hubert d'Iré, who was a daughter of Gui the Treasurer, had given Ronceray at her death three acres of vineyard that were exempt from wine dues, at Châtaigniers, near Beaumont. Constant, seeing that they were acquiring these lands, free of dues, asked the nuns for a lease of them. They granted this. He further obtained three acres of meadow near la Roche de Chanzé by a purchase disguised as a charitable gift; they adjoined three other acres which belonged to the cellarer's office.

Finally, in his old age, he exacted a promise from Agnes the Cellarer that the nuns would take his nephew Walter into their service, and that she would arrange a marriage between his niece Yseut and Rohot the cellarer. In return for this promise, he gave Agnes a pair of fox skins.

Since Constant had no direct heir and felt himself growing old, he decided that he would become a monk, while his wife would also enter into religion. Being a serf of Ronceray, he had to ask the nuns' consent. He became a monk at St. Aubin, and all the property that he held from Ronceray, in addition to what he owned personally, went to the abbey.

However, Constant sought to secure his nephew's future. From his cloister at St. Aubin, he despatched another monk, Renaud the Grammarian, whom he charged with a mission to Dame Beliart, the Abbess of Ronceray. Through his messenger, Constant assured the abbess that he was praying for her, and thanked her for permitting him to become a monk. He protested that he did not wish to claim any rights over the property he had held from her, but he begged the nuns to remember that he had always shown himself to be a hard-working serf and a faithful administrator, and to give his nephew Walter some rights over the property he had held from the abbey. A life-term lease would do, and at Walter's death the property would go back to the abbey; his heirs would not claim any of it. Walter then entered the nuns' service until they should let him hold his uncle's former lands. He refused to marry one of the serf-girls of Ronceray, but chose a woman of free birth, by whom he had two sons and a daughter. Now Walter had originally been someone's serf, and his uncle Constant had bought him, and had him made one of the Ronceray serfs. By a decision of the chapter, Walter now received several pieces of property under a deed of lease which expressly stipulated a life-term only; some had been his uncle's and some not. By a special arrangement the abbey acquired a gift from Constant of lands which were his personal property, and these were added to Walter's life-term leasehold. As for Gosberga, Constant's wife, she took the veil at Ronceray.

NOTES

1 This story is taken from notes written down, doubtless by a nun of Ronceray; see *Cartulaire du Ronceray,* no. 34, in Marchegay, *Archives d'Anjou,* t. III, pp. 27–30. [As told here, it is merely one portion of Professor Boussard's article on Angevin life in the 11th and 12th centuries. EDITOR'S NOTE.]

Forms of State

I O

Carolingian Administration

EDOUARD PERROY

The State and the Palace

Long studied by historians and erudite specialists, the political and administrative institutions of the Carolingian Empire present fewer problems and uncertainties than the social structure or the economic climate of the age. However, they have by no means been always correctly understood. What has struck authors above all has been the vigor with which the sovereigns of the new dynasty sought to give the Frankish State a solid framework, to enforce order, to ensure obedience to the royal commands. That they made such an effort cannot be denied. A careful reading of the capitularies conveys the very distinct impression that when the Carolingians came to power, they faced a desperate situation, one of profound anarchy, with authority almost completely dissolved. Pepin the Short and, in particular, Charlemagne tried to bring a little order into this almost universal disorder, to use and to develop the too feeble instruments of government that they had inherited from their Merovingian predecessors. One has to admit that for a time they partially succeeded, under conditions so unfavorable that what they accomplished even looks like a brilliant success.

But we must not be deceived. At no moment of its history did the Carolingian Empire possess the solid armature of a true State. A huge collection of peoples, there is no way of holding it together save through the goodwill of a Frankish aristocracy of great proprietors and warriors who are more concerned to enrich themselves than to back up the sovereign's authority. In a predominantly rural world, in a society in which the bonds between the different classes of producers and proprietors are essentially a matter of personal relationships, there is no room for more than a rudimentary administration; the agents of power are never, or almost never, professional officials: the organs of government are reduced to means as elementary as they are ineffective. Only through his personal prestige does a sovereign contrive, as best he can, to maintain some authority in an empire lacking firm organization. Even Charlemagne wears himself out in overcoming periodic political "crises", suppressing conspiracies and crushing the revolts that constantly threaten his work of restoration. Even the idea of the State, which has become thoroughly blurred, no longer serves to bolster power or keep subjects obedient. One begins to doubt whether the concepts of "administration", "institutions", or of a "State" are adequate to grasp the reality.

The Idea of the State

It is a commonplace to recall that at the beginning of the 5th century the Roman Empire still possessed, even in the already anaemic provinces of the West, a large body of specialized administrators. The offices of the Prefecture of the Gauls, located first at Trier and later at Arles, were still in command of some 2000 officials. A competent personnel, then, could still to some extent ward off internal and external dangers to the State, guarantee the security of property and persons, and above all ensure prompt execution of the orders of the prince. These conditions continued or were restored, in the Eastern Empire; in the West, on the contrary, and especially in Gaul, the Roman administrative edifice disintegrated during the 5th century in consequence of the Germanic invasions and the setting up of the barbarian kingdoms. What remained of it crumbled away in the course of the 6th and 7th centuries. In respect of administration, what the Carolingians inherited from the Merovingians amounted to practically nothing.

Worse still, along with its organs of administration the idea of the State, as it had found expression in the Roman Empire in the word *respublica,* had also wasted away. The term summed up the idea that all citizens formed a group under a supreme authority constituted for their good and embodied in the sovereign. In the Roman view—theory was far removed from practice—the imperial authority, although it might at times appear to be despotic, was in no way personal or arbitrary: its sole purpose was to promote the good of all, to strive to uphold the abstract concept of *respublica.* Obedience to the emperor derived from the public good and helped to further it.

All of this vanished in the barbarian kingdoms. Instead of a State, one undoubtedly tyrannical yet based on the idea of the public good, there was a personal and absolute monarchy. Under the Merovingians the kingdom, at least in theory, becomes the personal property of the sovereign; at his death his children divide it up in equal shares, as they would divide a private patrimony; there is no moral concept of the good of his subjects to restrain the king-despot in the exercise of his authority. The concept of the sovereign is the direct opposite of the concept that Roman public law had developed. But the new concept, too, was wholly theoretical: in reality, the theory of Merovingian absolutism was much at variance with the facts, mainly because of the social structure. The growing powers of the landed aristocracy kept the sphere of unchecked absolutism within very narrow limits. Yet this aristocracy, whose ambitions were simply for material wealth and the satisfaction of its hunger for power, showed itself incapable of developing any political theory. It produced not a single positive or constructive idea to set against the idea of the State as *respublica,* with which the jurists of the Late Empire were familiar. The very word *respublica,* as Fustel de Coulanges remarks, passed out of current vocabulary. When it occurs in writings of the 7th and 8th centuries, it refers to the Eastern Roman Empire, not to the Frankish kingdom. If the word went out of use, without being replaced by any equivalent term, it is because the idea of the State had disappeared from men's minds.

We have to admit that the Carolingians tried to fill this vacuum and to revive, under a new form, the idea of the State. They tried to replace the old Roman idea by one that stressed the collective duties of all subjects to the sovereign and the duties of the sovereign, a newer concept, to his subjects. The theory took form in Charlemagne's entourage and it is in his capitularies and in those of his son Louis the Pious that we find it most clearly expressed. The idea is new. It is entirely independent of the Roman idea, having arisen among clerics and being bathed in a religious sentiment that was naturally lacking in the political structure of the Late Empire. Contrary to the Merovingian sovereigns' view of their power, the Frankish king is no longer merely the owner of territories to be exploited for his material benefit. He speaks and acts in the name of the community of the peoples placed under his authority. He holds this sovereign power from God who, according to the Davidian and sacerdotal view of monarchy dear to clerics brought up on Holy Scripture, has designated the king to lead the newly elect people to salvation. The king reigns over all Christians; the king and his people have reciprocal obligations which flow from divine law.

This new conception of a kind of Christian monarchy is nowhere better defined than in the instructions the emperor gave to his *missi* in 802, charging them to exact a new oath of loyalty to the sovereign from all his subjects. Charlemagne states that many of his subjects felt that earlier oaths they had taken were merely personal, like those of a vassal, creating only negative obligations: not to do the sovereign wrong, not to make any alliance with his enemies nor with men who had broken their oath to him. The emperor rejects this interpretation as too narrow. For him, the oath imposes positive obligations much more extensive than mere fidelity to the sovereign. And he is careful to list them: the *fidelis* should in the first place pledge himself to serve God, "because the emperor cannot personally supervise each man". In other words, the emperor, who has the duty of guarding the faith, relies on each man to help him, to the best of his abilities, in maintaining strict observance of the Christian moral law. Similarly the *fidelis* must do no wrong to churches, widows, orphans or strangers, "because the emperor, after God and his saints, is their protector and their defender": he can protect them properly only if all his subjects help him. Finally, to take only the more significant clauses, the oath of fidelity binds the subject who has taken it not to deviate from the path of justice, and to aid the emperor, with all his might, to ensure the triumph of justice.

This idea of collaboration between the sovereign and his subjects for a common end, which is peace on earth and the salvation of as many people as possible, had the effect of infinitely multiplying the obligations stemming from the oath of fidelity. One can make a list of these by going through the capitularies issued after Charlemagne's imperial coronation, the date at which he takes the role of leader of the Christian people, in which his clergy had cast him, seriously. For example, it is forbidden to harbor a thief, since "every thief is disloyal both to us and to the Franks, and so is whoever gives him shelter". In so far as he is able, every *fidelis* is in duty bound to assist the poor, in order to suppress the social and moral scourge of vagabondage. For analogous moral reasons, he must refrain from cornering food supplies or conniving at illicit raising of prices, both of which are counter to the common good. All these obligations will be found repeated and justified in a capitulary of Louis the Pious dating from 823–825, in which the sovereign very clearly defines the reasons for these reciprocal rights and duties: it is the emperor's personal duty to watch over the Church and to maintain peace and justice "for the whole of his people" but, he adds, "although this command may appear to rest wholly on our person, it is really, however, by God's authority and human organization, divided in such a way that each of you, wherever he lives and in whatever social rank he is placed, may know that he bears a part of our burden; it follows that I must be your admonisher in all things and that you must be my helpers". The purpose of each man's duties is then to help the sovereign provide for "the common utility", to avoid "common harm", to work for "the common salvation of all".

There can be no denying the nobility of the sentiments behind this concept of the sovereign as the supreme guide of the Christian people, who demands the cooperation of each for the good and the salvation of all. But, if we find this idea in Charlemagne's legislation and in that of his son Louis the Pious, we may properly ask what resonance it evoked in their subjects: to what extent could it have been translated into action? Let us repeat, the idea came from the clergy; it was based on the Scriptures and on Christian morality, and represented the aspirations of moralists. Surely there is something illusory in believing, as L. Halphen did, that this idea sustained the political equilibrium of the Empire up to the time of troubles in the 830's? Actually, it could have been of practical use only in a truly Christian society, one pervaded by deep faith and an impeccable morality. These conditions plainly did not exist. One may even go so far as to say that the whole scheme was constructed in a void, with nothing to support it. Neither the sovereigns nor the clergy in their entourage could possibly have made it work.

In the first place, the social structure of the Frankish Empire was unfavorable to it. In a rural world, primitive in its customs and habituated to violence, the king's *fideles* were unable to grasp an abstract idea of the common good for which they would feel themselves responsible as a group. Even the development of relationships of dependence, which the sovereigns themselves encouraged, created none but purely personal obligations; their moral and compulsive value was strictly limited to the fulfilling of reciprocal duties between *fideles* and their lords. In such a society, held together by a multiplicity of oaths, there was no room for an abstract idea of the State and of the common good, even when it was upheld by a religious ideal and spiritual sanctions.

In the second place, the Christian monarchy of which Charlemagne dreamed could only be effectively realized if the sovereign, who was the representative of God on earth, the apex of the system, had the physical means to make his will known and respected. But he did not possess such means. In an immeasurably sprawling empire, there were not enough agents even to execute decisions taken at the summit. There were no true officials, men of experience and professional zeal; in short, there was no administration at all, in the proper sense of the term. A quick view of the chief mechanisms of this so-called "administration" will more than prove this.

The Palace

It would be extremely deceptive to speak of a "central administration" around the sovereign to which any important port of his functions were delegated, with specialized powers and with offices handling current business and issuing orders. Such a central administration existed in Charlemagne's time in the Eastern Roman Empire and, in a less highly developed but still very complicated form, at the headquarters of the Abbasid Caliphs of Baghdad. We can be quite sure that nothing like this existed at the court of the Frankish sovereign. What some historians by slipshod error call "the central administration" of the Carolingian Empire is the Palace, which can be defined as the private household group including *fideles* and servants who live with the sovereign and follow him around as he moves from place to place.

Details of the Palace organization, which elude us entirely prior to the reign of Charlemagne, are still only imperfectly known over the greater part of the 9th century. Many historians have been deceived by a celebrated work, the *De ordine palatii,* having uncritically taken its description as factual (L. Halphen, in the *Revue historique,* 1938). The author is the famous Hincmar, Archbishop of Rheims. Writing in 882, towards the end of a long career, he was trying to instruct the young King Carloman, sole ruler of Western Francia, who next to his uncle the Emperor Charles the Fat was the last survivor of the Carolingian dynasty. Hincmar looks back nostalgically to the grandeur of "the kingdom" in the preceding age —a veritable golden age—when he was young, and still further back, to the age of the glorious Charlemagne. He professes to be drawing on personal memories and on those of his elders, and even to be using a treatise since lost, by a contemporary of Charlemagne, Abbot Adelhard of Corbie. In fact, the picture he puts together is purely an ideal, altogether idyllic: he depicts a perfectly smooth organization of domestic and administrative services, where all the officials and serving-men were "joyous and laughing", lively and alert, where everyone knew exactly what he had to do. He puts his own political concepts into this figment of imagination; in particular, he gives the high clergy a leading place in the government of the kingdom, a place which they certainly did not hold under Charlemagne. He ascribes a firm and solid maturity to institutions which were on the contrary still very fluid, for example the great assemblies or *plaids,* the holding of councils, the procedures employed in the promulgation of capitularies. As L. Halphen says, "We see a truly idyllic scene: a program of carefully thought out deliberations that were yet kept secret; a body of councillors incapable of favoring private interests above the general interest, wholly incorruptible and deaf to flattery. . . ." This enchanting picture does not precisely correspond to any of the realities, at any moment, of the Carolingian Empire. It is best to ignore such biased writing and to keep to the facts, scant though they are, that the documents bearing on administrative practice disclose.

Like most of the institutions of the age, the Palace, under the first Carolingians, is a legacy from the Merovingians. From the reign of Charlemagne, the kings of the new dynasty gave it a new orientation, improving and extending some of its services. This Carolingian work deserves a close look.

The Chapel.   The first of the services in which we see a change is the body that is beginning to be called the king's "chapel". It comprises all those priests and clerks whose duty is to hold divine service and meet the religious needs of the king and his following and also to guard the precious relics the king owns and to venerate them by prayer. Indeed, it is from this latter function that the word "chapel", unknown in the primitive Church but destined to spread throughout the Christian world, derives. Among the precious relics to which the Carolingians laid personal claim, the celebrated cape (*cappa*) of St. Martin, which at some unknown date in the 7th century the Frankish kings had managed to remove from the Abbey of Tours to their personal oratory, was held in special veneration. Subsequently the mayors of the Austrasian palace had appropriated it, at the beginning of the 8th century. The diminutive, *capella* (the little cape), as it was familiarly called, quickly became attached to the sovereign's private oratory where it was kept. (It was with this new meaning, of a place of private prayer, as distinct from a church, that the term usually came to be used in the middle ages.) Finally, the clerks in charge of the oratory naturally came to be called *capellani* (chaplains).

This rather large group of clerks was placed under the direction of their principal member, who in Charlemagne's time still had no definite title. Under Louis the Pious he began to be called the chief chaplain or archchaplain. Already by Charlemagne's time he was an important person, always chosen from among the highest dignitaries of the Frankish Church. After the death of Fulrad, Abbot of Saint-Denis, who had held this position, in 782, Charlemagne gave it to Angilram, Bishop of Metz, who died in 791, and then to Hildebald, Bishop of Metz, who served under Louis the Pious up to 818. For these "absentee" bishops, it had been necessary to get a papal dispensation from the duty of residing in their diocese, on the excuse that the king's need to have them constantly at his side was a true need of the Church. The pope even conferred on Hildebald the personal dignity of archbishop; the records of a council held in 818 entitle him pompously, "Archbishop of the sacred palace". It goes without saying that this high dignitary of the Church and the Palace was the sovereign's chief ecclesiastical adviser, having a place of honor above all other prelates. But the "services" of which he took charge were in no sense administrative except in one case, which modern historians, in too much of a hurry to anticipate later developments, have called those of the "chancery". They refer to embryonic official work that was marginal to the chapel itself; the head of the latter had no part in it; those who conducted it, being clergy, are sometimes found helping with the religious duties incumbent on the chapel staff.

The term "chancery" (*cancellaria*), as describing a true administrative department, does not actually appear in the feudal monarchies until the 12th century. But under the Carolingians there is something that resembles this department and is progressively detached from the chapel. From the time of Pepin the Short the habit had grown up of recruiting the few scribes needed for the government of the palace from among the chapel clerks. This was quite natural; Latin remained the only official language of administration, to unlettered laymen it was almost incomprehensible, and clerks were the only people who could speak or write it with any correctness. In their capacity as clerks of the chapel, these scribes remained under the jurisdiction of the arch-chaplain. But in their capacity as scribes, they were called either *notarii* or *cancelarii*, and were under a chief scribe chosen from their ranks. His principal role was to write, on the acts and charters drawn up in this embryonic department, the validating sentence that diplomatists call the *recognitio*. Towards the end of Charlemagne's reign, this chief of the royal notaries or scribes has a definite place in the palace hierarchy. Henceforth the title of chancellor is reserved for him alone, for in the eyes of the sovereign he is the chancellor *par excellence* (*cancellarius noster*).

There is, then, a chancellor in the Carolingian palace. One cannot say that he directs a true chancery, for the little group of scribes under his orders has only a very restricted competence, has no centralized control over the issue of royal commands, and creates no important administrative archives.

It would be a mistake to look on the chancellor's office as a kind of central secretariat for the Carolingian monarchy. Indeed, the chancellor had only a limited responsibility for public "writings", and the sphere of the latter was in turn very narrow. It is not his business to take down the decisions of judicial pleas, which the parties to suits want carried out. Nor is it he who drafts capitularies or writes the king's letters. His work is limited to seeing that charters, that is, the solemn record of royal gifts, are properly written and validated. And in Charlemagne's reign a custom was appearing that was to spread during the 9th century, by which the churches and abbeys that were the principal beneficiaries of royal charters preferred to draft the text of the privilege in their own *scriptorium* and simply present it to the chancellor for validation. This considerably reduced the work of the royal notaries; the chancellor did not need a large staff.

Besides, let us not forget that the prevalence of illiteracy among the laity, consequently the very slight use that was made of writing, minimized the value of the written word. The king's will is expressed by mouth, by oral commands; the king's word (*verbum regis*) is identical with the king's edict (*bannum regis*), that is, with the right to govern. The king gives his orders orally to the *fideles* who approach him in his palace or when he hears pleas. And it is orally that his orders are communicated, by his great men, to the mass of the people whom the king cannot reach. In most cases a written order is not, properly speaking, an order, but merely a reminder of what the king had ordered orally. No doubt some of the chancellor's notaries drafted some official orders (*praecepta*) in a stereotyped common form. Again, if the king happened to send letters to men charged to carry out his orders, this way of transmitting the king's wishes had some secondary value. To conduct administration through writing would have required that the local agents of power have scribes about them capable of corresponding with the central power and of translating the king's written orders to the counts. Yet in spite of the advice Charlemagne gave them to this effect (he himself perceived the administrative value of regular correspondence), most of them did nothing about it.

This bankruptcy of writing enables us to understand the purpose and the variety of forms of the documents that are commonly classed together as capitularies. They bear little relation to authentic legislation. Very rarely, and only when their importance made it necessary, they take the form of "precepts" issued in the name of the emperor and formally validated. Much more often they are merely more or less detailed "minutes", not validated by the royal seal, of decisions announced or read by the king at his judicial sessions. More often still, they simply summarize, point by point, royal decisions. Sometimes only the headings of these were copied out, these being considered sufficient to refresh the memory of all who had been charged to execute the king's oral orders. One letter sent by Charlemagne's *missi* to the counts specifically defines this role of the capitularies as reminders: "We admonish you to reread your capitularies and to recall the verbal orders that were given you; then apply yourselves to show such zeal that you may be rewarded by God and by your master, the great emperor". It follows that only the oral transmission of royal orders is legally binding. The adage, "ignorance of the law is no excuse" had no currency in the Carolingian Empire, for no one who had not heard the law was bound to obey it. A letter of Charlemagne to his son Pepin, King of Italy (806–810), implicitly admits this: the Italians, he says, will not obey the capitularies that the emperor has ordered incorporated in their law, because they have not been so notified by the emperor in person. He then orders his son, who had been present at the judicial session where these capitularies had been orally proclaimed, to have them publicly read throughout his kingdom, in order that everyone should obey them.

In a society with so little need for writing, the chancellor's "department" remained quite embryonic. In consequence it was not impelled to keep any complete file of records. Only those capitularies that were written out in full and were in the form of precepts, could be kept in the archives. In the case of a capitulary relating to the organization of the army (808), Charlemagne orders that four sets of copies be made: one for the *missi* sent on tour, one for the counts who would have to do what it ordered, one for the *missi* of the army; the fourth was for the chancellor, evidently for safe-keeping at the palace. Louis the Pious gave a similar order in 819, for the capitularies recording the decisions taken at the last judicial session. But the collection remained small. In the reign of Louis the Pious, Bishop Angesise went to the chancellor's archives at the palace to get a set of the capitularies copied for his own use. It seems safe to say that he took copies of all he could find, which amounted to twenty-nine. Yet, for the period covered by his collection, modern specialists could easily triple this number. Better still, a little later it happened that a certain Benedict the Levite had the imagination to enlarge Angesise's collection by interpolating some false capitularies of his own composition. The palace archives were so badly kept, and people were so ignorant of the content of capitularies, that up to the reign of Charles the Bald these forgeries were regarded as authentic. Can one still speak of the Carolingian administration as having a "central secretariat"?

Lay Dignitaries. There is still less sign of any well-organized administrative service among the sovereign's lay entourage than in the work attached to the chapel. In this area the Carolingians made few important changes in the embryonic organs of government bequeathed them by the Merovingians. The Frankish kings' *domus* was managed by a cluster of "palatine officers" who were really only domestic officials. Domestic and public functions were intermingled, in utter confusion. The household managers, being in the sovereign's immediate following, on occasion were engaged on what we would call public business. This remains the rule in the Carolingian palace.

Of all the offices surrounding the Merovingian royalty, only one disappeared in the course of the 8th century, that of the *major domus* (which historians have dressed up in the ludicrous name of "mayor of the palace"), the chief administrator of the sovereign's whole household. His disappearance is obviously due to the fact that after he acceded to the royal dignity he was not replaced. After his usurpation in 751, Pepin the Short had no wish to have a powerful personage around who might overshadow him. The management of the royal domestic affairs passed to an officer with the German title of seneschal (Latinized as *senescalcus*). Literally, the word means "the old man, the chief of the servants". His main job was to procure food for the Palace. Writers and poets of the Carolingian renaissance paraphrased his title, which to their ears sounded barbarous, into "the prefect of the royal table". Alongside him was the butler, who enjoyed almost similar rank, and was responsible for keeping the Palace supplied with drink. Since the bulk of these provisions came from the royal domains, either through transport of their surplus or through the Palace moving around to consume this on the spot, the seneschal and the butler naturally exercised a certain authority and even control over the administration of these fiscal domains. (See articles 16 and 17 of the Capitulary *De Villis*.) The seneschal may even in Charlemagne's time, as was the case in the feudal age, have been responsible for examining the accounts of the domain stewards. Since the fisc was the sovereign's personal property, these functions were still of a domestic character.

The duties also of the constable (*comes stabuli,* count of the stable) were mainly domestic, being concerned with the royal stables. His functions, however, assumed special importance during military campaigns, for he was in charge of supplying remounts for the cavalry, the essential part of Frankish armies.

All of these high officials had numerous humbler servants under them:

servants to clean the royal apartments, door-keepers, porters, a swarm of cooks and pantrymen, grooms, and hunters and falconers. From the circumstance that they were his chief household officers, the seneschal and butler and constable were among the king's most trusted advisers. He employed them in many other capacities, on diplomatic missions and in positions of military command. The fact remains, however, that they were domestic officers. One should by no means think of them as "ministers", in the modern sense of the term, nor as heads of administrative departments.

But there were some lay officers in the Palace who did manage embryonic departments, for example, the chamberlain (*camerarius*), who was in charge of the king's private rooms. This part of the palace, being the most secret and the best guarded, was naturally the place where the king's treasure was piled. The word *chamber* comes to be synonymous with *treasure*; it is not in the least like a modern treasury. Lacking proper administrative institutions, the Frankish kingdom has no administrative expenses. It pays no salaries. All the king's servants, even those at the palace, get their living through allowances from his supplies, through free distributions of food and clothing, and through prebends, that is, fixed claims on the produce of particular lands. The monarchy incurs no costs in the public or collective interest, for public works are carried out through requisitioning materials and demanding service from those who will use them; military defence is on a similar basis. On the other hand, the kingdom has very little revenue, just enough for its modest needs: the remnants of public receipts over and above what is taken by the local agents as their allowance and for costs; surplus revenues from the fiscal domains; and finally the gifts that great men of the realm, or foreign rulers and their ambassadors offer the king. All this goes into the sovereign's chamber, or treasure. These reserves, on which the king draws to reward his followers or to meet unavoidable expenses, are not entirely in money. There is more gold and silver in the form of bars, hoarded; it is the chamber which on the occasion of Charles the Bald's monetary reform, under the Edict of Pîtres (864), lends the mint directors the mass of silver required to start minting the new coins. There were also jewels, gold crowns, ornaments, pieces of goldsmith's work, and even a store of luxury textiles: ceremonial robes, silks, colored cloth and furred cloth.

This treasure is the king's private hoard, it never plays the role of a public treasury. We should not be deceived by the erroneous description of it by Latinist writers in the sovereign's following, who dip into the classical past to speak of it as a public treasure (aerarium publicum). Certain modern historians have gone still further astray in seeing the chamberlain as a joint minister of finance and foreign affairs, simply because it was his duty to receive ambassadors! All we can say is that the management of this hoard required him to employ a few subordinate officials to take inven-

tories and keep rough accounts. True, we know very little about these arrangements, only that they could not have been at all highly developed. To
repeat, the sovereign regarded the treasure simply as his personal property,
to be used and disposed of as he pleased.

Einhard tells us how Charlemagne, three years before his death, made
arrangements to divide his possessions among his children, legitimate and
illegitimate. Two-thirds were placed under seal and set aside to be divided equally among the twenty-one metropolitan churches of the empire.
The other third was divided into four parts, one for churches, one for his
bastards and their descendants, one for the poor, and one for gratuities to
the palace servants. Thus the emperor's successor would start with no
treasure at all; he would have to build it up again. In the circumstances it
is hardly surprising that when Louis the Pious came to the throne he refrained from executing Charlemagne's will, which, to make it more solemn,
had been signed by eleven bishops, four abbots, and fifteen counts. If we
may believe his nephew and biographer Nithard, Louis contented himself with reserving one third for his father's funeral and for alms to the
Church and kept the other two-thirds for himself, paying out of it, however, the dowries of his two legitimate sisters. Nothing better reveals the
extremely rudimentary nature of this supposed "financial administration".

A much more important role was that of the "Count of the Palace",
the only addition to this group of offices (which was older than the Palace).
Despite his title, he is not a successor of the defunct *major domus*. The few
texts which refer to him show that he had a much more limited and better
defined role. He was the normal president of the palace tribunal, where
he rendered justice by virtue of a permanent delegation of power from the
sovereign. The volume of business coming before the royal tribunal seems
to have risen considerably under Charlemagne, at first because of the increase in the territory controlled by the Franks, and later through the prestige and authority that accrued to the sovereign. The emperor can no
longer take part in the debates except occasionally, as sovereign justiciar
then making a judgment from which there is no appeal. Procedural texts,
as well as legislative decisions, show that the count of the palace presided
over almost all cases, as the sovereign's lieutenant. His power soon became
so great and so discretionary that Charlemagne himself sought to limit it:
a capitulary from the end of the reign prescribes that in important suits
involving men of power, that is, suits between counts, bishops, abbots and
other great vassals, the count of the palace cannot in future make a final
judgment without first consulting the sovereign. He will however retain
full power to decide cases concerning lesser subjects and the poor. Einhard
portrays this great officer visiting the sovereign when he gets up in the
morning, to inform him of major cases that call for his decision; the emperor then summoned the suitors, heard a summary of the case, and
immediately gave judgment. The count of the palace was, nevertheless, de-

spite this limitation, the uncontested head of the royal tribunal. He therefore necessarily found himself directing an embryonic administrative service; it was to this that the party who won a suit applied for a transcript of
the decision, and it was here that applications to plead (*placita*) were
drawn up. There must have been several scribes. Thus Charlemagne made
the central administration of justice a little less amorphous than it had
been at the beginning of the Carolingian era.

Yet what was accomplished does not amount to very much. Our brief
survey obliges us to conclude that none of the palace work even distantly
approached what we would call a central administration. A mixing of domestic and administrative duties, an almost total lack of differentiation of
governmental responsibilities—these are the two leading characteristics. At
best, we can glimpse a little rudimentary organization, consisting of a
handful of subaltern employees in the services of the chancellor, the chamberlain, the count of the palace. To interpret these as actual "ministries"
of the interior, of finance or of justice is to go too far, and we should be
careful to shun any such false analogies.

Local and Regional Organization

Despite appearances, the local framework of Carolingian "administration"
is hardly any firmer nor better equipped than the central services of the
Palace. What is at first striking, however, is its apparent uniformity.
Whether we look at territories anciently occupied by the Frankish
monarchy, or at more recently conquered regions (Lombard Italy, Saxony),
at territories under the emperor's direct control or temporarily entrusted
to one of his sons as an autonomous kingdom, or constituting a "duchy"
or a military "march", the land is uniformly divided into counties.

Counts and counties. These districts are all administered by a personage whose office is a legacy from Merovingian institutions and whose
name is borrowed from classical Latin as was the custom in the Late Empire. The count (*comes,* companion of the prince) is also the equivalent of
the Germanic *graf,* Latinized in the documents of the period as *grafio*. Under his authority is a territory that contemporaries sometimes call county
(*comitatus*) but more usually *pagus* (region). It has been the equivalent,
since the barbarian kingdoms were set up, of the Germanic *gau:* we know
of these *gau* at least among the Lombards, the last of the Germanic peoples
to enter the Roman world.

Historians have tried to enumerate all the counties in the "great"
empire set up by Charlemagne, but owing to inadequate documentation
they have only partially succeeded. It is besides averred, as is too often for-
gotten, that the boundaries of the *pagus* or the *gau* were not in all cases
stable through the centuries. From one generation to another there were

variations due to subdivision of areas that were too large or to the temporary or lasting merger of adjacent areas that were too small. Though it is impossible to give an exact figure for any given date, we cannot be far wrong in placing the number of counties contained in the empire in Charlemagne's time at from 200 to 250.

The size of these districts varied considerably from one region to another and even within the same region. In general they were larger in southern Gaul and in Italy, where they quite often coincided with the bounds of ancient Roman city territories, and thus with a diocese; but the largest city territories were divided into several *pagi*. In the northern regions of Gaul, where the population was almost wholly Germanic, the *gau* were generally smaller, some not exceeding the size of one or two modern cantons. But there was no less inequality elsewhere; one thinks, for example, of the huge *pagus* of Brabant (reconstituted by Bonenfant) and of the spread of little *pagi* to the west of the Scheldt, dividing up French Flanders. Can we suppose, under these conditions, as does Halphen, that the counties were divided according to some logical system, taking account, say, of the greater or lower density of population? We have to confess that the principles behind the administrative geography of the Carolingian Empire escape us.

Administrative Personnel of the County.   Before we identify the count too hastily as an "administrator" in the modern sense of the word, we should know what subordinates he had at his disposal through whom he could make a delegated authority felt among the population of the *pagus,* large or small. In this respect he was no better off than the central services around the king in the Palace; he had no real organization, not enough servants to allow him to carry out his multiple functions efficiently. He had nothing like the retinue of the *strategus* who exercised military control and directed the administration of the provinces of the Byzantine Empire at this period. His subordinates can be quickly listed.

Charlemagne advises his counts always to have at least one notary with them, a scribe able to write out important administrative orders. The fact that the advice was expressly repeated indicates that many counts did not have this one indispensable secretary. There is never any proof that the advice was generally followed.

We should perhaps also credit Charlemagne with what seems to be an innovation, the creation of a proxy for each count, called the viscount, nominated by the count, the appointment being confirmed by the emperor. But this kind of permanent deputy, competent to act for the count at any time, seems to have had an effective existence only in the western regions of the Empire, that is, in Gaul. There is no example from Germany or from Italy.

When it was large enough, the country was in fact subdivided into secondary districts known either as *vigueries* (*vicaria*) or as hundreds (*centena*). The count appointed agents, *viguiers* or *centeniers,* to exercise authority over these, but we know little of their powers. A deputy of the count in his little district, as the count was of the sovereign, in his, the *viguier* or *centenier* had however a limited competence, at least in judicial matters. The tribunal over which he presided could consider only minor cases or petty misdemeanors, important suits and major crimes being reserved for the count's tribunal. We know even less about the geography of these districts than we do about the counties. It is not certain whether all *pagi* were so divided; again, the boundaries may have altered from one generation to another.

To put the best possible face on things, that is, to suppose that the count had several notaries, that he was flanked by a viscount and that his *pagus* was divided into several hundreds, gives him at most from ten to twelve subordinate officers. On such a basis the administration of the huge Carolingian Empire would have depended on from 2,000 to 3,000 persons, including both the Palace services and the little *centeniers*. A skeleton force, whose numerical inadequacy was aggravated by extreme incompetence. Scarcely any of these agents of power were professional officials, qualified administrators. In spite of appearances, then, the Carolingian Empire possessed no proper administrative organization.

The Count's Jurisdiction. With the aid of his clearly inadequate staff, the count has to exercise jurisdiction over a wide range of affairs. Like his Merovingian predecessor, he is the local representative of the sovereign in the plenitude of his powers, possessing complete authority in the whole bundle of forms that public power assumes. These were not differentiated; to classify them according to modern style as administrative, financial, judicial and military would be futile. It is his duty to proclaim and enforce all royal commands that reach him, whether as legislative capitularies, administrative rulings or other orders, oral or written, relating to problems peculiar to his county. He levies the various dues, taxes and "gifts" that the sovereign demands from his subjects in the *pagus;* he assembles the proceeds and is responsible for their utilization, for they have to cover all local expenses. He requisitions the labor and materials required for what we might call "public works", supervising the more or less regular repair of roads and bridges. In certain cases he is required to take surplus receipts to the royal chamber. He is also responsible for the maintenance of order, for local policing, and he presides over the public tribunal or *mallus,* where he pronounces sentence and subsequently collects the fines imposed. Finally, it is he who summons, recruits, and commands the armed contingents that his pagus has to raise for the royal host. We could easily extend the list of his duties: the count is in every way the sovereign's representative in his district; he exercises the undivided totality of public power.

This depositary of sovereign power is however far from being a government official in the proper sense of the word. Since he is not a paid official, and receives no regular salary, it is all too easy for him to evade the control that the central government would otherwise have over him. The count's remuneration included two main elements. In the first place he was endowed, for the duration of his term of office, with an "honor", that is, with a portion of the fiscal domains within his territory. His landed revenue was sometimes swollen by the right to hold the lay abbacy of some monastery in his *pagus*. He therefore enjoyed a considerable revenue over and above what he drew from his patrimonial possessions and from benefices the sovereign may have given him. All of this combined to make him the richest of the landed aristocracy over whom he presided. This mode of remuneration, through partial and temporary alienation of landed capital, was extremely prejudicial to the sound maintenance of the sovereign's resources.

In addition to this fixed endowment the count enjoyed "perquisites". He was entitled to keep a third of the fines levied in the courts of his district, both in his own tribunal and in the hundred courts. And these fines imposed for the benefit of public authority were considerable. In all suits, the losing party had not only to pay his adversary a pecuniary composition but also to pay a fine (*freda,* in the Germanic term) as a kind of fee to the royal justice; this fine as a general rule was a third as large as the composition. The count thus kept one-ninth of the judicial payments. Besides, at least from the reign of Charlemagne, capitularies multiplied the number of misdemeanors, even minor ones, which were to be regarded as an offence against the royal power (*ban*). These were punishable by the heavy fine of 60 shillings (720 penny pieces). Since this fine belonged entirely to the public power, the count naturally kept a third of it. His perquisites also included the right to keep a portion—usually a third—of all the taxes he levied, the most profitable of which were customs and market dues. His total cut was therefore far from negligible. Inevitably he tended by corruption to increase it. In the absence of any regular system of accounting or other effective control, he could readily retain more than his legal share of taxes and judicial fines, thus appropriating large amounts of royal revenue. He could abuse his usufructuary rights in the fiscal domains with which he was endowed during his term of office, through too intensive exploitation. Finally, he could and did exploit the people under his rule by multiplying occasions for the levy of fines, part or all of which he would keep for himself. The occasions were over-frequent summons to military service in order to levy the *heriban* fine for non-appearance, and over-frequent summons to the judicial sessions to which all free men of the county were bound to come on pain of a fine (*bannum dominicum*) for default. Charlemagne's capitularies are filled with provisions denouncing such abuses of power and threatening to punish the guilty, as an example, unless they treat their people less arbitrarily. The repetition of these complaints is peremptory proof that the sovereign authority was quite incapable of checking the abuse of power by its local agents; it was unable to establish justice and equity in a local administration exercised in its name by autonomous potentates.

However, the sovereign was not wholly helpless in the face of "officials" who did not choose to comply with his orders. The capitularies to which we have just referred constantly threaten counts who behave too independently or are too oppressive, with total loss of their "honor", that is to say, not only with the loss of their lucrative office and its comfortable landed endowment, but with probable loss of benefices and possible confiscation of their patrimonial property. These brutal deprivations were not a mere threat. There is proof that under Louis the Pious one such threat was actually carried out, and many more examples of this are known from the period of the civil wars between this emperor's sons. But were a few dramatic cases, occurring in particularly horrible circumstances or during the troubles of a political crisis, sufficient to ensure the loyalty, let alone the honesty, of counts? For that, the sovereign would have had to be in a position to dismiss or recall his agents at any moment, and to replace a weak or prevaricating man, without any difficulty, by a more reliable and competent candidate.

In principle, to be sure, the count held office only at the will of the sovereign, who appointed men of his own choice, and dismissed and replaced his administrative personnel at pleasure. In practice, this arbitrary power was severely limited. To begin with, the sovereign did not have a large enough supply of able men at his disposal from which good administrators could be drawn. It has long been noticed that the counts were recruited exclusively among the high Frankish aristocracy; it would be more accurate to say, from Austrasian aristocracy who were relatives of the ruling family. It has been ascertained that of 110 men who have been identified as holding important administrative positions and playing a major role in the government of the empire under Charlemagne and Louis the Pious, 70 were Austrasian Franks; of these, 52 were related to the Carolingian dynasty by some kind of family tie. All important matters, then, were in the hands of a few dozen great families, almost all of whom had intermarried. Even when a count's office was not passed on to his heir—the custom of hereditary succession appeared only gradually, in the latter half of the 9th century, and did not become universal—the successor of a count who died or who was removed, even when the dismissal occurred as a brutal punishment, was almost always a close relative. The best-known example of this is the countship of Autun, which for over a century was held by members of only three great families, all three from Austrasia. Scholars have been able to prove, through genealogical research, that all of the counts of Autun were near relatives of their predecessors.

Obviously the sovereign could not risk alienating so tightly knit an

aristocracy by arbitrary removal of counts. In a society thoroughly vassal-
ized, the honor was as a matter of fact assimilated to the benefice. It could
be taken away from the beneficiary only in case of flagrant misconduct.
This is why, even under Charlemagne, and contrary to what has sometimes
been affirmed, the count is often left in office so long that one can regard
him as really irremovable. He has time to acquire property of his own in
his county, to create a personal clientele of vassals there; sometimes he
marries there; in short, he becomes rooted there and founds a family. He
can be moved only by offering him advancement, that is, by offering him
more profitable honors elsewhere. The fixity of the counts dignity, temporarily destroyed during the civil strife between the sons of Louis the
Pious, was resumed and accentuated under their successors. When, from
856 on, we see the magnates of western Francia entering into an alliance
and promising each other mutual aid should the king unjustly deprive
them of their benefices and their honors, this amounts only to the explicit
formulation of a rule already implicitly recognized: the removal of a count
is justified only in case of outright rebellion. In these circumstances, can
we speak of him as though he were an official, a docile instrument in the
king's hand? The truth is that local administration was as non-existent as
central administration.

I I

A Note on State Organization: Segmentary States in Africa and in Medieval Europe

AIDAN W. SOUTHALL

Some writers on the subject have assumed that state organisation might emerge as a result of either external conquest or internal diversification.[1] Others have stressed conquest as an invariable concomitant. Genuine ethnographic evidence is poor, but Oberg and Gluckman assume a conquest origin for the Banyankole and Zulu, as Nadel tends to do for the Nupe.[2]

On the basis of the Alur evidence which I have already given,[3] I would suggest that, under certain conditions, the interaction of diverse ethnic groups of contrasted social structure may predispose them to coalesce into a composite structure of dominance and subjection out of which state forms develop. This process cannot adequately be described as conquest. There are two general conditions which favour it, the one structural and the other cultural: first, one ethnic group is politically organised only on a small scale, order is enforcible only within very small groups, and the degree of violence which is only restrained by the free balance of forces between conflicting groups is very considerable; another adjacent ethnic group presents the aspect of political organisation on a wider scale, securing a minimum of peace and order to communities which are thus less restricted in numbers and territory. Second, the one society offers to the other leaders of a charismatic type.[4] I use this term from Weber because his tracing of the "routinization" of pure into hereditary charisma is the only really relevant discussion of this problem, and among the many writings on sacral chiefship there are none which appreciate this aspect of its significance.

I have shown how, on the one hand, peripheral non-Alur groups invited or welcomed Alur chieflets in as rainmakers, arbitrators and finally as enforcers of the peace; and on the other hand how Alur of chiefly rank were imbued with a sense of political destiny and of spiritual mission which provided a traditionally sanctioned pattern for constant re-application in new situations. From the point of view of an unassimilated non-Alur group the Alur chieflet received amongst them was not so very far removed from the qualities of the pure charismatic leader. However, his position became "routinized" immediately on establishment, and from his own point of view, that of his few companions and that of the Alur community from which he sprang, his qualification was that of hereditary charisma from the start.

I cannot agree with Weber's exclusive emphasis on the king as war lord,[5] since this is only one of the possible forms, and conflicts with Weber's own more balanced statement that "the chieftain of early history, the predecessor of kingship, is still a dual figure. On the one hand, he is the patriarchal head of the family or sib, and on the other, he is the charismatic leader of the hunt and war, the sorcerer, the rainmaker, the medicine man —and thus the priest and the doctor—and finally, the arbiter." [6]

The Alur chieftain among the Lendu was revered more for his power to stop than his power to make war, and the sanction to his ritual authority which is always uppermost in people's minds is his power to make or withhold rain rather than his power to call in overwhelming force to crush the disobedient. These same ritual powers sanctioned his authority as an arbitrator. Had his position depended on the command of force or on personal prowess in war it appears that many units of Alur domination over other peoples would never have come into existence, for no irresistible force was brought to bear in their establishment. Once an institutionalised relationship had emerged, based on rainmaking, arbitration, sanctuary, and the chiefly initiation of cycles of production and consumption to the advantage of the whole group, force might be used to redress offences against the system which had already been accorded legitimacy by the group as a whole. Subsequent conflict between several such groups then led to a process of increasing definition of specifically political powers.

Groups entering this system exchanged a lower for a higher order of political organisation, and exchanged a system of values which left them without any refuge from vagaries of climate and resulting famine for one in which they put confidence in the oecological control of the dominant group to which they had freely given their allegiance.

The widespread occurrence of comparable structural and cultural conditions elsewhere suggests that this type of domination process may not have been unique to the Alur. In that case it must be considered as an alternative to internal diversification or external conquest in the analysis of political systems of the state type.

The distinction between state and segmentary organisation is theoretically valid, and at this abstract level intermediate forms demand no separate category. But in any scheme of classification which claims empirical relevance the criteria of legitimate isolation are different, and any empirical form which has a certain frequency, stability, and structural consistency must receive due consideration. The morphologically transitional is not necessarily the empirically transitional form.[7]

This discussion turns at first upon the definition of the state. For present purposes the most illuminating discussion of this is that of Nadel,[8] whose criteria of statehood may be summed up briefly as: territorial sovereignty, centralised government, specialised administrative staff and monopoly of the use of legitimate force. This is in line with Weber's treatment already referred to, and very largely with that of a number of other writers, granting differences of phrasing.

It is noteworthy that there is no important difference of principle between the more penetrating definitions produced by social anthropologists such as Nadel, and those of political scientists such as Laski.

Nadel recognises that "obviously, there exist transitory forms in which only one or two of these political principles are manifest" and leaves the matter there. This is surely to miss a point of some significance. I propose to examine, as briefly as possible, the incidence in space and time of that form of state which I term segmentary, which cannot be said to fulfil the criteria of statehood as given above, and which may tentatively be defined by the following characteristics:

(1) Territorial sovereignty is recognised but limited and essentially relative, forming a series of zones in which authority is most absolute near the centre and increasingly restricted towards the periphery, often shading off into a ritual hegemony.

(2) There is centralised government, yet there are also numerous peripheral foci of administration over which the centre exercises only a limited control.

(3) There is a specialised administrative staff at the centre, but it is repeated on a reduced scale at all the peripheral foci of administration.

(4) Monopoly of the use of force is successfully claimed to a limited extent and within a limited range by the central authority, but legitimate force of a more restricted order inheres at all the peripheral foci.

(5) Several levels of subordinate foci may be distinguishable, organised pyramidally in relation to the central authority. The central and peripheral authorities reflect the same model, the latter being reduced images of the former. Similar powers are repeated at each level with a decreasing range, every authority has certain recognised powers over the subordinate authorities articulated to it, and formally similar offences differ in significance according to the order of authorities involved in them.

(6) The more peripheral a subordinate authority is the more chance it has to change its allegiance from one power pyramid to another. Segmentary states are thus flexible and fluctuating, even comprising peripheral units which have political standing in several adjacent power pyramids which thus become interlocked.

Durkheim [9] used the term segmental to denote the lateral repetition of like units at the base of a society, equating it with his stage of mechanical solidarity. Subsequent anthropological fieldwork has revealed the importance of social structures based on the pyramidal articulation of segments rather than the mere lateral repetition envisaged by Durkheim. . . .

The more civilised states in any historical period have attracted the most careful study, and it is often only as an indirect result of interest in their early origins that attention has been paid to political systems which may in fact have been far more prevalent in time and space. From this point of view the great historical empires at the height of their power are, as political systems, atypical. For a sociological study of political structure there is nothing abnormal in periods of chaos or disintegration. If we abstract the great empires of the Ancient East, of Alexander in the Near East and of Asoka in India, of Rome and Byzantium, of Charlemagne, of Islam and the Moghuls, and of all the nation states of Western Europe, we are still left with the conclusion that, in many parts of the world, and at most times, the degree of political specialisation attained has been of the segmentary rather than of the unitary type.

One very interesting exception to the range of variation between the segmentary and the unitary state seems to be the type of state organisation reported from the Lozi by Gluckman.[10] The political division of the nation into non-localised and widely dispersed sectors seems effectively to limit the tendency to autonomy of component segments. Such a system appears to be consonant with the strong bilateral emphasis in Lozi kinship organisation, although these two features are not invariably associated.[11] For example, the Anglo-Saxon state remained segmentary in type until a very late date, although the Anglo-Saxon kinship system was bilateral.

At the time when the Roman authorities came into contact with the Germanic peoples of north-western Europe they noted the tendency to autonomy of the different provinces and subdivisions of a tribe. There were no common rulers, but princes of different regions and districts administered justice and settled disputes among their own people. As time went on, continual military operations not only forced tribes to form larger leagues, but also to submit to more concentrated and active authorities.[12]

In Anglo-Saxon England we find that the political system was still operating on segmentary principles. Order was secured by self-help rather than by any centralised authority. The degree of monopoly exercised by the king over the use of force corresponded closely to that exercised by an Alur chief.

The Saxon plaintiff was to demand justice of his foe before fighting him. If justice was refused, the plaintiff could legally lay siege to his foe for seven days, and, if he surrendered, could keep him in custody for thirty days, sending word to his kin to come and pay the mulct. "What is to happen if the surrender does not take place at the end of seven days, or the payment at the end of thirty, we are not informed, but it seems to be implied that the claimant may then fight and even slay his enemy without guilt."[13] If the plaintiff was not powerful enough to lay siege, he must "ride to the ealdorman and demand his aid, or, failing that he must seek redress of the king, before he takes it upon himself to fight his foe."[14]

A man could fight for his lord or *his kinsman* without incurring blood guilt, and it was lawful for him to make war upon a seducer of his wife, sister or mother. "We see that the ideas of the old blood feud and of the so-called 'Fistright' still lingered in the mind of even so wise a legislator as Alfred. Redress of wrongs by the action of courts of law might be the ideal, but in the actual Saxon world *private warfare must still be allowed*,[15] and all that the king could hope to accomplish was to confine it within narrow bounds and regulate its procedure."[16]

Jolliffe shows how political authority was divided between kings, lords, underkings and ealdormen, and how the jural system depended on central, shire and folk moots. There was, he says, no king's peace, but only innumerable local folk peaces, no rigidly defined territorial boundaries and no enforcement of authority from the centre, except *in extremis*. The maintenance of order still depended on the joint operation of local and kinship ties. The striking parallels with the level of political specialisation among the Alur need not be pressed further.[17]

Even feudal France in the eleventh century exhibited an essentially segmentary political system. The Capetian kings, it is true, had a titular over-all sovereignty, which was not challenged in principle. The great feudatories usually fulfilled their military obligations under the system. They were too weak to challenge the sovereign power because they were fully occupied in maintaining their own more limited jurisdictions. But, on the other hand, the kings took no steps whatever to maintain order, restrict bloodshed or protect the rights of persons within the fiefs of the feudatories. The counts fought amongst themselves, usurping and annexing, without any control from above. Within the great fiefs, also, similar conditions obtained. In many parts there was an active process of political segmentation.

Flanders was divided into castellanies or circumscriptions under military chiefs who tended to become hereditary. The Count of Flanders was, in the main, a vassal of the King of France, yet for Zeeland, Quatre Métier and Alost he did homage to the Emperor. "In reality (the Count of Flan-

ders) enjoyed almost complete independence." [18] Of the territories of the
Counts of Champagne it was said "there is no unity; the lands ruled by the
count have no cohesion whatever." [19] The Dukes of Burgundy, "although
theoretically they were masters of very extensive territories, . . . saw the
greater part of their possessions slip from under their control to form
genuine little semi-independent principalities." [20] "The very name of
'Kingdom of Burgundy' covered a whole series of territories without unity,
without mutual ties, and over which the king's control was quite illusory." [21]

It is obvious, therefore, that feudal France at this time came nowhere
near the definition of a unitary state in practice, and it seems doubtful
whether the application to it of the theory of the sovereign state can be
meaningful. The political structure was based on a pyramidal series of
mutually opposed segments rather than on powers delegated from an absolute authority at the centre.

Feud-right remained in the Lombard state of the seventh century.
While the king and the nobles made counter claims it is evident that the
political system worked on segmentary principles. "On the whole, the
dukes endeavoured to found their power on inherited rights, and to exercise in their own territory the same authority which belonged to the king
in the whole state, whereas the king claimed for himself the right of nomi-
nating the dukes and treated them as his officials."[22]

I shall conclude by drawing attention to some of the factors involved
in the transition from the segmentary to the unitary type. But we must note
the distinction between intermediate theoretical types and transitional
empirical types, and remember that the segmentary state is no more transitional in relation to the unitary state than the latter is in relation to
modern attempts at international systems which do not fit the concept of
the nation state with its absolute sovereignty.

Wheras the unitary state is a structure in which there is a central monopoly of power, exercised by a specialised administrative staff within defined territorial limits, the segmentary state is a structure in which specialised political power is exercised within a pyramidal series of segments tied
together at any one level by the oppositions between them at a higher level,
and ultimately defined by their joint opposition to adjacent unrelated
groups.

Segmentary states are, indeed, fragile structures of great flexibility.
But they may under certain circumstances last for a very long time. They
may later develop into unitary states or can revert to the segmentary feud
pattern. Transition from the segmentary to the unitary type must be associated empirically with such factors as the decreasing efficacy of ritual
powers, the abolition of the feud system, the definition of feudal obliga-

tions, fiscal development, royal landholding, and the general elaboration of the bureaucratic idea especially as concerns the passage from hereditary subordinate authorities with generalised political powers to transferable officials with restricted and closely defined powers.[23]

Ritual supremacy is often accepted where political control is not, and segmentary states may characteristically be more highly centralised ritually than politically. If powers of a more substantial and specifically political kind are successfully exerted, the ritual validation of the political structure naturally plays a less vital rôle. If the central authority can tie the subordinate authorities to defined feudal obligations this is a sign that the central authority has acquired legitimacy in the political field, and this may be regarded as the most elementary prerequisite of the unitary state. As long as feuding is regarded as a lawful mechanism for the ultimate redress of wrongs, it is clear that the central authority has failed to monopolise political powers, which remain in the hands of subordinate segments, the latter being in this context very often organised on extended kinship principles or at least oriented to a kinship ideology. The abolition of feuding presupposes the successful establishment of a formalised system of courts, and this implies sufficient subordination of the segmentary authorities to permit effective appeal from local to central justice.

Even under the feudal system, many states remained essentially segmentary. For, until the central authority can prove its efficacy to the average individual in terms of personal security, the individual must cling to kin or other traditional local units, and even to feudal authorities, in such a way that the distribution of power is segmentary in type.[24]

Fiscal development is both cause and effect in relation to centralised power. The latter depends fundamentally on a degree of economic independence of subordinate segmentary authorities. This is not satisfactorily achieved by the feudal system alone, for as long as political obligations are primarily defined in terms of personal service the independent action of feudal lords tends simultaneously to strengthen their authority and leave their superior helpless. If personal service can be commuted for cash, the central authority immediately acquires the means of maintaining an administrative staff dependent on itself and therefore dependable in its loyalty over against all subordinate segmentary authorities.

In the segmentary system tribute is received in direct return for ritual and jural services rather than in recognition of any regular fiscal obligation. This type of tribute does little more than enable the central authority to fulfill its obligations when called upon by subordinate segments. The next stage, from the analytical point of view, is the definition of fiscal obligations as between any segment and its component segments at the next lower level, though the fiscal exactions of the latter on their own account are not effectively limited from the centre. This increases power at the centre by regularising its economic basis, while leaving the powers of subordinate segments essentially unimpaired and still does not fulfill the conditions for the emergence of a unitary state. The latter depends upon the enforcement of a centralised fiscal system to the exclusion of subsidiary systems operated within subordinate segments, and ties up closely with the development of the jural system to the point at which appeal from local to central justice is effective.

Landholding provides another index of power centralisation. Landholding according to customary and hereditary principles deriving from the kinship system is typical of segmentary states, and often persists at the base of the system long after other types of tenure have been introduced at the top. When the ritual relationship of central authorities to land is extended to specific political and economic rights, land can be used both directly and indirectly to secure and reward faithful followers and to extend and maintain the centralised administrative staff. In Alur society this was impossible because land had acquired no economic value, and its use was restricted to subsistence occupation with accompanying political and ritual obligations. In Norman England the king was able to use the distribution of feudal land rights as a means of hampering segmentary powers by allotting lands in many different parts of the country to all the greater vassals. Charlemagne's holding of extensive lands throughout his empire enabled him to secure the economic basis of state organisation. Likewise, in the traditional system of Buganda, there is sufficient evidence to show how the royal use of land assisted the transformation of a segmentary state composed of hereditary authorities with independent powers into a unitary state in which subordinate chiefs were transferable appointees of the king.[25]

All the changes outlined above may be said in general to favour or depend upon the growth and elaboration of the bureaucratic element in the state. It is the establishment of such a specialised non-hereditary administrative staff which emancipates the central authority from its segmentary limitations through the definition of jurisdictions and the creation of a unitary power structure.

NOTES

[1] H. H. Gerth and C. Wright Mills, *From Max Weber* (1947), p. 252.

[2] K. Oberg and Max Gluckman, in *African Political Systems*, M. Fortes and E. Evans-Pritchard, eds. (1940), and S. F. Nadel, *A Black Byzantium* (1942), pp. 69–70.

[3] In chapter VIII of Southall's book from which these excerpts are taken: *Alur Society: a Study in Processes and Types of Domination* 1956. EDITOR'S NOTE.

[4] See Gerth and Mills, *op. cit.*, pp. 245–52, and the translations from Max Weber's *The Theory of Social and Economic Organization*, ed. Talcott Parsons (1947), pp. 329–42.

[5] "The king is everywhere primarily a war lord, and kingship evolves from charismatic heroism." Gerth and Mills, *op. cit.*, p. 251.

6 *Ibid.*

7 In this connection note Harold Laski's remarks on the theory of the modern state in *The Grammar of Politics* (1941), pp. 44–5: "The modern theory of sovereignty is, thirdly, a theory of political organisation. It insists that there must be in every social order some single centre of ultimate reference, some power that is able to resolve disputes by saying a last word that will be obeyed. From the political angle, such a view, as will be argued, is of dubious correctness in fact; and it is at least probable that it has dangerous moral consequences. It will be here argued that it would be of lasting benefit to political science *if the whole concept of sovereignty were surrendered.* That, in fact, with which we are dealing is power; and what is important in the nature of power is the end it seeks to serve and the way in which it serves that end. These are both questions of evidence which are related to, but independent of, the rights that are born of legal structure. For there is, historically, no limit to the variety of ways in which the use of power may be organised. The Sovereign State, historically, is merely one of those ways, an incident in its evolution *the utility of which has now reached its apogee.*" (Italics are Southall's.)

8 See Nadel, *op. cit.,* p. 69.

9 See E. Durkheim, *The Division of Labour in Society,* tr. by G. Simpson (1947), p. 175: "We give the name *clan* to the horde which has ceased to be independent by becoming an element in a more extensive group, and that of *societies with a clan base* to peoples who are constituted through an association of clans. We say of these societies that they are segmental in order to indicate their formation by the repetition of like aggregates in them, analogous to the rings of an earthworm, and we say of this elementary aggregate that it is a clan, because this word well expresses its mixed nature, at once familial and political."

10 M. Gluckman, "The Lozi of Barotseland", in *Seven Tribes of British Central Africa,* 1951.

11 *Id.,* "Kinship and Marriage Among the Lozi of Northern Rhodesia and the Zulu of Natal", in *African Systems of Kinship and Marriage,* 1950.

12 P. Vinogradoff in *The Cambridge Medieval History,* vol. II (1913), p. 639.

13 T. Hodgkin, *The Political History of England,* vol. I (1920), pp. 302–3.

14 *Ibid.*

15 (Italics are Southall's.)

16 Hodgkin, *loc. cit.*

17 E. A. Jolliffe, *The Constitutional History of Medieval England* (1948), pp. 1–139.

18 See L. Halphen in *The Cambridge Medieval History,* vol. III (1922), p. 122.

19 *Ibid.,* p. 123.

20 *Ibid.,* p. 124.

21 *Ibid.,* p. 145.

22 See L. M. Hartmann, *ibid.,* vol. II, p. 208.

23 See the discussion of bureaucracy in Gerth and Mills, *op. cit.,* chapter VIII.

24 Cf. Vinogradoff in *The Cambridge Medieval History,* vol. III, p. 460.

25 A. H. Cox, "The Growth and Expansion of Buganda", *The Uganda Journal,* vol. XIV, no. 2. Cf. Sir Apolo Kagwa, *The Customs of the Baganda* (1943), p. 87: "There were two reasons for the resolution of the chiefs of Buganda and Sese never to go to the royal court or to see the king. History shows that these chiefs were originally as much rulers as the king himself. Eventually several tyrannical kings reduced their power to that of mere chieftainship, which made them very indignant."

12

Primitive States

PHYLLIS KABERRY

The great majority of the Alur chiefdoms were small (1,000 to 8,000 members); they were based not on conquest but peaceful assimilation; and their political boundaries were indeterminate in so far as outlying chieflets did not automatically refer disputes and render tribute to the central authority. The Alur (who speak a Nilotic language) moved into what is now the western part of Uganda and the adjacent Belgian Congo some twelve generations ago. Like the surrounding peoples such as the Okebo and the Lendu, they had segmentary agnatic lineages; unlike them, they had chiefs who acted as rainmakers, dispensed justice and received tribute. The Alur chiefs not only attracted dependents from other tribes; they were also called in by neighbouring groups to arbitrate and settle feuds. Sooner or later such groups would request a chief to send a son to be a chieflet over them, to maintain order and make rain. To begin with, a chieflet confined himself to curbing excessive feuding and protecting his subjects against independent neighbours. Later he intervened more frequently in internal disputes, exacted fines, and built up his own little court of retainers and councillors. Any one chiefdom might be viewed, then, as a series of zones in which chiefly authority tended to vary in incidence as one moved out from the headquarters of the chief, surrounded by Alur clans owing him direct allegiance, through settlements with long established chieflets, to those that had recently acquired chieflets of their own and who were not completely "Alurized." Ukuru was the largest of the chiefdoms and, with an estimated population of 60,000, included one-third of the highland Alur as well as Lendu, Okebo, Madi, Abira and Palwo groups. The chief had his serfs and advisors but no special administrative officers; he sent his envoys to collect tribute and install chieflets; he received fines, labour and tribute;

and he had more armed men at his disposal than any chieflet though he had no complete monopoly of force.

. . . Southall elaborates a conceptual distinction between what he calls "hierarchical power structures" or "unitary states" and "pyramidal power structures" or "segmentary states." In the former, there is territorial sovereignty, centralized government, specialized administrative staff, and a monopoly of the use of legitimate force; in other words, certain powers are reserved solely to the central authority. In the "segmentary states", very similar powers are exercised at several levels of segmentation. Southall tentatively lists some of the main characteristics of such systems: (i) "Territorial sovereignty is recognized but is limited and essentially relative, forming a series of zones in which authority is most (sic) absolute near the centre and increasingly restricted towards the periphery, often shading off into a ritual hegemony. (ii) There is a centralized government, yet there are also numerous peripheral foci of administration over which the centre exercises only a limited control. (iii) There is a specialized administrative staff at the centre, but it is repeated on a reduced scale at all the peripheral foci of administration. (iv) Monopoly of force is successfully claimed to a limited extent and within a limited range by the central authority", and so on (p. 248). "The more peripheral a subordinate authority is, the more chance it has to change its allegiance from one power pyramid to another. Segmentary states are thus flexible and fluctuating (p. 249), even comprising peripheral units which have political standing in several adjacent power pyramids which thus become interlocked" (p. 249). Southall then suggests that this type of structure has a very wide distribution not only in Africa but also in early medieval Europe (e.g. Anglo-Saxon England and feudal France in the eleventh century) and in some Indian states such as the Maratha.

In isolating a particular type of state which has a widespread distribution and in attempting to define its main characteristics, Southall has made an important and original contribution to political studies. Whether he has selected the most appropriate term to describe it and the contrasting type—the unitary state—is another matter. "Unitary" is an unfortunate choice since any political system is by definition unitary, and it might be better to speak of "sovereign states". What, then, of the term "segmentary"? Southall has argued, and I think rightly argued, that there must be a clear analytical distinction between the form of the political structure and the variation of powers exercised at different levels within it (p. 250); but he himself is in danger of obscuring this distinction when he passes from political systems such as the Shilluk, Zulu and Alur, which morphologically display the characteristics of continual segmentation and in which authority is of a restricted kind, to those systems in which authority is restricted but in which the constituent political units do not continuously segment, e.g. feudal France and Anglo-Saxon England.

There is a further point. In the latter type of political structure, the unequal incidence of authority may not correspond with a series of geographical zones. The boundaries of territorial sovereignty and military hegemony may be clearly defined and coincide, but there may be a considerable delegation of judicial and co-ordinating powers to the lower levels of administration irrespective of geographical location. The central authority may merely act as titular and/or ritual guardian of the state resources; he may constitute a final court of appeal and intervene directly only in those cases which are deemed to be offences against his person. Factors underlying the distribution of authority in any one system are the ethnic composition of the population and its distribution, density of population and pattern of settlement, facilities for communications, external relations, and lastly and not least the nature of economic resources and the extent to which they can support an elaborate administrative and executive machinery and a permanent military organization.

Basic to any classification of political structures is an explicit formulation of the tasks of government to which the factors I have listed above may then be related. The tasks of government are the enforcement of law and settlement of disputes; the defence of the territory and its inhabitants against external aggression; the safeguarding of natural resources; the control and co-ordination of those activities deemed to affect the welfare of the society as a whole or large sections within it; and, lastly, the validation and maintenance of the structure of authority itself.

Within the broad category of states or centralized political systems, we can then distinguish between those states in which the central authority is of a sovereign kind and in which therefore there is congruence of jurisdiction in all or most of the tasks performed by government; and those states in which the central authority exercises a monopoly of power in only certain fields of government, or only exercises more power than that wielded by the heads of constituent units. It is obvious that the fully-fledged sovereign state is a relatively rare phenomenon in human history (Nazi Germany and the U.S.S.R. are cases in point); and that even in the United States of America the federal authority possesses effective monopoly in only certain departments of government. The same holds true for all federations in which the component units are territorial groups exercising considerable autonomy in internal affairs. Any one of these component groups may have a segmentary political structure (e.g. an Ashanti *oman* or a village or group of villages under an Alur chieflet). We should, then, restrict the category of segmentary political states to those in which continuously segmenting unilineal or quasi-unilineal groups are vested with political functions. We should also recognize that in such systems there may be a progressive weakening of the central authority as one moves out towards segments on the territorial boundary; but in others, again, there may be a specific delegation or enforced relinquishment of some of the major tasks of government to groups irrespective of geographic location, and a reserve of only certain powers to the centre authority. A segmentary political organization does not exclude the possibility of key administrative posts being held on the basis of achievement rather than as a hereditary right; ...

Towns

13

Residence and Capital in the Early Middle Ages (Ostrogoths and Visigoths)

E. EWIG

A capital is defined by Larousse as "a principal town, seat of the public powers of a State". Essentially an urban phenomenon, the capital seems to have vanished from the western world at the close of the Roman era, to reappear only with the flowering of towns in the second half of the middle ages. The agrarian economy of the early middle ages had hemmed people in within a local or regional milieu. Central authority, tied to landed property, could not make itself felt at a distance. The king was obliged to be incessantly on the move, his court became itinerant. This situation altered in the 12th century. The renascent urban economy once more grouped countries around central points. By putting liquid funds at the disposal of the central power, which enabled the country to be governed indirectly, through salaried officials, it made possible the establishment of governments with a fixed residence. Center of the new life, the town inevitably drew the court to itself, or at least those parts of it which were in course of being transformed into organs of central administration.[1]

In broad outline, such seems to be the historical evolution which led to the reappearance of the capital in Europe. Far from denying that the central power underwent important transformations in the 12th century, in part provoked by the urban renascence, I propose merely to correct the picture that is sketched for the early middle ages. Contrast between itinerant courts in the first medieval period, and modern capitals, is too crude a formula. The kings of the early middle ages were not nomads, kingdoms were not lacking in centers which gave them cohesion and structure. The heritage of Rome made itself felt in many areas. In certain respects, the royal towns of the early middle ages recall the capitals of the Late Empire.

The Roman Empire had possessed a capital in the modern sense—Rome "the head of the world"—and a great number of administrative capitals, provincial metropolises. From the time of Augustus, the emperors had contributed a great deal to the splendor of the Eternal City. However, the terrible crisis of the 3rd century brought a divorce between court and capital. Political troubles and the barbarian menace on the frontiers obliged the emperors to move about frequently. Headquarters near the frontiers were turned into imperial residences. Under Diocletian, Nicomedia and Sirmium, Milan and Trier began to rival Rome. The last great imperial building at Rome dates from the time of Diocletian, Maxentius and Constantine. From 364, the emperors were concerned merely to repair Roman monuments threatened by decay.[2]

The true rival of Rome was not any of the residences of the tetrarchs, but the second Rome founded by Constantine on the shores of the Bosphorus. In the West, the role of the Eternal City was by no means ended. She still had a privileged place in the Empire; above all she continued to harbor the Senate, which despite its political decline enjoyed immense cultural and social prestige. Rome had remained the center of pagan cults, and the Senate in the 4th century took the role of defender of the religious traditions of the Empire. At the end of the century, civil-military conflict at the court of the Emperor Honorius enabled it to regain political influence. Stilicho leaned on it in 397 and in 407; in 408 and 409, Alaric played the senatorial card against the court of Ravenna.[3] Despite the failure of Attalus, the last pagan emperor who was not ashamed to embrace Arianism to please the Visigoths, the recovery of senatorial influence over affairs of state in the 5th century is obvious.[4] It was without doubt facilitated by the victory of Christianity within the Senate, which put an end to the religious conflict between Rome and the court.

In the 4th century, the role of Rome as capital of the Christian religion, promoted by imperial decrees,[5] was gradually becoming clear. The Roman Church appeared alongside the Senate on the scene of public affairs. In the spring of the year 409, the senators sent an embassy to Ravenna presided over by Pope Innocent I.[6] In the course of the 5th century, collaboration between the Senate and the Church became closer. But the roles were reversed. Thanks to the work of the great popes St. Leo and St. Gelasius, Rome became the City of the Apostles.

...During the last decades of the Western Empire, Rome, and Ravenna alternated as imperial residences. The mausoleum of the Theodosian dynasty, built by Honorius near the basilica of St. Peter, was a stirring witness of this return of the 5th-century emperors to Rome. It seems that Honorius was buried in the tomb; Galla Placidia, Valentinian III, and other members of the dynasty followed him there.[7]

"For the formation of a capital, the installation of the royal administration was more important than the king's residence." [8] This pertinent remark of A. Schulte regarding the western capitals of the middle ages applies also to the Late Empire, since the four capitals of the tetrarchy were at first general headquarters. The emperors set up central administrations there which continued even during vacancies in the four prefectures of the praetorium created by Constantine. The personnel of these administrations was considerable, the offices being no doubt near the royal palace. The tetrarchs and their successors all maintained a mint, factories, warehouses, and barracks in their capitals. The emperors of the 4th century, being heads of the army as well as of government, often went on campaign or on a tour of the Empire, thus to a certain extent prefiguring the itinerant kings of the middle ages. Just the same they tried to give their capitals all the splendor of court towns. At Trier, the imperial residence took up a whole quarter, flanked by baths built by Constantine in sumptuous style. Other palaces were ranged around the town or in the neighboring countryside, by members of the dynasty.[9] Constantine also founded the cathedral of Trier. At Ravenna, Galla Placidia had the churches of St. John the Evangelist and Holy Cross built, as well as the mausoleum which bears her name.[10] The emperors even founded universities in their towns of residence,[11] which gained a very real ascendancy in the areas of which they were capitals. The Gallo-Roman senators were so attached to the capitals of Gaul that they never forgave the Theodosian dynasty for having abandoned Trier and Arles.[12]

Of the two great administrations of the West, only that of Ravenna survived the disasters of the 5th century. It passed from Odoacer to Theodoric, who maintained it almost intact. The reign of the Ostrogothic king and of his immediate successors prolonged the Western Empire, in narrowed form, up to 535–540. The dualism of the capitals lasted also. The mosaic on the door of the palace of Ravenna shows Theodoric surrounded by effigies from Rome and Ravenna.[13] In 500, the king celebrated the tricennial festival at Rome, living in the emperors' palace on the Palatine.[14] The Senate voted him a statue.[15] But the Gothic king could not pretend to fill the place vacated by the emperors at Rome. Theodoric quietly abandoned the cradle of the Empire to the Senate and to the Church, though assuring his control over Rome through the Master of the Offices. While the imperial mausoleum by the Vatican was turned into a church, the king had his palace, his palatine church (St. Apollinare Nuovo) and his tomb built at Ravenna.[16] The town-residence, seat of the central administration, was also the center of Arian worship. The Goths built the Arian cathedral of the Holy Spirit there, the Arian baptistery of St. Mary in Cosmedin, and the churches of St. Anastasia and St. Eusebius.[17]

Theodoric stayed also at Verona and at Pavia, where he built palaces and amphitheatres, baths and warehouses, and restored the walls.[18] In this there was nothing new. The emperors, too, had favored certain provincial towns. They had lived in country palaces and hunting lodges as summer homes.[19] If the memory of the Ostrogothic king attached to Pavia, to Monza, and especially to Verona, as well as to Ravenna, that is explained by later development. There is nothing to indicate that Ravenna had any rivals during his lifetime. The town kept its rank as capital of Italy under the Byzantines. Around 700, the exarch had another palace built there which became the seat of the imperial government.

The splendor of Ravenna as the emperor's residence and its role as administrative capital of the West explain the attraction that this town had for the Ostrogoths. One notes, however, that all of the Germanic kings chose towns as residences. The Vandals installed themselves at Carthage, the Suevi at Braga, the Visigoths at Toulouse, the Burgundians at Lyons and Geneva, the Franks at Paris, Soissons, Rheims, and Orleans, the Lombards at Verona, Milan, and Pavia. Apparently the kings lived in the palaces arrayed by provincial governors in the metropolises and cities of the Empire. Like the Emperors and the Ostrogothic kings, they sometimes left these to stay in other palaces they inherited on the Roman fisc.[20] The towns that we have just mentioned nevertheless remained royal cities par excellence.

In the series of royal seats one finds Roman metropolises (Carthage, Lyon, Braga, Rheims). Others, without being archiepiscopal centers, were counted among the great towns of the age, such as Toulouse.[21] But the historical circumstances at the moment of the foundation of a kingdom were often decisive for the choice of a capital. This explains the choice of secondary towns in the list. If the Visigothic kings from 418 took up residence at Toulouse and not at Bordeaux, the metropolis of the second Aquitaine, which was assigned them by the emperor, it is because they had their eye on Narbonne and the Mediterranean coast. After the victory over Syagrius, Clovis doubtless settled in Soissons, his adversary's headquarters. After the victory of Vouillé, he chose Paris, where the roads leading from Frankish Belgium to Spain and from Rouen to Lyons crossed. His new place of residence was a defensive and offensive bastion against his rivals in Gaul, the Visigoths, and the Burgundians. The strategic importance of Orleans, Attila's chosen objective in 451, equalled that of Pavia, whose growth dates from the Franco-Gothic war of 508. The choice of residences was thus largely determined either by the prestige of a metropolis, or by reasons of a political or military order.

In their residence-towns the kings installed a rudimentary administration, represented by household services of Germanic origin and a chancery of Roman provenance, no doubt copied from that of the provincial governors.[22] A palatine clergy appears first around the Arian kings, then also in the Catholic courts.[23] The rudimentary governments of the West offered some analogies with the imperial government, which the kings emphasized by borrowing insignia and titles from the imperial court. The royal entourage, composed of dignitaries of the court and the king's companions (military companions and senators of the realm), in its capacity as the king's council resembled the emperor's consistory. In the Vandal and Visigothic kingdoms its members were entitled counts (*comites*). The household ministers could be compared to the "private chamber" (*sacrum cubiculum*), the chancery to the staff of the Master of Offices. However, one hesitates to speak of a central administration. For the Germanic-Latin kingdoms had none of the great administrative organs, nothing of the civil bureaucracy which in the ancient imperial capitals existed independently of the *cubiculum* and represented the public authority. The central administration of the kingdom was more or less absorbed by that of the court. Consequently the grading of honors (*cursus honorum*) was inverted. The dukes and counts who were governors of provinces achieved a higher rank than that of the king's "ministers", with the exception of the Merovingian majordomo. One began a career at court to finish it in the provinces.

The capitals of the West were therefore court towns rather than administrative centers. Nonetheless, we shall see that they exercised a profound influence on the history of our countries.

In the kingdom of the Visigoths, the three crises of 508, 531, and 551 each provoked a shift of the royal residence: from Toulouse to Narbonne, from Narbonne to Barcelona, from Barcelona to Toledo.[24] Theodoric the Great chose Narbonne as the seat of his grandson's court, for the Narbonne region, leading to Provence, was then a bridge between the kingdoms of two peoples enjoying a fraternal relation. Theudis settled at Barcelona in order to reconquer the Narbonne region. Later he undertook the conquest of Baetica, and after 542 he launched an offensive against the Byzantines in Africa. These expeditions no doubt led him to establish a general base in the south of Spain. Theudiscle, Theudis's son and successor, died at Seville, but Barcelona was still the royal seat. The kingdom's third crisis opened in 551, when the Byzantines landed in Baetica. King Agila set up his headquarters at Merida, where he died in 554. It was then that his successor Athangild (551–67) settled at Toledo, which remained the capital of the kingdom up to the time of the Arab invasion.

The influence of political and military reasons on the choice of Visigothic residences is undeniable. But for the choice of Toledo, other reasons had to come into play. Visigothic settlement did not extend over the whole peninsula. It was centered around Segovia, fanning out to Soria,

Burgos, Palencia, Valladolid, Toledo, and Alcalá.[25] In this region of Visigothic settlement we know of three royal palaces outside Toledo: Recopolis, built by Leovogild in 578 for his son Reccared, probably on the Tagus north of Arcavica (Cabeza de Griego); Gerticos, where Reccesvinth died and his successor Wamba was elected (672), in the diocese of Salamanca;[26] Pamplica, no doubt Pampliega near Burgos,[27] where Chindasvinth was elected in 642 and where King Wamba ended his life in a monastery. It is in this region, again, that Reccesvinth in 646 founded the church of St. Juan de Baños (the province of Palencia),[28] and that one finds the celebrated votive crowns of Svinthila and of Reccesvinth (at Guarrazar, in the province of Toledo) apparently coming from a monastery dedicated to St. Stephen which maintained close relations with the court.[29] Narbonne and Barcelona, the first residences, were in deeply Romanized provinces. The kings there leaned on the aristocracy. In settling at Toledo, they came closer to their own people without breaking contact with Baetica, the richest and most highly civilized province of Spain.

Toledo became dominant in Spain in the reign of Leovigild (568/69–586), the creator of Gothic-Spanish unity. But Visigothic Gaul remained jealous of its traditions. On two occasions, in 568 and in 631, it succeeded in imposing a king of its choice on the kingdom. Two usurpations—in 672 and 673—failed. The usurper Paul, who was recognized also in the Taracona region, seems to have proposed a partition of the realm. He called himself the Eastern King and accorded the king of Toledo the title of Western King. When King Witiza was making ready for the succession of his son Achila, he ceded him the Taracona region. In 700, in analogous circumstances, he himself had been named governor of Galicia, that is, of the ancient kingdom of the Suevi. The autonomous character of the Narbonne region, of Suevian Galicia, and even of the Taracona region had therefore remained very much alive, perhaps nourished by the tradition of ancient royal seats, but all the same without disturbing the position of Toledo.[30]

Toledo was not an ancient metropolis, it was a dependent of Cartagena. But after the occupation of Cartagena by the Byzantines in 554, the new royal residence "became, without having the title, the actual metropolis of the ancient region of Cartagena".[31] The episcopal city was thereafter endowed with new ecclesiastical foundations. Besides the cathedral of Our Lady [32] and the church of St. Leocadia-without-the-Walls, the basilica where the bishops were interred,[33] four abbeys are mentioned in 7th-century sources: St. Michael's, Holy Cross, St. Eulalie's, and St. Côme's or the monastery of Agalí.[34] The monastery of Agalí, a nursery of bishops since the beginning of the 7th century,[35] was located in a suburb. Dating from the middle of the 6th century, it was without doubt the city's oldest monastic foundation. The kings apparently played a part in the founding of the principal churches of Toledo, but the sources give no details. All that we know, is that the abbey of St. Leocadia was also the site of royal tombs.[36]

As well as the cathedral and these five abbeys, we find in the 7th century the "praetorial" church of the Apostles or of SS. Peter and Paul.[37] The title indicates that this was the palatine church, which must have been close by the royal palace.[38] Wamba (672–80) and Egica (687–702) were anointed there by the archbishops.[39] The title of palatine church recalls the church of the Apostles founded by the first Christian emperor at Constantinople. Writing of the conversion of the Goths to Catholicism, Jean de Biclare points to the parallel between Reccared and Constantine, between the third council of Toledo and the first Council of Nicaea.[40] From 589, Toledo was given the title of the "royal city".

The royal city became the true center of the "national" life. The assemblies of the Visigothic people had formerly been held near Toulouse. We lose sight of them in the period of "the Ostrogothic interval". We know of two Catholic councils convoked in 516 and 517 at Tarragona and at Gerona, proof of the reorganization of the kingdom on the ecclesiastical plane. A third council met in 527 at Toledo, three others at Barcelona (about 540), Lerida (546), and Valencia (546).[41] After the fixing of the royal residence at Toledo, Leovigild in 580 convoked there the famous Arian council which was supposed to prepare the religious unification of Spain.[42] The attempt miscarried, but the council of 580 was nevertheless a forerunner of the Toledan councils of the Catholic era, of which there was a series of fifteen between 589 and 694. The episcopate, sitting in general council, when the business had to do with the affairs of the kingdom joined with the great men of the "royal Hall" or simply with the high dignitaries of the palatine Office. Thus a new style of general assembly came into being, whose decisions were ratified by acts of the council. The composition of this assembly was defined by canon 75 of the council of 633.[43] The tenth canon of the council of 653 laid down that the assembly should meet to elect the king "either in the royal town or in the place where the *princeps* shall have died".[44] The assemblies were at first held in the basilica of St. Leocadia, the kings' necropolis and from 653 in the praetorial church, where the kings were anointed.[45] Only provincial councils met in the cathedral.[46]

The growth of the royal city raised the prestige of the count and of the Bishop of Toledo. The count of Toledo was always among the great dignitaries in the general assemblies, although his role in the court is not clear. A mere suffragan of Cartagena, the Bishop of Toledo from 554 became the metropolitan (the archbishop) of Carpetania, that is, of those parts of the province remaining under Visigothic rule after the Byzantine invasion. He continued to hold metropolitan rank after the reconquest of Cartagena, with the title of Metropolitan of that region.[47] After 656, the bishops of the royal city presided over the councils of the realm.[48] In 681 they obtained the right "of installing in vacant bishoprics in any province of the realm, candidates they judged worthy, after royal approval."[49] This prerogative, defined in 683 as the right of ordination,[50] was copied from the patriarchal law of Constantinople.[51] The primacy of Toledo was created.

King Wamba enlarged the town in 674 and fortified the walls.[52] The royal city also asserted itself on the cultural plane. During the "Ostrogothic interval", the center of intellectual and artistic life lay in Levantine Spain, at Gerona, Tarragona, and Valencia.[53] Arts and letters then passed to Baetica, from Justinian of Valencia and his brothers Justus, Nebridius, and Elpidius to Leander of Seville and his brothers Isidore and Fulgentius, as d'Abadal relates.[54] Up to the beginning of the 7th century, Toledo was indebted to Seville, Cordova and Merida. It was from there that the torch passed to the great metropolitans, to the two Eugeniuses, to Ildefonse, and to Julian, the principal artisans of the mozarabic liturgy.[55] The land of the Goths, the royal province par excellence, became covered with churches and monasteries, often founded by the help of the kings. The monastery of Servitanum in the diocese of Arcávica, the first center of monastic culture in Castile,[56] developed close relations with Reccared.[57] St. Fructuosus, the legislator for the monks of Spain, came from Palencia. Reccesvinth entrusted him with the bishopric of Dumio, later made him metropolitan of Braga.[58] The Toledan monuments of the age have disappeared; but the art of Toledo survives in a good number of Castilian churches and in the celebrated treasures of Guarrazar and Torredonjimeno.

To sum up, we see that Toledo, in its character as royal residence, had no rival among the cities of Spain. The sources show several country palaces; the king doubtless had other palaces in other towns, but we know of no other city residence worthy of the name outside Toledo. It was in the royal city that the great officers of the court normally resided, it was there that the councils and assemblies of the realm were held. The basilica of St. Leocadia seems to have been the royal necropolis, although kings were sometimes buried near palaces where they had died. The palatine church of the Apostles became the principal shrine of the realm, where the great ecclesiastics and laymen assembled to discuss public affairs. We are ill informed as to the buildings constructed by the kings, but it is certain that the town grew in the 7th century and that it was also in that period a center of arts and letters. The bishop of the royal city ended by becoming metropolitan of the region of Cartagena and even primate of Spain, on the model of Constantinople. Nothing could better illustrate the dominance of the capital over the realm.

* * * * *

[The remainder of Professor Ewig's article deals in equal detail with the role of royal towns among the Lombards and the Franks. EDITOR'S NOTE.]

NOTES

1 W. Berges, "Das Reich ohne Haupstadt", *Das Haupstadtproblem in der Geschichte.* Festgabe zum 90. Geburtstag Friedrich Meinecke (Tübingen, 1952), pp. 1–29.

2 *Storia di Roma*, XXII: *Topografia e urbanistica di Roma.* Bologna, 1958.

3 V. A. Sirago, *Galla Placidia e la transformzione politica dell' Occidente* (Louvain, 1961), pp. 77 ff.

4 E. Stein, *Histoire du Bas-Empire*, I (1959), pp. 223 ff. and 337–42. S. Mazzarino, *Stilicone. La crisi imperiale dopo Teodosia*, Rome, 1942. J. Sundwall, *Abhandlungen zur Geschichte des ausgehenden Römertums*, 1919.

5 H. Lietzmann, *Geschichte der alten Kirche*, IV, part 2 (1953), p. 63. Fliche-Martin, *Histoire de l'Église*, III (1947), p. 468.

6 Sirago, *op. cit.*, pp. 95 ff.

7 H. Koethe, "Zum Mausoleum der weströmische Dynastic bei alt St. Peter", *Mitteilungen des Deutschen Archäologischen Instituts*, Römische Abteilung 46 (1931), pp. 22 ff.; Sirago, *op. cit.*, p. 260.

8 A. Schulte, "Pavia und Regensburg", *Historisches Jahrbuch*, vol. 52 (1932), p. 472.

9 For example, that of Conz, about ten kilometers above Trier, up the river.

10 Sirago, *op. cit.*, p. 260. M. van Berchem and E. Clouzot, *Mosaïques chrétiennes du IVe au VIe siècle*, Geneva, 1924.

11 J. Steinhausen, "Die Hochschulen im römischen Trier", *Trier, ein Zentrum abendländischen Kultur. Rheinischer Verein für Denkmalpflege und Heimatschutz* (1952), pp. 27 ff.

12 K. F. Strohecker, *Der senatorische Adel im spätantliken Gallien* (Tübingen, 1948), pp. 41 ff.

13 W. Ensslin, *Theoderich der Grosse* (1947), p. 260.

14 *Ibid.*, pp. 111 ff. and 116.

15 *Ibid.*, p. 269.

16 *Ibid.*, pp. 258–9. Cf. Koethe, *op. cit.*, p. 27, n. 7.

17 Ensslin, pp. 261 ff., 266.

18 *Ibid.*, pp. 147, 152, 197, 268, 312, 317. Theodoric built a palace and an amphitheatre at Pavia, a palace and baths at Verona, where he also had the aqueduct repaired. The building at Pavia was done after the Frankish war (508–10), during which the king made the town his headquarters. He stayed at Verona in 520 and 523.

19 Some edicts of Valentinian I are dated from Conz and from Nassogne on the western side of the Ardennes. Theodoric had a palace probably for summer use at Monza and a hunting lodge near Galeata in the province of Forli.

20 The Vandal kings lived at the palace of Byrsa on a hill at Carthage and lived also near Maxula, at Alianae, Hermiana, and at Grassa (north of Hadrumetum-Sousse, some 73 kilometers from Carthage). See Chr. Courtois, *Les Vandales et l'Afrique* (Paris, 1955), p. 250.

21 The area of the Roman town (97 hectares) equalled that of Cologne (96 hectares) and of Mainz (100 hectares). See H. Büttner, "Frühmittelalterliches Städtewesen im Frankreich", *Studien zu den Anfängen des europaischen Städtewesens. Vorträge und Forschungen*, IV, Th. Mayer, ed. (1958), p. 153.

22 P. Classen, "Kaiserreskript und Königsurkunde", *Archiv für Diplomatik*, II, 2 (1956), pp. 1 ff. and 86 ff. The Germanic kings imitated certain formulas of the imperial acts, all concerning rights and forms reserved for the emperor. Among Roman councillors who were organizers of Germanic chanceries we note: Leo of Narbonne, councillor of Euric. See K. F. Strohecker, *Eurich König der Westgoten* (Stuttgart, 1937), pp. 90 ff.; *id.*, *Der senatorischer Adel*, p. 90; K. Zeumer, "Westgotische Gesetzgebung", part III, *Neues Archiv*, vol. 24 (1899), p. 119; *Ennodius, Vita Epiphanii*, in *Monumenta Germaniae A. A*, VII, p. 94. Also Syagrius, the Solon of the Burgundians. See Sidonius Apollinaris, *Epistolae* V, *ibid*, vol. III, p. 80; A. Coville, *Recherches sur l'histoire de Lyon du Ve au IXe siècle* (Paris, 1928), pp. 23 ff.; Strohecker, *Senatorischer Adel*, p. 98. On Aridius and Laconius, councillors of the Burgundian kings, see Gregory of Tours, *Historia Francorum*, book II, chapter 32; *Chronicle of Fredegar*, book III, chapters 18, 19, 23; Strohecker, *op.*

cit., p. 98. On Aurelian, councillor of Clovis, see Fredegar, book III, chapter 18. On Parthenius, the powerful minister of Theudebert I, who died in 548, see Strohecker, pp. 125 ff. On Heyschius, minister of Childebert I, then bishop of Lyons, see L. Duchesne, *Fastes épiscopaux de l'ancienne Gaule*, vol. II, part 2, p. 19. On Paul and his son Peter, councillors of the Lombard king Agilulf, see G. P. Bognetti, *Santa Maria di Castelseprio* (Milan, 1948), pp. 104–12 and *Storia di Milano*, vol. II, pp. 115 ff. There is evidence of an independent administration of the patrimony among the Visigoths. See C. Sanchez-Albornoz, "El aula regia ye las asambleas politicas de los Godos", *Cuadernos de Historia de España*, vol. 5 (1946), pp. 65 ff.

23 J. Fleckenstein, *Die Hofkapelle der deutschen Könige*, Schriften der Monumenta Germaniae Historica, No. XVI, vol. I (1959), pp. 3 ff.

24 R. de Abedal Y de Vinyals, *Del reino de Tolosa al reino de Toledo*, Madrid, 1960.

25 *Id.*, "A propos du legs visigothique en Espagne", *Caratteri del secolo VII in Occidente*, Settimane di studio del centro italiano di studi sull' Alto Medio Evo, No. V (Spoleto, 1958), pp. 541 ff. J. Werner, "Die archaologischen Zeugnisse der Goten in Südrussland, Ungarn, Italien und Spanien", *I Goti in Occidente*, Settimane di studio . . . III (1956), pp. 127–30.

26 *Historia de España*, III, pp. 102, 121; *Vita Wambae*, in *Monumenta Germaniae Historica, SS. rerum Meroving.*, V, pp. 502 ff.

27 *Monumenta. A A., Chronica Minora*, II, p. 260. Identified by Mommsen with Pampeluna, without doubt in error.

28 P. Palol de Salellas, "Esencia del arte hispánico de época visigoda: romanismo y germanismo", *I Goti in Occidente*, p. 96.

29 J. Pérez de Urbel, *Los monjes espanoles en la Edad Media* (Madrid, 1933), p. 512. *Historia de España*, III, pp. 625 ff.

30 R. Gibert, "El reino visigodo ye el particularismo español", *I Goti in Occidente* (1956), pp. 537–38. R. Menéndez Pidal, *Historia de España*, III (Madrid, 1940), pp. 97 ff., 116 ff., 123 ff., 133, 135.

31 Fliche-Martin, *Histoire de l'Église*, vol. V (1947), p. 237.

32 References in Migne, *Patrologia Latinae*, vol. 84, columns 451, 433, 505.

33 Migne, *P.L.*, vol. 84, col. 363, 389, 393, 551; vol. 96, col. 205 ff.; vol. 44. col. 451–2.

34 *Ibid.*, vol. 84, col. 468; vol. 96, col. 201 ff.

35 *Ibid.*, vol. 96, col. 201–4, 43.

36 Pérez de Urbel, *op. cit.*, p. 512.

37 Migne, *P.L.*, vol. 84, col. 411, 467, 487, 509, 528. *Vita Wambae*, chapter 4. *Praetorium* and *civitas regia* were synonymous.

38 For mention of another royal palace to the east of the city see Quadrada y Vicente de la Fuente, *España. Sus monumentos y artes, su naturaleza y historia*, III (Barcelona, 1886), p. 53, but according to A. González Palencia (*Les mozarabes de Toledo en los siglos XII y XIII*, vol. I, Madrid, 1930) there is no documentary evidence for this.

39 *Vita Wambae*, chapter 4; *Chronica regum Visigothorum, Monumenta Germaniae Historica, Legum Sectio*, I, pp. 460–1; H. Löwe, "Von den Grenzen des Kaisergedankens in der Karolingerzeit", *Deutsches Archiv*, vol. 14 (1958), p. 363, n. 89.

40 E. Ewig, "Zum christlichen Königsgedanken im Frühmittelalter", *Das Königtum. Vorträge und Forschungen*, Th. Mayer, ed. (Lindau-Constance, 1956), pp. 26 ff; id., "Das Bild Constantins der Grosse in den ersten Jahrhunderten des abendländischen Mittelalters", *Historisches Jahrbuch*, vol. 75 (1956), pp. 26 ff.

41 D'Abadal, *op. cit.*, pp. 57, 63 ff.

42 J. Orlandis, "El cristianismo en el reino visigodo", *I Goti in Occidente*, pp. 163 ff.

43 Migne, *P.L.*, vol. 84, col. 384.

44 *Ibid.*, col. 425.

45 *Ibid.*, col. 363, 389, 393, 551. The proceedings of all councils held in the church of the Apostles carry the signatures of "illustrious men".

46 *Ibid.*, col. 465, 505, 433 ff.

47 *Ibid.*, col. 392.

48 *Ibid.*, col. 447.

49 *Ibid.*, col. 475 ff.; Fliche-Martin, *Histoire de l'Église*, vol. V, p. 255.

50 Migne, *P.L.*, col. 475 ff.

51 The 28th canon of the Council of Chalcedon gave the bishops of Constantinople this right in the dioceses of Thrace, Asia, Pont, and in missionary lands. H.G. Beck, "Kirche und theologische Literatur im Byzantinischen Reich", *Byzantinisches Handbuch*, vol. II, part 1 (Munich, 1959), pp. 30 ff.

52 *Historia de España*, III, p. xlviii.

53 Pérez de Urbel, *op. cit.*, pp. 95 ff.; Palol de Salellas, *loc. cit.*, pp. 76 ff.; D'Abadal, *op. cit.*, pp. 57, 86 ff.

54 *Ibid.*, p. 65.

55 J. Fontaine, *Isidore de Séville et la culture classique dans l'Espagne visigothique* (Paris, 1959), pp. 864 ff.; Palol de Salellas, *loc. cit.*, pp. 85 ff., 92 ff.

56 St. Ildefonse said of its founder, the African, Donatus, that he was said to have introduced the rule of monastic observance into Spain (*Liber de viris illustribus*, chapter 4, Migne, *P.L.*, vol. 96, col. 200). This passage becomes intelligible when interpreted as referring not to the whole of Spain, but to the province of Toledo. Ildefonse had been a monk of Agalí, the earliest of the Toledo monasteries. In insisting on the priority of Servitanum, he seems to me to indicate a link between Servitanum and Agalí.

57 The king gave Abbot Eutropis of Servitanum the bishopric of Valencia. Pérez de Urbel, *op. cit.*, p. 204.

58 *Historia de España*, III., p. 423.

14

The Different Types of Formation
of European Towns

An historical typology of the medieval town has to take into account all of
the forms that urban life assumes and the conditions under which they
arose: the physical plan, the social structure, the multiple functions of the
town as an economic, administrative or religious center, its law and constitution. For all of these things were inter-related, mutually interde-
pendent. If we look at these inter-relationships, we perceive that they fall
into a certain number of general patterns, or types, which were always the
product of historical circumstances.

To understand how the urban culture of medieval Europe came to be
so extraordinarily widely diffused, one has to appreciate the great diversity
of circumstances in which the towns originated. One has to go back to the
contrast between Romanized regions and Germanic regions and try to
evaluate the influence of the opposite forces inherent in the two cultures.
Numerous types of town emerged within Europe's vast space, the process
of differentiation occurring under a combination of influences that varied
from one region to another and through time. This paper can do no more
than indicate the main lines of differentiation.

At the start, the problem is that of the relation between the medieval
town and the ancient city. The fall of ancient civilization has often been
viewed as a dramatic catastrophe caused either by the invasion of the Germanic "barbarians" or by that of the Arabs, which supposedly closed the
Mediterranean. The catastrophic picture has now been abandoned in favor of the generally accepted view that there was in fact a gradual transition from the Roman world to the medieval.[1] Scholarly discussion of the
nature of the transition, of how to interpret it, has obliged us to look

much more closely into the actual course of events. We have learned how to make the necessary chronological distinctions. As to the fate of the towns, our aim is to be able not merely to describe it in much greater detail, but to analyze it, to show which of the many urban functions disappeared and which survived.

Keeping in mind the continuity of civilization, the urban historian can divide Europe into three broad zones. The first includes the northern Germanic area east of the Rhine, and Scandinavia, neither of which experienced any direct influence from Mediterranean urban culture. The second stretches over what is now northern France, through the Rhineland, and down the Danube valley; here the Mediterranean urban civilization had penetrated, and though it suffered a serious setback, it was not wholly destroyed. (Pre-Norman England, where one also finds a few vestiges of Roman cities, is more nearly related to the north Germanic area.) The third is the Mediterranean zone, where Roman urban traditions persisted, urban centers continuing to be occupied, continuing to provide a characteristic habitat and mode of life. In Italy, social and economic development went on without a break, as has recently been demonstrated again from the Po valley.[2] There is a real possibility that there was even a rudimentary continuity of the Italian urban community in its juridical form. On the other hand, in the middle zone mentioned above—Gaul, the Rhineland, and the Danube valley—and also in Spain[3] and in the French Midi,[4] we know for certain that Roman municipal organization disappeared.

Obviously, most of our problems refer to the towns of the middle zone, which has now to be subdivided. On the lower Rhine and along the Danube there was an almost total collapse of urban life, while in the Moselle country and the middle Rhineland the ancient urban heritage was better preserved. Again, in the upper Rhine and the province of Helvetia, the Roman cities fell into ruin.[5] The Alemans made much more of a clean sweep with the past than the Franks did.

If we ask how well the various urban functions were maintained in the central region, we notice important differences of degree. The ancient Roman municipal organization, as has been stated, died out completely. The town, as such, ceased to be an essential organ of the public life of the State, and the countryside acquired a political significance of its own. When we look at the economy, we find that although certain technical activities, such as the manufacture of pottery and glass, were still carried on, industrial organization is no longer urban, as it had been in Roman times. The landed estate, the seigneury, for the most part took over the industrial functions of the town. Those Frankish ceramic works in the hills between Bonn and Cologne that were engaging, as we know from archeological research,[6] in large-scale export to Scandinavia, were probably under seigneurial direction. The manufacture had certainly not sunk to the level of mere cottage industry.

When we want to study the continuity of settlement patterns, a problem that can be resolved only through case-studies, we again have to call on the archeologists for help. The evidence has to be examined very carefully: even when at first sight a town seems to be an example of perfect continuity, one often finds that its center of gravity moved. In Bonn, for example, this center was displaced from the site of the Roman fort, north of the present town and outside the medieval wall, to the site of the tombs of the Christian martyrs of the Late Empire, a kilometer to the south. Sanctuaries had been erected here,[7] and it was here that the medieval town began to grow. The shift is like the swing of a pendulum. The case of Bonn, which is far from unique, is a very important one, both historically and from the point of view of historical method. Thanks to the evidence of Bonn, Aubin was able to discover this phenomenon of the displacement of the urban center of gravity.

That the site of the tombs of Christians martyred under the Late Empire should become the embryo of the medieval town is very characteristic and is explained by a factor that was the decisive element in the transition from Antiquity to the Middle Ages: the Christian Church. The excavations that have been carried out since 1930, first at Bonn and at Xanten, more recently at Cologne and Trier, reveal the importance of Rhenish Christian communities at the end of Antiquity. We owe our knowledge of the situation at Trier to Kempf, an archeologist, and to Ewig, an historian.[8] The Constantinian cathedral here has been shown to be a double church, in its grandeur and size comparable with any of the larger religious edifices of early Christianity. It could have served a Christian community of several thousand people. It is from Trier, indeed, that the ecclesiastical organization of the Rhineland was begun, about 250 A.D. It is very likely that Eucharius who according to the most reliable of the episcopal lists drawn up in the 10th century was the first head of the Church in the Moselle region, lived at this period. These episcopal lists, which show no gaps, offer positive proof that ecclesiastical organization survived the Germanic invasions, just as the sanctuaries and the Christian communities did.

The Church of the Martyrs of Bonn also survived the invasions, and we know from K. Böhner's excavations in the cemeteries of Andernach and of Bonn that a provincial Roman population continued to live alongside the Frankish conquerors.[9] Christian communities did more than just preserve the habitat and technical knowledge; they kept a spiritual force alive. This spiritual force embodied some of the classical heritage, though not all of that heritage nor even, it is said, its essential core. Still, in the shadow of the Church, many urban traditions were carried on: the habit of living in groups—a custom adopted by the clergy—the use of writing in every manifestation of culture, the use of the town as a religious center and as the center of ecclesiastical organization. In the Carolingian era, however, all these traditions weaken. As Pirenne stressed, this era is much more differentiated from Antiquity than the Merovingian period. The use of writing comes to be restricted to the clergy, lay instruction in it being dropped, and among remote monasteries and the ever-growing number of rural churches we find religious centers that are independent of urban episcopal authority. Nevertheless, episcopal organization, which possessed that superior power to conserve and to create which we think of as properly urban, persisted throughout Christian Europe. So also did popular fascination with the saints' cults at urban shrines. The fact that the bishop had his seat in a city moreover gave it a dignity far above that of any settlement on seigneurial land. This is true wherever we look, and even in the deepest decadence of urban economy. It is true of the cathedral cities both in the Rhineland and in the old Roman province of Narbonne; [10] in the valley of the Meuse, Liège had to be promoted to the rank of city because the bishop lived there; in the valley of the Rhone the same circumstance could cause a *villa* to be promoted to a *civitas*.

Besides noting these early differentiations, urban history has also to deal with the play of forces apparently pulling in opposite directions. In the north Germanic zone, for example, the sparseness of the population and the fact that the nobles, the dominating class, were utterly rustic, would on the face of it seem to be highly unfavorable to the development of urban life. Trade was carried on by itinerant merchants, organized for the purpose in associations, and operating out of a special type of small settlement known as the *Wik*. Here we have a potentially creative element, but by itself the *Wik* could not become a town. Its creative potential first appears in the central zone where the Roman urban tradition had partially survived. In this environment it grew in importance and was able to link itself either with what remained of a Roman city, or with a lord's castle. Thus at Ratisbon a merchant settlement took shape beside the old Roman fort. Outside the walls of the old Roman city of Cologne Rhenish merchants built their own suburb. Just across the river from the cathedral city of Verdun on its rock, a settlement of rich slave-merchants appeared. Right in front of the Count of Flanders' castle at Ghent, a trading-post grew up. This dualism, peculiar to the towns of the Northwest of Europe from the start and just as apparent in their constitutional history as in their topography, has received a great deal of attention from Belgian and German historians. Particular emphasis has been laid recently on the respective roles of the unfortified merchant colony and the lord's castle in creating the town, and on tracing the evolution of the two elements. The fortified, protective element is likely at first to be the bishop's palace, inside an old Roman city; later it may be a dynastic castle. The colony of merchants busied with long-distance trade evolves into a market for the handiwork of artisans. The textile industry of Northwest Europe in fact dates from the very same period as the so-called renaissance of commerce; [11] it matures precociously, soon producing for export. This economic progress is favored by a considerable rise in population and consequently in the density of settlement.

The power relationship between the walled *civitas* and the *Wik* then undergoes radical change, a change that proceeds more rapidly to the north. Indeed, it can be stated as an absolute rule that the further north one moves along a northwesterly axis, the more the power of the *civitas* declines while that of the *Wik* grows. One of the signs of change is in the character of the churches. In the westerly towns, the majority of these are old collegial or monastic foundations, antedating the merchant colony. In the northerly towns, more and more of the churches are built for associations of merchants: [12] it is the wealthy exporters who are determining the conditions of religious life. Thus it is through a process of fusion, of the intermingling of functions, that the northwestern towns are formed. As the wandering merchants become settled business men they decide that the *Wik,* like the *civitas* or the lord's castle, also needs stone walls for defence. When the commune appears it is through a fusion of the forces of association represented in the merchants' gilds and in the juridical traditions of the local Frankish community. This results in the sworn association which ultimately wins control of the town.

Northwestern continental Europe is distinctive also in the fact that the countryside retains political autonomy. The persistence of the seigneurial organization of rural society is reflected, visibly, in the castles that the nobles own outside the towns.

The above sufficiently indicates the general type of town formation to be found in the Northwest, with its regional variations dependent on the respective weight of the *civitas* and the *Wik*. In England, however, the course of development was different. While on the Continent the towns are foreign bodies, as it were, in the surrounding seigneurial organization, which restricted rural economic development, in England both State and manor were early oriented towards a money economy. The Normans, who were of a mercenary and calculating temperament, had a marked influence in this direction. The circumstances of their conquest of the island enabled them to institute a remarkably advanced system of fiscal accounting, through the royal Exchequer and its records, and they also perfected State control of coinage and of weights and measures. The royal policy of limiting the development of seigneurial justice drove the lords, in turn, to wring as much money as possible from their lands. The large role of money rent in the English manorial system early led to leasing, and the network of roads favored the diffusion of enterprise. In short, in England trade was never thought of as being narrowly restricted to towns. Nor did the fact that the towns were based on associational ties separate them, as it did on the Continent, from the general public life. In England, feudalism never

destroyed the popular juridical base of the monarchy. The towns therefore received only a limited juridical autonomy.

The Mediterranean town, sharply distinct from the town of Northwest Europe, is a special type of medieval urban civilization. It attained its
most remarkable expression in Italy, where, as has been seen, urban life
had never died out. In contrast to the dualism that characterized the northwestern towns, in Italy we see the *civitas* remaining a unity. Here, although
in the early middle ages urban communities engaged in agriculture, they
were already embryonic regional markets. By the 10th century, both in
Italy and in Spain, they were receiving legal grants of the right of sanctuary,
and of privileges of immunity. Socially, they were stratified by wealth, not
by distinctions based on birth. Free merchants, who had always existed
here, are already buying land in the *contado* (the country district around
the town) by the 10th and 11th centuries.[13] The nobility moves, voluntarily
or otherwise, into the town. The town houses of nobles become one of the
characteristic features of the Mediterranean urban type: their towers rise
in all the towns of Italy, Spain, and southern France. Genoa made a series
of contracts binding nobles to live in the city. In this way the *contado* lost
its ruling class and became a territory governed by the town. The urban
republics of northern Italy were born as city-states. What is important
above all is that they were merchant city-states. Their existence prevented
the formation of the kind of territorial state that we see emerging in France
in the 12th century, and in the German territorial principalities, which had
the effect of hardening class distinctions. In Italy it is the rich who form
the upper class; money obliterates differences in birth. While in the North
itinerant merchants become citizens, in the South urban landowners become merchants.

Although medieval urban history involves so sharp a contrast between
the North and the South, communication between the two zones nevertheless brought outside influences to bear upon the rise of the northern towns.
The very custom of grouping houses close together, and the techniques of
building in stone, spread originally from the South. Southern types of
habitat design are still noticeable in the valleys of the Meuse, the upper
Moselle, the Saar and the Rhone—the traditional routes of Mediterranean
cultural influence. What a strikingly urban impression the city of Namur
gives—a solid mass of stone houses and other buildings pressed between the
cliff and the Sambre and the Meuse; while an hour's drive away, the city of
Brussels fans out into suburbs and into the open countryside of Brabant.

The Mediterranean zone significantly affected also the constitutional
history of the northern towns. Not only was the bishop's domination of the
cathedral city a legacy of the Late Empire, but the decisive forces that
transformed the personal bond between merchants as members of a gild
into a communal authority, corporate and territorial, flowed from the
Mediterranean towns. In these, urban law had always been territorial. In

my opinion, the critical region through which these forces filtered was the region of the Meuse, where Roman and Germanic institutions had long been in contact. It was here that the northern town was first envisioned, on the model of southern towns, as a place of liberation. The German saying, "Town air makes free" (*Stadtluft macht frei*) came from Spain and from Italy.

The territorialization of town law had also its models in local Frankish communities.[14] But it was under encouraging currents of influence from the South that it found effective expression in the towns.

The new institution of consular government in towns was soon on the move, spreading from Italy. Even in northern towns there are instances of nobles participating, as they did in Italy, in town government, and there are similar instances of nobles building towers for town residences. The later institution of the *podestà,* although it spread to southern France, and was tried out in Ratisbon, was not generally accepted north of the Alps. The northwestern towns preferred to keep their own form of urban government and administration under a mayor or burgomaster.

In reality, the constitution of the medieval town is everywhere original; the stamp it bears is that of the irresistible forces of association. The sworn association, though said to be Germanic in nature, is found all through Europe and was certainly not always of Germanic origin. Indeed, its northern and southern forms are very different. The Italian form, the *conjuratio,* did not, like the northern form, grow out of the gild. It was from the merchant gild conceived as a society, from the fraternal relations depicted so vividly in the statutes of the gild of St. Omer, that the sworn associations of the Franks drew their revolutionary sense of human brotherhood. There is nothing of this in the statutes of Italian towns.

From the economic point of view the medieval town stands out as according supreme importance to commerce and industry, from the institutional point of view as organizing public life entirely through associations. Here, for the first time in history, the economic man enjoyed full political rights.[15] A multiplicity of social types were merged into one: the citizen. The medieval town was a unified entity. As such it is something quite different from the ancient city that preceded it, for the latter was governed simply by a town-dwelling aristocracy, and was always primarily a political, military, and religious center.

The typically medieval elements of urban life naturally occur in their purest form in the towns of the Northwest. The type that these represent was moreover the most widely diffused: one finds it in Germany east of the Elbe, in Poland, Moravia, and in northern Hungary. The town of southern Hungary, like that of Russia, is of still another type, a non-European type.

The towns of ancient Germany used to be styled organic in contrast to the artificially created towns of colonial Germany. There is still a certain validity in this distinction, although it has to be qualified when one realizes that a new merchant colony or a new seigneurial castle was also created as it were out of nothing, and became a town in the full sense of the word only through a process of organic evolution. The town that is founded by a lord belongs to a special type. In Europe this is true of all periods and all countries; it makes no difference whether the founder be a king or a lord, nor even if the foundation is merely a juridical decree raising a village to the dignity of a town. The founding brought new urban groups into existence. Towns were ideal points of crystallization for the institutions of a territorial state, serving both as fortified strongholds and as administrative centres, and at the same time attracting population. The attraction was due to the principle that "Town air makes free", and to the fact that townsmen came under the exclusive jurisdiction of the town court. In the countryside there was always a tangle of seigneurial rights; the town was a juridically autonomous unit. Since it attracted population, the creation of an urban center enabled a lord to consolidate his hold over newly conquered territory and might facilitate further conquest of contested areas. Ample examples may be cited from the founding of Spanish towns after the Reconquest, of *sauvetés* and *bastides* in southern France, of *villes neuves* in northeastern France, of royal and seigneurial towns in Germany. All of these were planned foundations, created all of a piece. To the historian with an eye for generic similarities, they not only form a general type but fall into sub-groups or families having an identical law or identical ground-plans.[16] In Germany, where the nobles traditionally built castles and were slow to think of themselves as town-founders, planned foundations date mainly from the 13th and 14th centuries. Consequently it is not enough to classify towns simply by region, one has also to take account of chronological changes.

These founded towns make up a high percentage of the little medieval towns. For medieval towns have also to be classified by size and population, as large, medium-size, and small. The large towns—this means those with over 10,000 inhabitants—are typically dependent on trade with other regions and on export industry. At Nuremburg, for example, the metal-work industry attained European renown because the city's trade was able to furnish it with raw materials. The economic structure of a town determined its social structure in the sense that it gave rise to a wealthy patriciate which kept control of political affairs. Although this control in the course of time often met with violent opposition, in many towns the patriciate managed to retain power for a very long run. The economic activity of the medium-size towns is more limited in radius. There may be a few lines of export to a distance, but the economy is really based on a regional market and on the products of independent artisans. The little towns, those with under 2000 inhabitants, have been the subject of new study recently by A. Ammann. They can no longer be regarded as mere fortified villages sunk

in rural egocentrism. They too, certainly in the later middle ages, had some
import and export trade.

As we have seen, at the beginning of urban history in the early middle
ages, the distinctions that have to be made are regional distinctions. It is
only when we reach the later middle ages that distinctions of size become
relevant. A map of the distribution of European towns at that period would
have to be completed by indicating their nature as large, middle-sized, or
little towns.

Medieval towns show no uniformity. It is their variety that makes
their history so interesting and at the same time so difficult. Only by looking for similarities, by distinguishing types of town, can we discover the real
nature of the many disconcerting differences between the history of one
town and another. Only in this way can we make any headway in understanding the supremely important role that towns have played in the
history of the West.

NOTES

[1] See H. Aubin, "Stufen und Triebkräfte der abendländischen Wirtschaftsentwick-
lung im frühen Mittelalter", *Vierteljahrschrift für Sozial- und Wirtschaftsgeschichte*,
vol. 42 (1955), pp. 1 ff.

[2] C. Violante, *La società milanese nell'età precomunale*, Bari, 1953.

[3] J. M. Font-Rius, "Neueren Arbeiten zur spanischen Stadtegeschichte", *Vierteljahrschrift fur Soz. und Wirtschaftsgeschichte*, vol. 42 (1955), pp. 137–151.

[4] A. Dupont, *Les cités de la Narbonnaise première depuis les invasions germaniques
jusqu'à l'apparition du consulat*, Nîmes (1942).

[5] E. Ewig, "Das Fortleben römischer Institutionen in Gallien und Germanien",
Comitato internazionale di Scienze storiche. Relazioni, vol. VI (Florence, 1955), p. 561.

[6] H. Jankuhn, "Probleme der rheinischen Handels nach Skandinavien im frühen
Mittelalter", *Rheinisches Vierteljahrsblätter*, vol. 15–16 (1950–51), p. 499.

[7] See the plan in *Geschichtlicher Handatlas der deutscher Länder am Rhein*, by J.
Niessen (Cologne-Lorrach, 1950), p. 420.

[8] E. Ewig, *Trier im Merowingerreich. Civitas, Stadt, Bistum*, Trier, 1954.

[9] K. Böhner, "Die Frage der Kontinuität zwischen Altertum und Mittelalter im
Spiegel der fränkischen Funde des Rheinlandes", *Trierer Zeitschrift*, vol. 19 (1950), pp.
82 ff.

[10] A. Dupont, *op. cit.*, pp. 217 ff.

[11] H. Ammann, "Deutschland und die Tuchindustrie Nordwesteuropas im Mittelalter", *Hansische Geschichtsblätter*, vol. 72 (1954), pp. 1 ff.

[12] See P. Johansen, "Umrisse und Aufgaben der hansischen Siedlungsgeschichte
und Kartographie", *Hansische Geschichtsblätter*, vol. 73 (1955), pp. 37 ff.

[13] Violante, *op. cit.*, pp. 41 ff.

[14] This is perfectly clear in F. Steinbach, "Der Ursprung der Kölner Stadtgemeinde",
Rheinische Vierteljahrsblätter, vol. 19 (1954), pp. 273 ff.

[15] F. Steinbach, *Der geschichtliche Weg des wirtschaftenden Menschen in die
Soziale Freiheit und politische Verantwortung* (Cologne-Opladen, 1954).

[16] C. Hase, "Gegenwärtiger Stand und neue Probleme der Stadtrechtsforschung",
Westfälische Forschungen, vol. VI (1943–52), pp. 129 ff.

Economic Life

15

The Circulation of Merchants in Western Europe from the 6th to the 10th Century: Economic and Cultural Aspects

FERNAND VERCAUTEREN

The subject which I have the honor of discussing before you concerns both economic history and the history of culture and civilization. This last notion is rather elusive; if we wish to pin it down, we have to emphasize that in the early middle ages culture and civilization were restricted to a very small elite. In the 6th and 7th centuries it is in the senatorial circles of Italy and the Frankish kingdom, and then in certain ecclesiastical centers, that we find evidence of the study and practice of literature, philosophy, and poetry.[1] The merchant world of which I am to speak did not belong to this intellectual elite. Does this mean that it in no way shared in the cultural life of the early middle ages?

It is not my purpose here to go into the history of trade. To keep to the subject assigned me, I wish to pose the following question: did merchants between the 6th century and the 10th contribute in any way, purposefully or not, to the diffusion of certain forms of civilization? To answer this question, we have to probe their mentality. Had these men no other interests save buying and selling, making a profit? Had they no cultural sensibilities, aesthetic or religious? Did their occupation influence their way of thinking and feeling? Or conversely, did their cultural aspirations more or less determine their behavior as men of business? Finally, did all those men whom the documents describe as merchants belong to quite the same social and economic milieu? It is decidedly easier to ask questions like these, if only to frame working hypotheses, than to supply satisfactory answers.

We are indeed obliged to admit that our sources are scanty, and further, that they are almost all one-sided and indirect. By this I mean that documents referring to merchants and mercantile affairs almost never emanate from the milieu of the merchants themsedves. These sources are nearly always of ecclesiastical origin; they are often hostile to merchants or at least indifferent, and speak of their activities only occasionally or by way of a selective illustration.

To be able to describe the movements of merchants and the regions they traversed would be very important. In an age when such traffic was assuredly minimal, when settlements were dispersed and often isolated, when regional differences were sharp, when the arrival of men from "outside" was a break in the monotony of a narrowly circumscribed life, when non-native products and articles not in current use were objects of real curiosity, it is obvious that the arrival of one or more merchants could itself have a psychic resonance. Such itinerant merchants would be certain to bring news, making the most of it, and the memory of their stories, true or imaginary, would linger on among their hosts and their listeners and among all who had seen them.

One can conceive, then, of the mere passage of merchants, in the periods we are considering, as having in itself some cultural significance. To appreciate this fully we would have to know more than we actually do about the itineraries of merchants, pilgrims, and other travellers. It is generally presumed that they continued to use the Roman roads; this is possible though not a certainty. It seems that from the 7th century, markedly so in the 8th century, waterway travel was more common than formerly.[2] Owing to deficiencies both of techniques and of state organization, many of the old Roman roads were no longer being kept in repair.[3] Besides, in the northern parts of the Frankish kingdom and in Germany, Roman roads formed less of a network or, in some areas, had never existed. In short, even small boats made possible the transport of far more merchandise than could have been carried by cart, especially since the techniques of harnessing remained very primitive, as we know, up to the 10th century.[4]

Thus, from the 7th and 8th centuries, merchants in Northern Europe will be moving chiefly by way of streams and rivers and coastal waters, and the same will be true in the plain of the Po and along the shores of the Adriatic.

In the 6th century, the Mediterranean area is still the center of maritime traffic and trade. This is well attested both for the Ostrogothic kingdom and that of the Franks: one has only to read the *Variae* of Cassiodorus, and the work of Gregory of Tours, to be persuaded of it. In a letter of Theodoric to one of his counts, written in 509 or 510, the king laments the loss of several ships which had been taking wheat from Sicily to Gaul. In another letter written between 508 and 511, he orders all the shipowners of the Campania, Lucania, and Tuscany to stand ready to take victuals to southern Gaul, where there was serious famine.[5] A similarly revealing notice in the *Liber Pontificalis* reports the Emperor Justinian as arranging for wheat to be shipped from Egypt to relieve a famine in Rome.[6]

In the writings of Gregory of Tours, too, one finds many signs of the frequency and importance of maritime traffic along the coasts of Spain, Provence, and Italy. It even seems that from the second half of the 6th century Italian-Frankish relations depend more on the sea route than on the land routes crossing the Alps. R. Latouche has lately drawn attention to this fact, which is no doubt due to the Lombard invasion of North Italy between 568 and 572.[7] Up to the middle of the 7th century the maritime route around North Italy is more frequented than the land route, a circumstance which greatly benefits ports such as Marseilles.

I shall cite and comment on some illustrative texts which have a cultural as well as an economic significance.

Gregory of Tours reports an anecdote relating to St. Radegonde which proves that people at Poitiers were informed about navigation conditions in the Adriatic and of the occurrence of storm threats to shipping there: Radegonde had one of the four keys of the Abbey of Poitiers thrown into the waves to calm them.[8] The Bishop of Tours notes, *à propos* of this personage, that in the time of King Sigebert clerks were sent *in partibus Orientis* to fetch relics of her.[9]

Henri Pirenne once devoted an article to the importing of papyrus into the Frankish kingdom; among the pieces of evidence on which it is based is a particularly eloquent passage by Gregory of Tours. In a crushing reply to abusive letters from his colleague Felix, Bishop of Nantes, the historian of the Franks expresses his regrets that Felix is not bishop of Marseilles: he would then have had all the papyrus he needed for venting his spite.[10] The point to note is the cultural significance of the import trade in this product.

Gregory of Tours occasionally credits the merchants who brought exotic goods to Gaul, with pious and benevolent feelings; it was they, he notes, who gave a hermit living near Nice "the roots of Egyptian plants" on which he subsisted through Lent.[11] I do not know to what plants our author alludes.

It was not only merchants who went to the East. Certain doctors who had learned their art in the Byzantine Empire lived in the Frankish kingdom. A notable case is that of Reovalis, known as *archiater* (the chief physician), settled at Poitiers at the end of the 6th century. He had performed an operation of an unusual kind, from recollections "of what he had once observed a doctor do in Constantinople".[12]

Mr. Lopez remarked here a few days ago, how regrettable it is that we know so little of the history of music in the early middle ages. Keeping within the limits of my subject, I would like to comment in this connection on a passage from Gregory of Tours. Describing in some detail King

Guntran's ceremonial entry into the town of Orleans, this author tells how the whole population of the town came to meet the sovereign, singing *laudes:* "here people were singing in Syrian, there in Latin, while in another place there were Jews chanting hymns in honor of the king".[13] To be sure, this is only an isolated text, but it calls to mind the story in the *Life of St. Caesarius of Arles,* of laymen singing psalms and hymns in Greek and in Latin, in Southern Gaul at the beginning of the 6th century.[14]

These linguistic feats are to be explained by the presence of numerous eastern merchants, ordinarily described in the sources as Syrians.[15] Among these were some who had ambitions outside commerce: according to Gregory of Tours, a Syrian merchant named Eusebius in 591 became Bishop of Paris and promptly distributed a great many ecclesiastical offices in his diocese among his compatriots.[16] The incident suggests that these Syrians had some degree of culture and of education.

There were sometimes other relationships, no less odd, between religious phenomena and trade. Again it is Gregory of Tours who tells us of an olive tree, green only at the top, whose leaves and bark had healing power, that was to be seen on the tomb of a saint at Nîmes. People said that a well-known merchant had collected a load of these leaves and was preparing to ship them to the Orient, but before he reached the port he was stricken with a serious illness.[17] On the other hand, a merchant of Poitiers was miraculously favored, his boat navigating the Moselle from Metz to Trier without trouble, because he had shown pious reverence to St. Martin.[18]

We may add that it was sometimes by the medium of travellers—merchants or pilgrims—that manuscripts passed from one country to another. It was in this way that Bishop Gregory of Langres (506–540) had received the story of the passion of St. Benigne, from travellers who were either going to or returning from Italy.[19]

Such are a few of the facts we have from the 6th century, referring to the Merovingian kingdom. To get information of this kind from the next centuries is much more difficult. It is true that we know the broad outlines of the structure of Carolingian commerce, even though specialists are far from unanimous as to its real importance in the economic activity of the 8th and 9th centuries viewed as a whole. But the documentation is far less explicit as to the cultural aspects of this economic life.

There is evidence of fairly wide economic activity around the North Sea. The Frankish kingdom is in touch with England, Ireland, and Frisia. Monastic expansion in these regions, as in the northern and eastern parts of *Francia,* must have been accompanied by some trade. The chief centers of northern trade at the end of the 8th century were Rouen, Amiens, Duurstede, Maastricht, and Quentovic; in the last-named port there was a resident official with the title of *procurator,* who levied customs tolls on merchandise in transit.[20]

We know almost nothing of the way of life or of the mentality of the merchants of these regions at this period, and little about their personal status. An 8th-century *Life* of a saint mentions a Frisian who had given himself with all he possessed to the Abbey of St. Maximin at Trier and who then, in order to make himself useful to the saint to whom he was vowed, went overseas to trade.[21] But it is not clear whether he was trading privately or for the Abbey. For at this period there were a good many merchants acting for abbeys or for churches, notably so in the case of the church of Verdun at the end of the 8th century.[22] There were also occasional merchants like those serfs to whom the Council of Frankfurt refers in the year 794: if they refuse the new royal coins, they are to be publicly flogged and forbidden to trade on their own account; but if it is proved that they are trading only by order of their master, the latter will be liable to a fine of 15 *sous*.[23] Again, there were palace merchants: they enjoyed special protection by the sovereign and if they devoted themselves "freely to commerce in their own interest and on their own account . . . (they were) also bound sometimes to conduct business for the palace". Monsieur F. L. Ganshof has made the latest study of them, in connection with the *praeceptum nego-tiatorum* which Louis the Pious issued in their favor in 828.[24] The sovereigns were thus concerned with the security of merchants; when in 873 the King of the Danes sent ambassadors to Louis the German to arrange for peace in the border zone between the Saxons and the Danes, he asked also that merchants of both countries traversing the zone be enabled to buy and sell the commodities that they were transporting, in peace.[25] This evidently refers to professional merchants making relatively long journeys. The existence of such men is attested by a considerable number of sources which there is no space to describe here.[26] We must however note that alongside the small *mercator*, who often traded only occasionally, and in addition to the abbey merchants who were really only doing transport service, these professional merchants—whose existence has sometimes erroneously been denied or slighted—had to conduct business on an international scale. They transported wheat, arms, silks, spices, and slaves.

We know, especially since the work of Monsieur Verlinden, the role played by those Verdun men who went regularly to Spain.[27] Commercial relations between that country and the Germanic regions of the Carolingian state—in particular, Mainz, which was an important business centre— are attested to in many documents, among them being a little-known one which came to my attention through the kindly erudition of Señor J. M. Lacarra. In 848 a Spanish priest, St. Eulogius of Cordova, was preparing to leave his country to join his two brothers, who for reasons unknown to us were "in ulteriores Togatae Galliae partes apud Hludovicum regem Bai-oariae", that is to say, in the kingdom of Louis the German (840–876). He thought he could reach the Frankish state by way of the Spanish mark but was hindered by military events. He then altered his itinerary and went to Pampeluna but found it impossible to cross the Pyrenees because a count

at war with Charles the Bald was devastating the countryside. Eulogius
then went to Saragossa; there was a rumor that his brothers, having joined
a troop of merchants from the further parts of *Francia,* had in fact arrived
there. On the way to the town, Eulogius actually met these merchants and
learned from them that his brothers were in reality still at Mainz. Later,
this report was confirmed as correct by the two brothers themselves, on
their return to their country.[28]

This document would deserve a lengthy commentary; suffice it here to
state that it refers to merchants who came, in about the year 848, from the
Rhineland or from Bavaria, to Saragossa. The most probable guess we can
make as to their business is that they were slave-traders.

Other texts of the 9th and 10th centuries attest to the export of slaves
from *Francia* to Spain, notably by Verdun men.[29] The mention of Bavaria
in Eulogius' letter is however interesting. It was through Bavaria, which
adjoined the Slav regions, that the main commercial route linking the
Frankish kingdom with these regions ran. And we know that in the Carolingian era they were the principal source of slaves. The presence of a
troop of slave-merchants at Saragossa may further be explained by the fact
that the city was a main centre of this trade: a Jew living there who specialized in it received important privileges from Louis the Pious.[30]

The invaluable detail in this letter therefore rounds out, in a vivid
and exact way, the documentation collected by Monsieur Verlinden, which
consists chiefly of juridical records and legislation.

It is relevant to our subject here to note also that the merchants of
whom St. Eulogius's letter speaks travelled through countries strikingly
different: the Slav border-lands, the Carolingian state, and the Moslem
regions of Spain. Surely such journeys involved cultural contacts? Reading
our text, we see that the merchants referred to were well informed, since
they were able to tell St. Eulogius that when they passed through Mainz
they had met or heard about his two brothers. In this age the presence of
strangers could not escape notice; it must have left some impression.

There are a good many other texts of the same kind which lead one to
the same conclusions. It is enough here to recall the story that occurs in the
Life of St. Gerald of Aurillac: a party of Venetian merchants, near Pavia,
offer to sell Gerald silks and spices; he buys nothing from them but he
shows them a piece of silk that he bought at Rome and tells them what he
paid for it; one of the merchants immediately remarks that the price was
very low and that even at Constantinople this silk would be worth much
more. This anecdote, on which Monsieur F. L. Ganshof has written a brilliant note,[31] confronts us with merchants who are perfectly informed as to
prices on different markets; this proves that they must have frequented
these markets, and shows also that they had the technical knowledge required in their business, in particular, the notion of there being a certain
"just price".[32]

This idea existed also among the merchants of the town of Verdun. When the army of Louis III, the Young, in 879 invaded Western *Francia*, the soldiers who had taken Verdun sacked the town because the inhabitants refused to sell them food "at the just price".[33] Here again we have to do with traders who through contact with strangers are aware of the market value of commodities and have a sense of professional ethic.

It might be possible to multiply examples of this. The evidence is sufficient to indicate that alongside the little merchant dealing only on a local market there were always, in the 9th and 10th centuries, a few men who did larger business of international scope. In this connection I think a remark on terminology is relevant. The term *mercator* is rarely used in the 6th and 7th centuries; for example, it hardly ever occurs in the work of Gregory of Tours, who prefers the word *negociator*. In the 8th and 9th centuries, on the other hand, the more common term is *mercator*. May not this be due to its link with the word for market (*mercatum*), and to the appearance of a body of market legislation?[34] The word *negociator*, so common in the 6th and 7th centuries, still occurs in Carolingian times, but much less frequently. It seems, at this period, to be applied almost exclusively to merchants engaged in long-distance trade. These suggestions are merely tentative; I propose to develop the subject further, elsewhere.

For the moment, however, I am posing a double-headed question. In the 9th century was there not a real as well as a terminological distinction between the *mercator* who operated on a local or regional *mercatum,* and the *negociator* who attended to international *negotia?* And was not this distinction inherited from earlier times, from the Merovingian period and from the late Empire?

Did the market regulation and the protection of merchants in long-distance trade that were introduced by the Carolingian state survive after this period? The question is difficult to answer. In the German regions, where monarchical authority was better maintained than in France, merchants seem still to have enjoyed protection.[35] Elsewhere, the commercial revival that is evident at the end of the 10th century and in the 11th century often arose independently of any action on the part of public authority. Most merchants were itinerant; they usually went about in groups and sometimes mingled with the throng of pilgrims. In 1027, Canute commended his subjects who were travellers, whether they should be merchants or pilgrims, to the bishops of his Anglo-Saxon realm.[36] There is an example of this link between the life of the merchant and the pilgrim in the 11th-century *Miracles of St. Ouen:* we read there of a paralytic going to Rouen on a donkey in the hope of being cured there through St. Ouen's intercession; near Paris, he is attacked by brigands who steal his mount; then some wayfarers and merchants come along, take care of him and carry him to Rouen in their boat.[37]

Documents of the 11th century usually mention merchants only when they have shown Christian piety or the lack of it. A very odd case was described lately by Monsieur Ph. Wolff, that of a *negociator* named Robert who was in Barcelona in 1009.[38] At his death, in that town, he left the canons there some merchandise he had imported, consisting of twenty pieces of cloth of various colors. Monsieur Wolff has aptly remarked that "this consignment of twenty pieces of cloth represented a veritable fortune and it was this unusual windfall that inspired the canons to plan the reestablishment of their chapter. The stock of Robert the merchant led to a series of enterprises attracting other gifts which made this restoration a reality, and similar restorations followed at Urgel and at Gerona." [39] Here we see an undeniable interaction between cultural and religious factors on the one side and economic factors on the other. A merchant's bequest is at the root of the restoration of the Barcelona canons' chapter in 1009. The story is all the more interesting since it is likely, in Monsieur Wolff's ingenious interpretation, that this merchant may have come from Flanders, or from that region.[40]

Most of the documents of this period are rather unfriendly to merchants, depicting them as animated by an acquisitive spirit which runs counter to the spirit of charity or piety. A text from the Meuse region, dating from the first quarter of the 11th century, shows us two merchants talking as they pass a church: one of them suggests that they go in to pray but the other refuses, saying he doesn't want to take his mind off business.[41]

The merchant is then characterized as a man who has hardly any time to spare for religion. It is felt, too, that his occupation, his "art", gives him a special cast of mind and necessarily engenders in him a love of gain; he is a man unable to resist the pleasurable impulse to drive "a good bargain". A passage in the 11th-century text of *The Miracles of St. Foy* is particularly eloquent on this point: it tells of a merchant of Auvergne temporarily enriching himself through illicit speculation in the wax used to make candles for the pilgrims who flocked to the shrine of St. Foy of Conques.[42]

But our best source as to the mentality and way of life of merchants is undoubtedly the well-known text of the chronicler Alpert of Metz, which refers to the lower Rhineland in the early 11th century. He describes the merchants here as tough men (*homines duri*), who resist almost any form of control, who scorn judgments awarded by virtue of law unless they happen to favor their own side. They are heavy drinkers, and the only people they admire are those who can tell indecent stories in a loud voice and incite them to laugh and drink. With the money they make, they hold banquets at which they become intoxicated.[43]

In interpreting this text we must allow for Alpert's moralizing tone; he has undoubtedly darkened the picture and rather exaggerated the crudity of these merchants' habits. These men nevertheless stand out as having a conception of life different from that of the society of their time, one that essentially rests on profit; this has moral and institutional consequences. Whether the documents come from central France or from the south, or refer to Lotharingia or to the zone of Frisian commerce, they all convey this same impression.

The above discussion is based, to be sure, on evidence that is fragmentary. The sources at our disposal are too thin, and lack detail. There is however ground for distinguishing, among the merchants mentioned in texts that run from the 6th century to the mid-11th, men who carry on only petty local trade and men who conduct long-distance trade. The presence of the latter is attested to over the whole period envisaged here: in the 6th century one finds them mainly in the Mediterranean area and in the southern and central parts of the Frankish kingdom; in the 7th and 8th centuries Frisian merchants are traversing the whole of the North Sea and its hinterland; in the 9th century an active commerce links the Slav countries and northern Europe, via the Carolingian state, with Spain; finally, in the 10th and 11th centuries, groups of merchants are to be found, often in company with pilgrims, on all the main travel-routes of France, Germany, and Italy. These shifts could not have occurred without cultural consequences, although the latter are difficult to discover. Some of the documents allow one to profile the mentality of the merchants, their attitudes towards the Church, their behavior in religious and professional matters.

To learn more, we have to wait through the next two or three centuries; then we can really gauge the degree of education, the ethics, the political and social reactions of the merchant world to cultural problems in general.[44] But one is tempted to think—if not to affirm—that the cast of mind demonstrated by the "business man" of the 13th and 14th centuries is already to some extent present in earlier ages, and that in this aspect there is no real break between the Syrian of whom Gregory of Tours speaks, the *negociator* mentioned in the Carolingian sources, and the *mercator* of the world of the 11th century.

NOTES

1 P. Riché, *Education et culture dans l'Occident barbare, VIe—VIIIe siècles*, Paris, 1962.

2 R. Latouche, *Les origines de l'économie occidentale* (Paris, 1956) pp. 155–61.

3 An 8th-century text mentions the dilapidated public road at Rouen. *Vita Ansberti episcopi Rotomagensis*, M.G.H., SS. rer. Merov., vol. V, p. 639.

4 R. Latouche, *op. cit.*, pp. 313-4, with bibliography.

5 Cassiodorus, *Variae*, IV, V, VII, ed. Mommsen, *M.G.H., SS. Antiq.*, vol. XII, p. 117.

6 *Liber Pontificalis*, ed. Mommsen, *M.G.H., Gesta Pontif. Rom.*, p. 159.

7 R. Latouche, "Les communications entre la Gaule et l'Italie sous le Bas Empire

et à l'époque mérovingienne", in *Studi in onore di Amintore Fanfani* (Milan, 1962), vol. I, pp. 473–80.

⁸ *Liber in gloria martyrum*, c. 5, *M.G.H.*, *SS rer. Merov.*, vol. I, p. 491.

⁹ Gregory of Tours, *Hist. Franc.*, IX, 40.

¹⁰ *Ibid.*, V, 5.

¹¹ *Ibid.*, VI, 6.

¹² *Ibid.*, X, 16 (15).

¹³ *Ibid.*, VIII, 1.

¹⁴ *Vita Caesarii Arelatensis*, c. 19, ed. B. Krusch, *M.G.H.*, *SS. rer. Merov.*, vol. III, p. 463.

¹⁵ R. Latouche, *Les origines de l'économie occidentale*, pp. 141–2.

¹⁶ Gregory of Tours, *Hist. Franc.*, X, 26.

¹⁷ *Liber in gloria martyrum*, c. 77. (See n. 8.)

¹⁸ *Liber de virtutibus S. Martini*, IV, 29, *SS. rer. Merov.*, vol. I, p. 656.

¹⁹ *Liber in gloria martyrum*, c. 50.

²⁰ *Gesta abbatum Fontallensium*, *M.G.H.*, *SS.*, vol. II, p. 291, Cf. F. L. Ganshof, *Histoire des relations internationales. Le Moyen Age* (Paris, 1953), pp. 51–2. For the relatively rich bibliography on Quentovic see J. Dhondt, "Les problèmes de Quentovic", in *Studi in onore di Amintore Fanfani* (Milan, 1962), vol. I, pp. 183–248.

²¹ *Acta S. Maximini episc. Trev.*, *A.A. SS. Bollandistica*, May, vol. VII, p. 24. For a slightly different version see the *Vita*, in *M.G.H.*, *SS. rer. Merov.*, vol. III, pp. 80–1.

²² *Gesta episcoporum Virdunensium*, *M.G.H.*, *SS.*, vol. IV, p. 44.

²³ Council of Frankfort, canon 5, *M.G.H.*, *Concilia*, vol. II, p. 166.

²⁴ F. L. Ganshof, "Note sur le *Praeceptum negotiatorum* de Louis le Pieux", in *Studi in onore di Armando Sapori* (Milan, 1957), pp. 103–112.

²⁵ See *Annales Fuldenses*, ed. Kurze, *SS. in usum schol.* (1891), p. 78.

²⁶ Some of these documents are discussed in E. Sabbe, "Quelques types de marchands des IXe et Xe siècles", *Revue belge de philologie et d'histoire*, t. XIII (1934), pp. 176–87.

²⁷ Ch. Verlinden, *L'Esclavage, dans l'Europe médiévale*, t. I (1955), pp. 707 ff.

²⁸ Letter from St. Eulogius of Cordova to Wiliesindus, Bishop of Pampeluna, 15 November, 851, recalling events from 848, when he had been in Pampeluna. Migne, *Patrologia, Latina*, vol. 115, pp. 845–52.

²⁹ Sabbe, *loc. cit.*, pp. 183–4; Ch. Verlinden, *op. cit.*, pp. 712–5.

³⁰ *Formulae imperiales*, no. 52, *M.G.H.*, *Formulae*, p. 325.

³¹ F. L. Ganshof, "Note sur un passage de la Vie de saint Géraud d'Aurillac", in *Mélanges Iorga* (Paris, 1933), pp. 295–307.

³² F. L. Ganshof (*loc. cit.*, p. 306, n. 3) does not believe that one can infer from this passage the existence of a theory of just price at this period; we disagree, and hope to return to the matter in another work.

³³ *Annales Fuldenses*, ed. Kurze, *SS. in usum schol.* (1891), p. 93.

³⁴ On the role of markets the most important discussion is that of the colloquium on urban history held at Constance in 1960, of which an excellent summary has been published by M. P. Schöller, "Das Marktproblem im Mittelalter", *Westfälische Forschungen*, vol. XV (1962), pp. 43–95.

³⁵ The problem was clearly summarized by M. H. Büttner at the Constance colloquium. See n. 35, above.

³⁶ *Receuil des Historiens de France*, t. X, p. 504, n. XXIV.

³⁷ *Miracula S. Audoeni*, *AA. SS. Bollandistica*, August, t. IV, p. 829.

³⁸ Ph. Wolff, "Quidam homo nomine Roberto negociatore", *Le Moyen Age*, t. 69 (1963), pp. 129–39.

³⁹ *Loc. cit.*, p. 133.

⁴⁰ This hypothesis rests on the name of Robert's brother, Truballe.

⁴¹ *Miracula S. Gengulphi*, *AA. SS. Bollandistica*, May, t. II, p. 649. Cf. *M.G.H.*, *SS.*, vol. XV, part 2, p. 794.

⁴² *Liber Miraculorum S. Fidis*, ed. A. Bouillet (Paris, 1897), p. 63.

⁴³ *Alpertus, de diversitate temporum*, II, 2nd ed., A. Hulshof, ed. (Amsterdam, 1916), pp. 49–50. See my comment on this passage in "Marchands et bourgeois dans le

pays mosan aux XIe et XIIe siècles", *Mélanges Félix Rousseau* (Brussels, 1958), pp. 659–660.

44 It will suffice here to recall the important article by Pirenne, "L'instruction des marchands au moyen âge", *Annales d'Histoire économique et sociale* t. I (1929), the works of A. Fanfani, especially his "La préparation intellectuelle et professionnelle à l'activité économique en Italie du XIVe au XVIe siècle", *Le Moyen Age* (Paris, 1952), and the fine book by Yves Renouard, *Les hommes d'affaires italiens du Moyen Age* Paris, 1949.

16

Natural Economy or Money Economy? A False Dilemma

MARC BLOCH

Premature hardening of concepts, a trouble well known in the physical sciences, is no less dangerous to the sciences of man. We too need to classify; we too have perpetually to combat the rigidity of our initial classificatory schemes. The following reflections are intended to illustrate, through one particular example, the necessity of this periodic recasting of our schemes. If the discussion is designed to stay within a relatively limited field of history, it is not from lack of awareness of the possibility of extending it to many other phases of economic evolution, noting a variety of subtle differences. How rewarding it would be, for example, to study the history of colonial economies, even that of the United States well into the nineteenth century, in the spirit of this enquiry! But it seemed that by concentrating it on one field the analysis would gain in clarity and conclusiveness.

First formulated in 1864 by Bruno Hildebrand,[1] the concept of natural economy has had notable success. It has been especially seized on, again and again, as providing the key to the economic civilization of the early middle ages, up until the great revival of the 12th and 13th centuries. On close examination, however, the concept turns out in this case to be a too simple tag which merely evades a fundamental problem. In effect it arbitrarily reduces a very complex system of payments to a simple matter of barter between producers or to unilateral payments by peasants obliged to set aside a part of their crops for their master. The historian then need never ask whether, in this type of social structure, vastly different from ours in every feature, the means of exchange, too, did not fill functions unlike those we see in them today, or saw in them yesterday. In a word, the concept invites one to a denial rather than to analysis—a facile but indolent solution which on further research breaks down.

In the first place it seems necessary to define our terms more precisely. The fact that a commodity is exchanged, not for gold or silver, but for another commodity, does not necessarily mean that the economy cannot be classed as monetary. In other words, money need not be metallic. As a generalization, this is a mere banality, to be found in any elementary textbook. The point, once we turn to the facts, is to discover the correct answers to the question why various early medieval societies were obliged to resort to practices of this kind. No single answer would fit all cases. Sometimes we have a simple case of the survival of a very primitive type of economy, as in Frisia, where pieces of cloth of a certain length, and no doubt of a certain texture, were long used as a measure of value and a means of exchange.[2] The custom persisted long after the groups concerned had become acquainted with metallic money. But payments in pepper raise quite different problems.

That this spice truly served as a form of money, at least between the 10th century and the 14th, is not open to doubt.[3] Let us guard against picturing a simple round of exchanges between a spicer and his neighbors, the spicer giving the shoemaker a few pinches of pepper from his pots in return for a pair of shoes. To cite just one example from a hundred at hand —the case of that Norman sergeant who, in about the year 1180, engaged to pay an annual rent of a pound of pepper for a piece of newly cleared land his master had granted him, the sergeant having no apparent connection whatever with the importing or sale of Eastern products.[4] It is even less conceivable that he could have planted pepper trees in his orchard. On the other hand, it is quite possible that the pepper-rent was gladly used to season sauces and roasts served at the lord's table. Even that, however, is not certain. There is nothing against supposing that it was set aside to be used in turn for other payments. Do we not find loans made in pepper at this time, especially in Genoa, both by private individuals and even by the commune?

The reasons that led to this particular choice, among all the possible substitutions for precious metal, are plain enough. Pepper actually satisfied almost all the conditions that classical theory requires of a monetary material. It was sufficiently scarce, and a quantity relatively small in bulk and weight in consequence represented a relatively high value. It was easy to keep. It could almost be classified as a fungible good, uniform in character, the variations of quality among different sorts of pepper being probably very slight. Finally, while serving as a kind of abstract medium of exchange, it was also a commodity with a use value independent of its monetary function. One could always be practically sure of finding a taker for accumulated stocks at need, perhaps even more so than if they had been gold or silver. Our ancestors, we know, liked their food highly flavored. In this partiality of their palates—due chiefly to poor stock-breeding, which left venison almost the only meat fit to eat—we find one of the reasons for their monetary habits.

However, the point to be emphasized is that the case of the societies using this curious money was very different from that of Frisia, with its pieces of cloth. There is nothing economically backward about it: the mere name of Genoa recalls one of the most vigorous centers of medieval trade and that of Normandy evokes the image of one of the most flourishing and well-developed countrysides of the time. Again, the very choice of an exotic product as a monetary instrument shows how far these groups were from practising or seeking a closed economy. Furthermore, a long tradition had familiarized them with the idea and the use of metallic money, and they never ceased to employ this too, alongside payments or credits in pepper. Why then were they not content to standardize their accounting in pounds, shillings and pence and to settle all payments with the sound of coin?

One is tempted at first to assume that scarcity of the precious metals was responsible. This indeed should be kept in mind, at least as a partial explanation. But on condition that we weigh its relevance with care, for this varies from one period to another. For the period before the great turning-point approximately at the end of the 11th century, there is no doubt. Not only was native production insignificant for gold and mediocre for silver. The balance of trade was then clearly deficitary, draining away much coin and bullion to the East; and the slackness of internal trade, by slowing down the circulation of money, reinforced the effects of its shortage. These last considerations do not, however, apply to the Genoese nor even to the Norman economy of the 12th and 13th centuries; [5] all the evidence is to the contrary. But even here it would seem that a condition of monetary famine made itself felt at quite frequent intervals. For the growth of the metallic stock, remarkable as it may have been, had not kept pace with the inordinately enlarged needs of commerce or credit. Medieval capitalism was under a constant handicap from its failure to invent the bank note. In a sense, the use of pepper as money was one of the results of this deficiency—a form, if you like, of necessary inflation.

Another reason, however, whose importance should not be overlooked, contributed to encourage the practice. This was the imperfection of minting. The responsibility, here, lies on political fragmentation, the origins of which lie outside our subject. There were a great many mints, and the coins in circulation varied widely according with their place of issue. Even the issues of each individual mint were constantly subject to wild variation. Hence the recourse to a commodity that was fairly stable in value. This flight from metallic money was never total; but, sporadically repeated, it was a highly characteristic feature of the medieval economy, occurring at times even in the most advanced areas. It amounted to a flight from the State. For though payments in pepper in many respects resemble payments in money of the more classic type, one feature is absent that would make them identical. Precious, durable, uniform, this commodity-money lacked the imprint of the public authorities. For this reason one is free to object that the custom of using it does not entirely conform to the concept of money economy. One would surely be still more reluctant to range it under the concept of natural economy.

Still, being a legacy passed on to the medieval age by the Mediterranean civilizations, metallic money never ceased to be familiar to it. But with variations in the manner of using it that need to be specified. It will be convenient here to recall the definitions, derived from the experience of the first age of capitalism, that current theory gives of the role of money. As we know, it distinguishes between three functions: that of storing value—which makes it, to quote Simiand, a wonderful means to economic "anticipation"; that of a means of payment; that of a measure of value. In the light of these three ideas, in turn, let us examine what the documents reveal about the practices followed in western and Central Europe from the Carolingian age to about the year 1200.

Obviously, during this period, the favorite means of storing value was always the precious metals. But most of the time not in the form of coin nor even of bullion. Certainly in church treasuries, and probably also in those of magnates and monarchs, the greater part of the metallic reserve was in the form given it by goldsmiths and silversmiths: goblets or liturgical ornaments, table-ware, a variety of jewelry. When obliged to make payments in excess of regular revenue, one put such articles in pawn to a money lender, in the frequently delusive hope of being able to redeem them later. Or one might take them to the foundry. There was nothing unusual, as there was later, in the age of Louis XIV, for example, or under the Revolution, in this behavior. It was accepted as perfectly normal. There, again, monetary instability was showing its influence. What use was it to store up a means of exchange that varied in value and might easily become old-fashioned in form? But a custom of this kind also attests to the low value which the economy of the time set on human labor: if people were so easily reconciled to see the value of the material fruits of their labor waste away, it was plainly because the loss did not amount to very much. In short, one can hardly doubt that hoarders were motivated at least as much by the desire to draw an immediate pleasure from their fortune as by any idea of "anticipation"; they assuredly were not simply looking to the future and they may well have been primarily interested in present enjoyment. The abstract voluptuousness of a Harpapon or a Père Goriot in gloating over their piles of coin is hardly an emotion that could have swayed men who were moved primarily by things material and immediate.

That, on the other hand, many payments of all sorts were handled in

coin, has by now been sufficiently proven. To the many examples given in
recent works I shall add only this little fact: besides giving quantities of
food to beggars who knocked at its door, the abbey of Corbie, in the first
half of the 9th century, was also distributing some alms in pennies.[6] This
is clear proof that these little coins were known to be of use to a starving
wanderer along the roads of Gaul at that time, enabling him to buy a few
necessities.

It must be admitted that one may question whether even the best attested of these payments in coin should come under the heading of money
economy, in the strictest sense of the term. Indeed, we know it to be a fact
that before coins were accepted they were often subjected to a test, by
weighing or some other means, in order to verify the content of precious
metal. The reason for this custom is obvious. People had reason enough to
be wary of the quality of minting and to fear the astuteness of coin-clippers,
whose scissors could adroitly shave the edges of a mancus or a besant. The
more vigorous administrative organs, like the English Exchequer under
the Norman or Angevin kings, even when they agreed to accept coins
simply by count, would deduct a certain percentage of their nominal value
to allow for the almost inevitable loss involved.[7] Now, as 19th-century
economists understood it, the essence of a true "money" is that its value is
inherent; a coin that needs to be weighed is more like bullion.

But here is another reservation which will doubtless seem more serious: much fewer payments were actually made in coin, weighed or not,
than a careless reading of the documents would suggest. An especially en-
lightening example occurs in the personal dues ordinarily known in France
as *chevage*. Originally a mark of a protective relationship and later, at
least in France, a badge of servitude in the new sense of that term, it was
assuredly, under various names, one of the most widespread types of seigneurial charge in the Europe of the first feudal age. One finds it commonly fixed at an annual rent of a few pence per head. To take these stipulations literally, it would seem that innumerable individuals of both sexes,
generally of the humblest classes, were in a position to pay out several
small coins each year. The truth is quite otherwise. Some of the charters
and descriptions, fortunately less reticent than the rest, show clearly how
the pennies could be replaced by payments in kind, the nature and quantity of these being sometimes specified, sometimes not, or even by a few
days of labor service. The documents making no reference to the possibility
of such a substitution are more numerous, but in the majority of cases they
contain nothing to indicate that it would be forbidden: the writers simply
saw no need to allude to a custom so universally familiar and resulting,
moreover, from ineluctable economic necessity. Everyone knew that a demand for payment in pennies meant, in pennies *or* in their equivalent—
their "price", as a Passau deed terms it.[8] Besides, it was plain that by insisting on the peasant always giving something that sometimes he was unable

to give, the lord would run the risk of getting nothing. What was the point, then, of describing such dues as money payments? Money was here filling the third of the functions enumerated above: it was serving as a measure of value.

Now, as all readers of cartularies know, there was nothing unusual about this procedure. Innumerable documents bear witness to it in this period, and even in the Merovingian period,[9] in connection with a variety of transactions. The value to be handed over is fixed in shillings and pence, later also in pounds. The possibility of a settlement in kind is mentioned or authorized, some documents specifying that the commodities handed over be duly "valued"—be in *apreçiadura,* the *Song of My Cid* put it,[10] more briefly. This recourse to a standard separate from the material paid over is what distinguishes the practice in question from the use of non-metallic moneys, described earlier. The lengths of Frisian cloth were both a means of payment and a measure of its value. The case of pepper, in certain respects, represents a transitional system. For the pepper was sometimes "valued" in monetary terms. Yet not always—our Norman contracts bear witness here—nor even in a majority of cases, at least not in the earliest examples.

The facts just related are well known; that is why it seemed superfluous to pour out a quantity of illustrations. The conclusions that they impose, on the other hand, are surely worth setting out clearly.

One conclusion touches the interpretation even of the documents. From the mere fact that a deed expresses a price or a tenant's dues in monetary terms, we cannot legitimately deduce that payment was really made in coin; obviously some more precise indication is needed. We have two successive records of the donation of a serf to the monks of Saint-Père-de-Chartres on November 2, 1107, by a certain Joselin de Leves. The first states that the donor's brother received 20 shillings as the price of his consent, the second states that instead of this amount in silver he had been promised a palfrey of the same value.[11] If the first deed alone had survived would we not have counted the transaction as evidence of monetary economy? In other words, in all statistics of medieval means of payment—how desirable it would be to have these collected on a massive scale—the cases, after being double-checked with extreme care, will have to be sorted according as payment was both measured and effected in money, or measured in money and effected in merchandise; and a third category will have to be set up, that of uncertainty.

Further, could anyone fail to realize that these monetary practices reflect one of the most significant and pervasive features of the societies known as feudal? I refer to their fidelity to a civilizing tradition which though it was often, to be sure, very dim, yet remained always accessible enough to consciousness to be capable, once the atmosphere become more favorable, of revival. Just as the political institutions of feudalism, characterized as they were by a profound enfeeblement of the State, nevertheless implied the memory of a past in which the State had been strong, and bore traces of this past, so the economy, in its most sluggish period, never ceased to cling to a monetary scheme based on principles inherited from the civilizations of the past. Thus it remained possible at least to relate the variability of payments to a general reference system.

This frequent dissociation of the standard and the means of payments seems in turn to have been destined to leave a deep and long-lasting imprint on economic mentality. Indeed, the regime of money of account under which Europe was to live for several centuries, at a period when the economy was already well developed, assumed its authentic form only with the great monetary revolution of the 13th century, with the return of gold coinage, the appearance of large silver coins, the reduction of the content of the penny, now definitely relegated to the role of small change. Only then did money that had hitherto been merely a unit in accounting detach itself as real money. The causes of this dualism and of its having been maintained for so long are very complex. It is difficult not to believe, however, that the habits of an earlier age, when money served as much for "accounting" as for paying, had not at least been a preparation for it.

To come back, finally, to the problem of classification: should an economic system in which money almost never ceased to hold the role of standard of value, but only imperfectly filled that of the means of payment, be termed a natural economy or a money economy? Or rather, is not its very existence enough to show up all the artificiality, and consequently the danger, of such a dilemma?

One last question arises: were the material objects that were used in making payments produced directly by the payer or his dependents? To put the question another way, if this method of payment is not one of the symptoms of "natural economy", must it be regarded as a sign of "closed economy"? When the payer belonged to the humble classes, there is no doubt that this was the most common situation. Yet it appears, here and there, that peasants who had no vineyard had to pay dues in wine.[12] Among dealings between persons of higher rank, the best known bring together an ecclesiastical group, paying out a price, and a member of the knightly classes, who receives it. Now in most of these cases it is obvious that the payment could not have come from purely domestic production. How many war-horses would have been bred in monastic stables? How much laymen's clothing, how many women's dresses, would have been hanging in wardrobes intended for the coarse robes of monks? Sometimes the document itself has been carefully enough worded to remove all ambiguity. When, at some time between 1090 and 1102, the monks of Saint-Vincent du Mans had received the consent of Hamelin the Forester to the gift one of his uncles by marriage had made them of the property of Ferrières, they were obliged also to compensate his wife, the donor's niece. It was agreed that they should give her "various furs". But obviously the monks had no furs. They sent one of their number to buy six Rouen pounds' worth of the fine things that had been asked, in the market at Falaise, and since the lady no doubt had little confidence in that holy man's taste, Hamelin ordered one of his own servants to go with the monk, "to choose the furs".[13] Thus a payment in kind had been immediately preceded by a money purchase especially prescribed, and made in a place especially reserved for such exchanges.

Then why, in a case like this, did the monastery not hand over the fine clinking pennies directly? To explain this curiously circuitous behaviour, we probably have to consider the preferences of the receiving party. Dopsch, some time ago, showed how it might be only as a last resort that dues were paid in money. The lord resigned himself to accepting it, for example, in the event of a poor harvest. In normal circumstances, he preferred to be paid in kind: this and other evidence would tend to prove that, among the aristocracy, "closed economy" was, if not always a reality, at least an ideal.[14] More imperiously still, in certain situations distinctly defined by custom, the social proprieties imposed their laws. This is nowhere more strikingly illustrated than in the deeds recording sales or gifts to churches. In the former we find, quite early, that the seller frequently received the sale-price in money—at least, on a literal reading of the text. On the other hand, when there is a question of obtaining the consent of relatives to a gift, whether this is really a gift, or a disguised sale, or to a transaction that is openly a sale, this consent is obtained by payments in kind, as a rule evaluated in money. At the extreme, we find stipulations like that in a deed concerning Saint-Martin-des-Champs, of about the year 1100: the other party having received hard cash, his daughter is assigned sixpence, but expressly "to buy herself some shoes".[15] The amount spent on these family "offerings" was always relatively small. It would no doubt have seemed improper to offer a person of rank a few miserable pennies. Even if it was worth no more, any little thing could be offered, and accepted, with more ease. So, today, a person who would scorn to receive a tip will not refuse a little gift.

The lesson of these last examples is clear: in their own fashion they recall a great truth. A study of payments, instead of being content simply to describe how their character varied with the time and the place, ought to concentrate at least as carefully on trying to discover the circumstances in which payments were differently motivated and why different classes of payers and receivers felt obliged to behave as they did. Not only because the possibilities vary with environment—everyone knows that monetary exchange spread more rapidly and became more nearly universal among the wealthy and in the towns—but also because the whole of a system of traditions and social conventions is eminently variable. The historian has only to look about him to realize the truth of this principle. In the French countryside, today, a small rural proprietor will in turn pay his architect with a bank check, his butcher with a postal note and his grocer in money. And if by chance one of his neighbors wants to make him a return for some service, the most imperious of all codes of civility demands that this take the form of a chicken or some butter. What is true of the present was true also, *mutatis mutandis,* of the past. In other words, all research on payments, if it is to attain its end, must become "social". So must all research in economic history.

NOTES

1 "Naturalwirtschaft, Geldwirtschaft und Kreditwirtschaft", in *Jahrbücher für Nationalökonomie,* Vol. II. The literature on the subject is immense, and there is no interest here in trying to list it. I will confine myself to citing the work of Alfons Dopsch, *Naturalwirtschaft und Geldwirtschaft in der Weltgeschichte* (Vienna, 1930), and the excellent critical review of it by Mr. Van Werveke, in the *Annales d'histoire économique et sociale* (Volume III, 1931) p. 428. See also my remarks concerning a memoir of Mr. Heckscher, *Ibid.,* p. 435, and my article, "Le problème de l'or au moyen âge", *Ibid.,* Vol. V, 1933.

2 Cf. H. Jaeckel, "Die friesische Wede", in *Zeitschrift für Numismatik,* XI, 1884. The use of cloth-money was equally widespread among the Slavs: cf. Helmold, *Chronica Slavorum* ed. Schmeidler, Vol. I, chapter 38, p. 77; G. Jacob, *Arabische Berichte von Gesandten an germanische Fürstenhöfe* (Berlin, 1927), p. 13. When in 1124 bishop Otto of Bamberg went to convert the Pomeranians, he had his wheat sold in order to buy some pieces of cloth, which would serve him as money to buy back Christian captives; Herbordi, *Dialogus* in *M.G.H. SS,* Vol. XX, p. 717.

3 Numerous texts, abundantly cited in literature, unfortunately very scattered. See, for example, P. F. Casaretto, "La moneta genovese" in *Atti della Societa Ligure di Storia Patria* (LV, 1928) notably pp. 3 ff.; the references assembled by A. E. Sayous in *Revue Historique* (CLXX, 1932) p. 9, n. 2; A. Schulte, *Geschichte des Mittelalterlichen Handels,* Vol. I, p. 73 and n. 1; J. Kulischer, *Allgemeine Wirtschaftsgeschichte,* I, p. 317. Late examples in H. du Halgouët, *La vicomté de Rohan* (Vol. I, 1921), p. 151. It would be easy to multiply references.

4 P. Le Cacheux, *Chartres du prieuré de Longueville,* no. LXIX (Publications de la Societé de l'histoire de la Normandie, 1934). Another example in the same region, at approximately the same date (reign of Henry II Plantagenet) and also concerning the grant of newly cleared land: S. Deck, *Etude sur la forêt d'Eu* (1929), p. 47.

5 C. H. Haskins, *Studies in Norman institutions* (1918) p. 45, notes that in the 11th and 12th centuries money rents are prominent in the donations made by the dukes, whereas the kings of France, at the same time, granted rents in kind more readily.

6 L. Levillain, ed., "Statuts d'Adalhard", in *Le Moyen Age* (1900), p. 355.

7 R. L. Poole, *The Exchequer in the twelfth century* (1912) p. 30 ff.

8 *Die Traditionen des Hochstifts Passau,* ed. Heuwieser (Quellen und Erörtergungen zur bayerischen Geschichte, N.F., Vol. VI), no. 108.

9 See the will of bishop Bertrand (March 27, 616) in G. Busson and A. Ledru, *Actus Pontificum Cenomannis in urbe degentium,* p. 137: "in gold or in horses five shillings."

10 Ed. Menendez Pidal, Vol. III, 1. 3236b ff. The whole passage is of the greatest interest for the history of payments.

11 B. Guérard, *Cartulaire de l'abbaye de Saint-Père de Chartres,* vol. II, p. 274, no. XVII. The brother later contested the donation, less, it seems, because he was assigned a horse instead of money than because of a delay in delivering the horse. Besides, he finally withdrew his objections.

12 Cf. Ch. E. Perrin, *Recherches sur la seigneurie rurale en Lorraine* (1935), pp. 303–304.

13 R. Charles and S. Menjot d'Elbenne, *Cartulaire de Saint-Vincent du Mans*, no. 802.

14 *Naturalwirtschaft und Geldwirtschaft*, p. 138. Prudent administrators, to guard against price fluctuations, judged it best to take dues simultaneously in money and kind, from each holding, in order to hedge against price fluctuations: see the remarkably intelligent explanations in the *Gesta abbatum Trudonensium* ed. de Borman, vol. I, ch. X, 6, pp. 176–177, concerning the abbey of Rodolphe (1108–1138). But, in 1184, these same fluctuations in the value of foodstuffs led to the substitution, at Saint-Denis, of rent in money for rent in kind: *Archives Nationales*, LL 1157, p. 57. On the inconvenience to a king obliged to buy provisions see Lambert de Hersfield, *Annales*, ed. Holden-Egger, pp. 100, 173.

15 R. de Lasteyrie, *Cartulaire général de Paris*, no. 127, and J. Depoin, *Recueil de Chartres et documents de Saint-Martin-des-Champs*, I., no. 102. Similar reference in *Cartulaire de Notre-Dame de Josaphat*, ed. Métais, no. 62.

17

Changes in Italian Agrarian Economy (from the Fall of the Carolingians to the Beginning of the 11th Century)

GINO LUZZATTO

I

Professor Grand has once again demonstrated that in agrarian economy, as it is true also in many other matters, the differences between one region of early medieval Europe and another are more and more turning out to be very slight. Everywhere we find fundamentally similar problems being dealt with in much the same way. The common elements are very numerous. In the first place, there is an obvious scarcity of population. This is a subject of remark and lament in the Europe of the early middle ages just as it has been in the last centuries of the Roman Empire. The scarcity of population is evident from the great extent of wooded plains, swampland, and heath; even if there were not ample documentary evidence of this in inventories of landed property, we have proof of it in the great number of places whose names refer to ancient forests. One has only to recall how commonly such place-names as Fagarè, Rovereto, Querceto, Quercianella, Carpineto, Saliceto, Ronchi, and many others of the kind, recur all over Italy, to realize how many forests have vanished; without this record in place-names, we would never even suspect they had existed. Again, as Professor Grand has observed, many documents mention vacant lands, holdings without a tenant. These were not necessarily uncleared, they may have been lands once cultivated but lying waste for lack of tenants. In any case, they show the low density of rural population.

Salvioli has stated—I do not know on what grounds—that two-thirds of the soil lay uncultivated. As Professor Grand said, it is utterly absurd to try to determine early medieval economy statistically. Yet the ratio of waste-land to arable was undoubtedly very high. Even so, there was a general shortage of labor: the provision of a large enough labor force to maintain tillage even of the small amount of land that was cultivated was a chronic problem. I will return to this shortly.

The system of property-holding, the distribution of property and the condition of the laborers, were also everywhere essentially similar.

However, alongside the numerous common features there were also marked differences, differences which depended primarily on soil conditions and climate. It would be idiotic to imagine that the same kind of agricultural conditions as prevailed in the plains around the Danube and the Rhine would be found in the Apennine range and its foothills, or in the Sicilian countryside. Within Italy itself, today, anyone who knows how local agricultural conditions affect farm leases is aware that there are deep differences between the Po valley and the Apennines, between regions with a continental climate and regions with a Mediterranean climate.

Another cause of differences within Italy, as also in parts of France and the Rhineland, was the survival of Roman cities. In Italy it is true that these had decayed, were very sparsely populated, having not only orchards and gardens within their bounds but even grain-fields and meadows. Nevertheless, they were still cities, administrative centers, the favorite residences of the *gastaldo* (local governor) or of the bishop, or of both, and in a great many cases they were market centers. Hence they had an economic importance which can hardly have failed to affect agriculture. For example, documents describing the property of the bishopric of Lucca reveal striking differences between the lands near the city gates and those at a distance.

On lands adjoining the city, we find a clear predominance of contracts under which the cultivator had to pay his rent, either wholly or in part, in money. On lands at a distance from the city, payment in labor services prevailed. Obviously, proximity to the city was the determining influence.

Proximity to a navigable river or to a sea-port exercised a similar influence. Geographical conditions were even more important than political conditions. The few comparisons that we are able to draw between territories remaining under Byzantine rule and those taken over by the Lombards reveal no great differences. Natural conditions and demographic necessity had the same effects in both. In this connection it is important to stress an underlying fact that many historians, especially amateurs, often forget, namely—as Professor Grand has already emphasized—the profound conservatism of the agrarian economy. Changes in the agrarian economy, until almost the end of the 19th century, are extremely slow.

Time and again, as we read the treatises of Cato, or Varro, or Columella, on rural life (*de re rustica*), we see that rural conditions, not today, but a century ago, were almost exactly like those described by the Roman writers. Yet it is regrettable that the history of rural economy has not been so well studied in Italy as in France. Fortunately, in the last thirty or forty years many monastic cartularies have been published. It should therefore be possible to arrive at a better understanding of the economic organization of monastic lands and of how this evolved during and after the 9th century. This will call for a certain number of students with the requisite training and enthusiasm—happily these are no longer lacking—to undertake what many scholars have proposed, namely, a patient study of the district around some one monastery. They must study it through the centuries, being careful above all to identify every place-name that occurs in the documents; in this way they can reconstruct every transfer of a piece of property, taking note of all changes either in modes of cultivation or in the relations between proprietor and cultivator. The abbey of Farfa, for example, which was one of the richest, with property extending from the region of Ravenna to the province of Rome, could offer a veritable mine of valuable data for monographic studies of this kind. Meanwhile, pending such studies, it is already possible to arrive at a few general conclusions that are fairly certain.

The property arrangements that are normally considered typical, and perhaps rightly so, of the period between the 9th century and the 11th are those of the so-called *curtis* system. Under this system various tracts of land—typically large tracts—were organized around a central courtyard. These lands formed the so-called demesne (Professor Grand called it the seigneurial reserve). There was also a much larger amount that was distributed to *coloni* (to use this term in the generic sense as referring to dependent cultivators), constituting the so-called *massaricio*. This system of dividing estates into two complementary parts undoubtedly dates from the end of the second century of the Roman Empire. It originated in the need of finding a substitute for slave labor, which, as the supply gradually diminished, became more expensive. Acordingly, free cultivators, and semi-free men, the so-called hutted serfs (*servi casati*), were granted small farms (*poderi*) from which they could wrest a meager living; at the same time, they were able to provide the lord with sufficient labor to work the seigneurial reserve. This system came to be very gradually adopted. Although one cannot regard it as absolutely dominant, we find it as the prevailing system, at least over a large part of Italy, by the end of the Lombard period. The letters of Gregory the Great, which are unique in giving us a glimpse of how estates at the close of the 6th century A.D. were run, make no mention of it. In contrast, documents of the 8th and 9th centuries show it as widespread.

The system of granting land in return for labor was nowhere standardized. Professor Grand spoke of free manses and servile manses, that is, of farm holdings assigned to free men or to serfs, the latter very probably being much like the men the Romans called *servi casati*, installed on a farm with a house. There were considerable differences in the amounts of labor required from the two groups, and in the ways in which the requirements were imposed.

A very common standard was that of requiring three days' work a week, which meant that half of a laborer's time would be devoted to his own land and half to the lord's. But this was not made into a general rule.

Agrarian contracts display appreciable variations in the extent of the labor services demanded. In France, as it seems to me Bloch has shown, the position of free laborers was protected by contracts requiring little or no labor service, while the relations between lords and serfs were regulated by custom, under which the half-time standard prevailed. Certainly the unfree were subject to much heavier demands. On the other hand we have a great many *livello* contracts with free men which call for a fixed proportion of their time: during the seasons of sowing, haying, harvest and vintage they were to work on the lord's land every other day, during the rest of the year every third day. In other cases the obligations were much lighter and were limited to specific jobs such as transport services, for example, and the carrying of letters and messages. But the major distinction was another one: in many cases, relating particularly to serfs, labor services were to be rendered at the will of the lord or of his administrator. There was no fixed agreement as to the number of days' service nor as to where the work was to be performed. The dependent cultivator was wholly at the mercy of the lord or of his administrator and had to serve whenever and wherever they chose.

Looking at the problem from a purely economic point of view, two calculations have been made for large estates in Italy—for the monastery of Bobbio, by Hartmann, and Darmstadter's, with some later revisions by myself, for the monastery of St. Giulia of Brescia. Hartmann, for Bobbio, estimated that 5,500 swine lived on the demesne, all that they produced being reserved for the lord. According to him, the demesne also produced 1600 loads of hay, 300 pounds of oil, 10,000 bushels of grain and from 600 to 800 amphora of wine. From the *massaricio*, on the other hand, although it was much larger than the demesne, the lord could take only 800 amphora of wine and 17,500 out of the 70,000 bushels of grain that it is estimated these tributary lands yielded. The relative insignificance of the revenue drawn from the tributary lands was compensated, on the other hand, by the large number of days of work that the land could obtain for the demesne. Hence the higher yield from the demesne really depended on the command of labor from the tributary lands.

For St. Giulia, which had sixty such estates, scattered over a vast territory, we have precise accounts from only one, that of Ponziano. On the demesne there were two mills, which ground 1500 bushels of grain, a few pigs (23), and meadows yielding 25 loads of hay. On its arable lands 1500 bushels of seed grain yielded a harvest of from 6,000 to 7,500 bushels. It had a staff of about 22 *prebendarii* (actually slaves, who received a prebend, or food allowance, from the lord, taken out of demesne produce). In contrast with the demesne lands were 41 tributary farms worked by 48 families of varying status: *servi, aldi, libellarii*. Generally, all were described as occupants or tenants (*manentes*). They gave the lord only 300 bushels of grain, 8 amphora of wine, and a few animals, but they gave at least 1200 days of work a year. On the sixty demesnes of the monastery of St. Giulia it is estimated that there were in all 5,000 swine, 2,000 sheep, and 300 cattle, and a harvest yield of 1600 amphora of wine and 200,000 bushels of grain over and above the food allowed the 740 prebendary serfs. From the tributary lands, on which there were about 8000 families, the monastic proprietor drew annually only 13,000 bushels of grain and 450 amphora of wine, but in compensation obtained 60,000 days of work a year. One sees how the division was the only possible means of ensuring a really high return from the demesne, far higher than the lord drew from the tributary lands. There is therefore no doubt about the existence of the system. It was probably very common. But it was not the dominant system, in the sense of being universal, because the documents themselves, few as they are, contain frequent records, especially in descriptions of property boundaries, of free cultivators who owned their property outright. These allodial properties, as they were called, continue to be rather numerous.

If, I say, we can speak of the regime of the *curtis* (manor) as prevalent in the 7th century and perhaps still later, as we have seen, in the 8th and 9th centuries, the idea that a manorial economy prevailed, on the contrary, cannot be accepted. In any case it has nowadays few defenders. What is meant by the term, "manorial economy"? It is all too commonly defined, following Bücher, as autarchy (to use a term that has become only too fashionable), as a closed domestic economy, one in which the great estate with its subdivisions became a self-sufficient organism, providing everything it needed, importing nothing from outside, and exporting nothing. This thesis is not only invalid for Italy, where one can very easily show it to be inconsistent with the facts, but its validity for Germany has come under most authoritative attack from Dopsch, and Bloch has brought excellent arguments to bear against it in France. The first argument rests on the fact that the lands making up a curtis did not lie together; great landed estates were always discontinuous. Not only the tributary lands but often the lands of the demesne itself were scattered in various localities and did not form a continuous entity.

Further, in Italy the survival of cities, which I have already mentioned, and the existence of some small degree of trade, triumphantly contradict the theory of such a type of economy. Hartmann, in an epoch-making little essay, long ago brought out the importance of a Liutprand's charter of 715 granting the inhabitants of Comacchio the right to ship salt and other products from the Adriatic, including Oriental imports, up the Po as far as Pavia and beyond, with the use of river-port docks along the way.

From the end of that century, and from the beginning of the 9th, we have equally firm evidence of trade by Venetians, who were at first competing with the Comacchi, and then, when the latter fell under Lombard rule, took over, almost completely, the role of their river boatmen. Thus we can be certain that both an import and an export trade existed. Not only did landowners in the Po valley buy salt, the first object of the trade and the most in demand, and along with it a few Oriental luxury products, there was also a flow of exports from the great estates of northern Italy to the Adriatic. Documents a little later in date show us that the great monasteries of north Italy had an enormous number of "cells" in Pavia where they stored and sold commodities, having their own boats, styled "ships", at first on the Ticino and soon on the Po, on which they transported these goods. Thus they both received goods from merchants coming from the Adriatic and sold, to the same men, agricultural products of which they had a surplus—a city like Venice was inevitably in need of these—but sometimes they themselves shipped produce down the river. All of which goes to show that the economy was not narrowly closed, not self-sufficient.

We have other proof of this in the existence of money: mints, far from being on the decline, were now multiplying. They were not yet minting gold, but Byzantine gold coins, followed soon by Arabic, were in circulation. Minting and the circulation of foreign money prove that we are not dealing with an absolutely natural economy. Certainly many exchanges would have been made in kind, as can still occur today, but money was always the standard of value and often served as the medium of exchange. We cannot speak of such an economy as closed, self-sufficient, or based on a purely natural autarchy.

I have referred above to some matters that Professor Grand did not raise, because the arguments have not, I believe, been discussed in our recent conferences, and because in my view there was an unbroken continuity between the Lombard period and the Frankish, and perhaps for still longer. With the Frankish occupation of Italy many of the great landed proprietors were displaced by new men, notably among great abbots and royal administrators: there were many new donations and grants of land, in the main at the royal expense, to followers of the new conquerors. But the property system remained practically the same.

A more controversial question is that of the influence that feudalism exerted over the property system. People speak of a manorial system and a manorial economy. Can we, in the same way, speak of a feudal economy? In reality the wording of the documents that refer to the great estates of the 9th and 10th centuries gives no certain support to the conviction that feudalism was of decisive importance in property arrangements. Feudalism was primarily a political rather than an economic phenomenon. The commendations on which so much emphasis is laid are a phenomenon going back into a much earlier age, a phenomenon due above all to the weakened authority of state power, to the situation of helplessness in which the small proprietors found themselves, their sense of having been abandoned; they preferred to put themselves under a great lord rather than remain utterly forsaken. Commendations sometimes finally acquired some feudal content, but this occurred only in extremely rare cases. Among many hundreds of documents from these centuries that I have had occasion to read, I have found only one, a lease of the year 808, in which besides promising small payments in money and wine, the lessee bound himself to serve on horseback in case of war—a strictly feudal service. But in the rest, there is no innovation at all.

An element which was, however, influential, especially affecting relations between lords and their dependents, was the spread of immunities. The grant of an immunity, particularly if it covered fiscal rights, certainly spurred commendations, reduced the number of free proprietors, and led to a growth in the size of great estates. It later affected the relations between lords and dependents in the sense that the lord was enabled in many cases to flout custom by imposing heavier obligations on his dependent cultivators than those due under the old contracts, or more often under custom, simply because he now enjoyed more power. Being the sole ruler in the district he had no fear of the remote and frequently impotent sovereign; his activities were not subject to any control. If the dependent cultivators tried to get the judicial authorities to uphold the old customs, as happened many times, they found themselves defeated by the circumstance that the lord could bring very strong pressure to bear on the magistrates. Although not a judge, he is always present in the court of justice that has the duty of hearing these cases. He has some judges completely in his hands: only in the rarest of cases do judges of this kind hear dependents' petitions with any sympathy. Besides, by means of the immunity the lord was authorized to impose charges due under public law, such as tolls; he could thus enforce use of the seignorial mill, demand labor services for the construction, repair, and maintenance of his castle, or for flood control in the public interest. In a word, he could assert a claim to everything that his dependents bewailed as excessive exactions (*superimpositiones*). In this way a new

body of custom, as it were, took shape, which invalidated the old contractual bonds and produced that stability in the condition of the dependent classes of which Professor Grand spoke.

All this, as I have indicated, could have a repercussion on economic
life, but did not substantially alter the way in which it was ordered. What
prevailed was what in France is called the seignorial regime, and here (in
Italy) the regime of the *curtis*.

II

This morning's discussion noted the improvement of agrarian production
in the 8th century and at the beginning of the 9th. This improvement
probably continued, in spite of the devastations caused by the Arab and
Hungarian invasions, and in spite of the profound crisis that the great
royal and ecclesiastical estates underwent in this century. The documents
that have been examined, in some regions, for the purpose of ascertaining
what crops were grown on arable land and what trees were planted, show
that all through Italy—in the plains, in all the Apennine regions, and in
the islands—the chief crop was grain, mainly wheat. Unfortunately this
continued to be so even among the woodlands of hilly regions and moun-
tain slopes. This made for inefficiency. Another handicap was inadequate
fertilization. This was due not so much to lack of livestock—pigs, sheep,
and other animals abounded—as to an almost total lack of stables, and to
the primitive state of agricultural techniques.

In this connection Professor Grand has spoken of the great importance
—perhaps rather exaggerated—of changes in the method of harnessing
horses. Actually, the plough was not very widely used, and the types of
plough known—to judge from later tradition—were quite primitive. Land
was usually worked with a spade or a hoe. Because methods were so primitive and labor so scarce, the yield of grain per hectare, seems to have been
poor, averaging about four times the amount of seed sown. This would
indicate a yield of from 6 to 7 quintals per hectare, in districts where it
now averages from 12 to 15 quintals, with maximum yields, in some places,
reaching 40 or 50 quintals and in exceptional cases, 60 quintals per hectare.

Cultivation of vines ranked next to grain-growing, being widely
distributed and of great economic importance. Our evidence of its wide
diffusion comes not only from the commonly-used generic formula by
which lands were described as wooded, arable, or set with vines, but also
from the very great number of agrarian contracts specifying that a certain
area, probably just a small plot, must be planted with vines. For the first
six years after planting the cultivator paid no rent for the vineyard, after
this as a rule giving half the produce to the landlord; occasionally it was
agreed that after the six years the vineyard would be divided, half becom-

ing the cultivator's property, half being returned to the landlord. Several of the surviving contracts fix the exact size of the area to be kept in vines: from 200 to 300 feet by 40 or 50. Yet in spite of their small size, vineyards were regarded as second only to the grain-fields in importance.

Often there is record of olive trees growing near the vineyard, not only in the regions that specialize in olive culture today, but in north Italy—in hilly country and sometimes even in the plains. But the groves were very small; for example, one contract that required the planting of olive trees set the number at 37. Production must therefore have been very modest. Finally, there is frequent mention of fruit trees, without indication of the species. Yet these usually remained very few in number even in regions that are now celebrated for their fruit. There is no record whatever, even in the South, of the growing of citrus fruit.

It has been affirmed, on the basis of a single document, that not only were mulberry trees grown but that silk-worms were reared and raw silk exported from northern Italy to the Orient. I confess that I am obliged to reject this testimony. I think it is a matter of mistaken interpretation, because not only is actual record of the rearing of silk-worms lacking for the 8th, 9th, and 10th centuries, but even in the 13th and 14th centuries we have firm evidence of it only for the country bordering the straits of Messina. Even Lucca, which became the chief center of the silk industry in the 12th and 13th centuries, did not produce its own raw silk but imported it. All through the records of Venetian trade there are very frequent references to the importing of silk from eastern regions, in particular from Syria. Therefore it seems to me absolutely out of the question that we could have been exporting raw silk. The great diffusion of silk-worm culture in Italy came after 1500, above all in the first half of the 19th century.

One industrial plant—flax—was however much more widely cultivated than today. It may be objected that flax is still quite common in Italy. But except in the province of Cremona, where I believe a little is grown in order to spin the fiber, it is grown for the linseed. In the early middle ages, on the other hand, the records show that flax was widely cultivated for weaving. Documents of the 10th century from Varesotto and from the region of Viterbo describe the ponds used for retting the fiber.

It is quite common in this period to find agrarian contracts stipulating that land shall be improved (ad meliorandum), sometimes by raising the yield of the accustomed crops, but more often by introducing new crops. Lizier, who in 1908 went through all the published monastic documents from southern Italy in search of material illustrative of early medieval rural economy, came to the conclusion that from 950 new plantings of vines stood in a ratio of 1/1 to new plantings of all other crops; between 950 and 975 this ratio became 2.50/1 and between 955 and 1025 it became 3.25/1. Thus most new planting came to be of vines. These figures are from southern Italy, but one would judge that the situation was not very different in other regions of Italy. A comparison between the spread of the vine and the olive is very suggestive: contracts calling for new vineyards outnumber those for new olive trees by seven to one.

Along with this gradual improvement, we observe a phenomenon very well known to all students of the early middle ages, especially in Italy —the frequent alienations, sometimes open but much more often disguised, of royal property and of the property of the great monasteries. Shortly after his nomination as abbot of Bobbio, the future pope Sylvester II, Gerbert of Aurillac, complained that his predecessors by certain writings (*codices*) called *libelli,* had alienated all the monastery's property; as he said, "I do not know how another abbot can be elected, my successor will find the whole of the property dispersed." After the death of Otto III the situation became still worse, and Gerbert obtained a charter by which all the grants of land made by the abbots over the past fifteen years were annulled. The state of affairs that the future Pope Sylvester II bemoaned at Bobbio was duplicated, on a larger scale, on the great estates of the Abbey of Farfa, which were depleted under several abbots, most notably under Abbot Campone. These alienations usually took the form of leases. On this point one must beware of a misunderstanding into which several students of the subject have fallen, that of confusing two different types of lease. The one type was granted directly to the cultivator, for the working of specified plots of land. The other was a lease to rich agricultural contractors, who were granted large tracts for a very long term, the land continuing to be worked by the existing occupants. The leases given by Farfa and all the other monasteries which within some fifty years were depleted of the greater part of their property were precisely of this second type which served to disguise veritable alienations. That this was their effect is sometimes very clearly revealed by the wording of the document itself, in which it is seen that the lessee gave the abbot what would seem to us an extremely small sum of money. In those that I have seen, the maximum was 200 shillings—in one instance, 300. But in many cases the figures are much lower—150, 100, 80 shillings. We must remember, it is true, that we are still very close to the monetary reforms of Charlemagne, when a lira was actually the equivalent of a pound of silver (by weight); as the documents show, silver still had a very high purchasing power. To cite a single rather significant example, one 9th century document informs us that the grantee gave the abbot, in gold, silver, and in horses, the value of 150 shillings. So, for 150 shillings one could get some gold, some silver, and several horses. The abbot who received this amount granted the land for an annual rent of two or three pence, purely fictitious. Actually it was a sale, the sale price being the sum that the grantee gave the abbot.

This morning the question of why these sales occurred came up for discussion. Now naturally contemporaries who protested against them and sought to stop them talked only of the abbots' greed and avarice. Professor

Grand spoke, correctly, of a political and military need, of the fact that the great monasteries were obliged to assure themselves of defense. Hence the grants of land to *milites*, to nobles, who could guarantee them some defense of their property. I believe, however, that in addition to this cause there were others of an economic nature. I am not alone in this. Among others who think so is the young scholar, Violante, who in his excellent book, *La società milanese prima delle origine del Comune*, has examined this whole economic development, especially in the 10th and 11th centuries. We are inclined to see the cause of the sales in the development of commerce, in the importance that markets assumed, and along with them the class that was now established in every large city, at least in Pavia, Milan, and Cremona, as well as in the maritime cities. The development of commerce increased the demand for at least some, if not all, agricultural products. This rise in the demand for products and the rise in their value came at a time when there were still complaints of a shortage of labor.

This shortage of labor, which I stressed earlier, is apparent from the wording of some of the records of the monastic alienations. For example, land was granted on the condition that the lessee settle a certain number of workers on the land. There is also frequent record of vacant holdings being given to the occupants of another farm to cultivate. One and the same tenant then worked two holdings, his own and another that had lacked hands.

Now this shortage of labor at a time when products were rising in value, through the increase in demand, pushed the man who had newly acquired an estate into exacting from the tenants settled on his tributary lands the whole amount of the labor services sanctioned by ancient contracts or custom, and sometimes still more than this amount. Consequently there was a state of unrest among the dependent cultivators, who viewed with growing bitterness the impossibility of devoting more than half the labor force at their disposal to their own lands. Unrest grew also among the lesser nobles—the *aldi* and *milites* of middling rank—who from this time on were living in the city and who were unwilling to tolerate the superiority of other ruling powers.

In reality a more fundamental change was in progress, one that goes a little beyond the limits of my subject. After the year 1000 A.D., as Lopez pointed out this morning, there was an undoubted rise in the population. Naturally we have no population statistics for any part of Europe. Not until the 14th century do we have relatively firm data, and then only for an individual city or for a very small region. Statistical data for entire states begin to appear only in the 16th century and even then are not numerous. But even without statistical data, there are unmistakeable signs of growth in the population of western and central Europe after 1000 A.D., and perhaps even in the last decades of the 10th century.

We see it in the greater mobility of the population, we see it in the beginning of the phenomenon of mass migration—a phenomenon best known in Germany, when the Germans crossed the Elbe, reversing the course of their original advance, a reversal later repeated in their retreat after the last world war. We see it in the emigration along the Baltic coast to the Neva. We see it all through the west, in the majestic phenomenon of the Crusades. Primarily religious, this had at the same time underlying demographic causes in a sense of malaise due to an excess of population, and in this need of movement reappearing for the first time in the Middle Ages since the barbarian invasions.

The consequences of this demographic change became apparent in the cities and the countryside at about the same time. In the country there are often complaints about the flight of dependents, attempts are made to prevent these escapes, and quarrels multiply between dependents who want liberty and proprietors who want to make certain of the dependents' labor services. In the cities the consequences of the change appear in the movements that led to the setting up of the Commune. As Lopez mentioned already, this movement is chiefly a matter of relationships among landowners. A middle class arose from the drawing together of small landowners and the class of merchants who had risen in the world; the latter in many cases had themselves become small or middling landowners. This citizen middle class found itself in conflict with the great lords, and often with the Bishop who had jurisdiction over the city. Of the two movements perhaps the basic one, the one that accounts for the other, is that of the dependent peasant class, but the first to appear openly, the first to lead to anything revolutionary, is the city movement. The urban Commune precedes the rural Commune, yet in the countryside or in the little Communes in the minor fortified centers, where rustics and members of the nobility live side by side, pacts are drawn up whose chief aim is to uphold the customs, to stop the constant breaches of custom by which it was always the rustics who suffered. These juridical pacts between rustics and lords arise in a variety of Communes, notably in the smaller ones and in those that Lopez calls agrarian Communes, achieving, or at least trying to achieve, some protection for the peasantry against the oppressiveness of the ancient feudal lords, of the heirs of feudal law, against their exactions, against unlimited obligations to work on the lord's land at his will.

On the other hand, the need for these labor services had appreciably diminished, since the demesne had almost entirely disintegrated. On the royal estates, the demesne lands have all, for military or other reasons, been given away to the kings' *fideles;* dissolution of ecclesiastical estates that we have already observed had occurred chiefly through grants of the demesne lands. In consequence, though labor services do not entirely disappear, they come actually to amount to very little. In some parts of Italy they never entirely disappeared. Even today, in some districts, peasants speak of "works" due, meaning that in addition to paying rent in money and kind they are under the obligation of giving their landlord a few days' labor, for which they are, however, paid. For a few days in the year they become wage-earners.

But the rise of the Commune, that general movement of renewal, of increased mobility, of aspiration to freedom certainly helped to loosen these bonds, and to start a movement towards the freeing of the serfs. We have with us Professor Vaccari, who has shown extraordinary skill in his work on the enfranchisement of the serfs. Now collective enfranchisement of serfs usually came through political action by the Commune. But independently of these collective enfranchisements decided by the Commune, it is clear that the rise of the Commune, and especially the rise to power of the strong commercial cities, had an enormous influence on the surrounding country districts, and brought about the almost total collapse of the old manorial regime and feudal estates. But the collapse was not definitive: with the weakening of the Commune, with the formation of a new aristocracy, the rural classes again sink into conditons that are far from happy. The villeins, those who were once known as the *manentes,* will become in effect, not by legal decree but through custom, again bound to the soil, they will enjoy only a very restricted liberty. But at any rate a first transformation preceding that of 1789 by seven centuries, had already taken place.

Humanism and Science

18

Centers of Culture in Frankish Gaul Between the 6th and the 9th Centuries

PIERRE RICHÉ

In the cultural history of Gaul, the period which runs from Clovis to Pepin the Short is one of the most sterile; set beside the Carolingian Renaissance, it seems like a poor relation. If one opens even an advanced textbook, the pages on it are quickly leafed through. The author speaks of barbarism, of mediocrity, of the decline of culture, and finally reaches the great "Carolingian Renaissance". Historians have perhaps taken too literally the famous opening sentence of Gregory of Tours' *History of the Franks:* "Literary culture in the cities of Gaul has declined and is even disappearing"; the bishop then dwells on the ferocity of nations, the violence of kings, the ruin of religious foundations. It is true that Merovingian Gaul suffered heavily from the invasions and the subsequent civil wars. How, in these conditions, can we conceive of there being centers of culture, in the humanistic sense, especially centers of lay culture, that is to say, schools where the first, preparatory form of culture could be acquired, of public or private libraries, of circles of educated people, of patrons playing the role of Maecenas? Is this sort of thing imaginable? And if we turn to the centers of ecclesiastical or monastic culture, how can we allege the existence of episcopal and monastic *scriptoria,* of monks and clerks enlivening schools, undertaking the writing of books to be sent out all over the kingdom, at a time when ecclesiastical literary production in Gaul was utterly mediocre? But the pessimism of Gregory of Tours should not deter us from looking into the matter. This research is difficult, for our documentation is very thin. We have to collect and test the authenticity of each piece

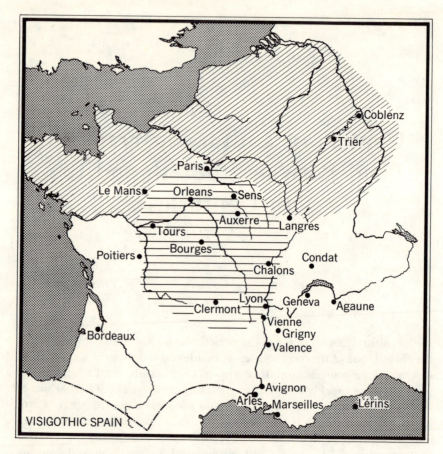

Figure 1. Centers of Culture in 6th-Century Gaul.

////// "Barbarian" Gaul

═══ Conciliar Zone

of information and try, like a worker in mosaic putting his separate stones together, to reconstruct the picture as a whole. Were there centers of culture in Gaul? What was their radius of influence? What was their role in the history of Western culture in general?

At the start I would like to observe—and this holds for all aspects of culture, both artistic and intellectual—that one cannot study Merovingian Gaul as though it were a single entity. Northern and Eastern Gaul are clearly different from Southern Gaul. For this reason I include a map (Figure 1) distinguishing the northern areas, which I have called "barbarian Gaul", from the south, which I call "Roman Gaul", the region where

Roman culture persisted; like Visigothic Spain and Ostrogothic Italy, it formed a part of the great Mediterranean world. Political unification of Merovingian Gaul was achieved through the conquest of Aquitaine by Clovis in 506 and through the conquest of Provence and Burgundy by his successors; but underneath this political unity lay a sharp cultural discordance. One can understand it on realizing that the Frankish population was mainly concentrated in the "barbarian" Gaul of the north. In the south, on the other hand, there was very little Frankish settlement; very few Germanic tombs have been found. Besides, in Aquitaine, Provence, and Burgundy, the Franks left the administration alone, the counts being in general chosen from among the Gallo-Romans.

This contrast between "barbarian" and "Roman" Gaul takes different forms. In the first place one has to note that urban civilization was much more alive in the south than in the north. There was more commerce: it is in the towns of "Roman" Gaul, at Clermont, Bourges, Orleans, Tours, and Bordeaux, that we meet foreign merchants, the Syrians. It is also in Roman Gaul that we find the majority of the inscriptions that have survived; we find these in the regions of Arles, Vienne and Lyons, and of Poitiers, Tours and Clermont; in the north, however, inscriptions are very scattered and there are many places without any. Inscriptions of course signify a civilization of the written word. Southern Gaul, like Italy and Spain, remains faithful to this civilization of the written word. Gallo-Romans drew up deeds in the 5th and 6th centuries, examples of which have been preserved in the formularies of Angers, Clermont and Tours; it would seem that these deeds were still being entered in the municipal registers, the last witnesses, as it were, to municipal life. Again, one can contrast the two regions by noting that the great aristocratic families known to have maintained Roman traditions are found, as one would expect, in that part of Gaul south of the Loire and the plateau of Langres. In searching for centers of culture in Gaul, we have to keep these opposite conditions in mind. I propose to treat first the centers of traditional culture in Southern Gaul in the 6th century and at the beginning of the 7th, then the centers of culture in the north, and finally the creation of new centers in the 7th and 8th centuries; these last were essentially monastic.

Within the Gaul that I call Roman, three regions stand out: Provence, Burgundy, Aquitaine. In all three, lay cultures of a Roman type survived. Let us start with Provence and Burgundy, which are linked by the Rhone valley. We discover Gallo-Romans bearing the titles of patrician and of rector, we discover inscriptions still dated by consular years up to the beginning of the 7th century and coins struck in a style that looks Roman or Byzantine. This Burgundy and this Provence are always in close communication with the other Mediterranean countries by the overland roads of Provence or by sea via the great ports of Arles and Marseilles, which are always very active. If we open the letters of Ennodius of Pavia, a Provençal who settled at Milan and then at Pavia, early in the 6th century, we see that he has correspondents in Provence and in Burgundy; if we read the letters of Bishop Avitius of Vienne, we see that he corresponds with men in Milan and Ravenna; we are back in the Roman cultural unity. In speaking of correspondence, one should not think only of the writer; the presence of the courier in a strange country and his opportunity for conversations there was a part of the mutual enrichment to which the exchange of letters give rise.

Centers of culture are always in towns, in those towns where traditionally public schools were maintained, no doubt up to the beginning of the 6th century. At Arles, at that time, in a little group of relatives and friends of Ennodius, whose members were friends also of Sidonius Apollinaris, we meet a certain Firmin who in 498 welcomes Caesarius of Arles. Firmin seeks to have him learn the liberal arts, especially rhetoric, by entrusting him to Pomerius, an African refugee in Arles. Later one finds educated men among those who heard Caesarius preach, for the bishop asks them "to bear with rustic language without complaining". One can imagine the hagiographers who write the *Life of St. Caesarius* asking scholars not to criticize the simplicity of their style. At Marseilles at the end of the 6th century, one finds another circle of educated men around the patrician Dynamius, who writes letters in a style much like that of Ennodius of Pavia, and also poems, unfortunately now lost. There is also, in this group of educated Provençals, a certain senator named Felix who according to Gregory of Tours was studying Virgil, Roman law and arithmetic with the help of a slave, like an ancient Roman.

Let us go up the Rhone to Avignon. In about the year 561, a monk of St.-Laurent in Paris declines the king's proffer of the bishopric of Avignon. Why? For fear he would be laughed at by sophisticated senators and philosopher-officials. Continuing northward, we come to Vienne; Vienne had a great period of culture in the time of Claudian Mamert at the end of the 5th century and again at the beginning of the 6th, under Avitius, and must have remained a source of culture throughout the 6th century. Indeed, towards 599, Didier, Bishop of Vienne, is accused of instructing certain people in grammar; now to teach "grammar" at this period meant to teach literature, humanistic culture. The information about Didier comes in a letter of Gregory the Great, a letter which in my opinion has been misconstrued. Gregory the Great did not mean to condemn classical culture, his intention was simply to remind the bishop of his duty as a bishop, which was to teach holy scripture or the moral law, not literature. The evidence in the letter has an important bearing on our subject, for it proves that there was a shortage of teachers at Vienne at the end of the 6th century, the bishop being forced into this role; it indicates also that there was still some interest in classical literature. We know from Didier's biographer, Sisebut, that he was himself a man of letters; he came from an aristocratic family, no doubt from Autun, and perhaps even from the family of the Syagrii. It was a tradition in these great families, up to the end of antiquity, to pass on the ancient culture from generation to generation.

We can make this point still more clearly if we turn into Aquitaine, where the towns may no longer be centers of culture, but where centers exist in the great families. Auvergne is the region furthest from the Mediterranean, but it was always in touch with the Mediterranean countries, for like Provence it formed part of the kingdom of Austrasia, and consequently Auvergne officials were quite often sent to Provence. Auvergne appears to have been a center of resistance to Germanic influences; it is there that we meet families who have kept a sense of Roman greatness and of Roman culture. We find them alike in Poitou, in the region of Bordeaux, in Berry, and in the Loire valley. Information is lacking only for the region of Toulouse. The great families, the descendants of Sidonius Apollinaris, the Leontii, the Sulpicii, cherish the ways of the old culture. Fortunatus and Gregory of Tours aquaint us with these men of letters: poets and rhetoricians such as Sulpicius, Bishop of Bourges, Felix, Bishop of Nantes, Gregory of Tours himself. Gregory is a most interesting case, for coming from a great senatorial family, he should have had the traditional culture, that is, the lay culture; but on account of his father's illness he was entrusted to an uncle who was a bishop, and therefore rceeived an exclusively ecclesiastical education. Later, however, he tried to make up for what he had missed by reading whatever was still available. In the next generation, in Sulpicius II of Bourges or Didier of Cahors, we find men who are still well-read. In the middle of the 7th century a last representative of these senatorial families of Aquitaine, Bonnet of Clermont, was trained in "external sciences", that is to say, in what remained of the liberal arts.

Thus we may say that there were centers of culture in Southern Gaul; assuredly they are modest, and do not give much light; the ashes of the past pile up as time goes on, but all the same they are centers where culture is transmitted. This culture consists primarily of grammatical knowledge. People can still distinguish literary Latin (*sermo scholasticus*), from spoken Latin; there is even an attempt to speak correctly. Virgil is still read, perhaps in excerpts, but he is read. People actually give children names taken from the ancient literature: we have men called Dido (a bishop of Albi, a bishop of Tours, a bishop of Poitiers), Hector (the patrician), Patroclus (the saint), Orestes (a bishop of Bazas and of Vaison), Virgil (a bishop of Arles) and even Cato (a priest at Clermont) and Plato (a bishop of Poitiers). People love to compose poetry, even though the .erses are sometimes rather lame. The tradition of rhetoric is kept up in the art of writing letters; this can be verified by reading the letters of Dynamius of Marseilles, at the end of the 6th century, or those of Didier of Cahors in the 7th century.

Thus the flame of the ancient tradition still burns; it burns all the better because there are no centers of ecclesiastical culture in Merovingian Gaul to take over the torch and replace this lay culture. In this regard the contrast with Spain is startling. Unlike 6th-century Spain, Southern Gaul at this period has no influential centers of ecclesiastical culture. You will tell me that at the beginning of the 6th century there was Arles. Yes, certainly there was Arles, but after the death of Caesarius (546) everything came to a halt as though didactic and canonical writing were dependent on one person. Religious life in Gaul has grandeur, the bishops are busy, councils meet frequently. But we must note, in connection with councils, that all of them meet in the same region, which I call "the conciliar zone", perhaps a debatable term. We find Orleans (councils there in 511, 533, 538, 541); Tours (a council in 567); Clermont (a council in 535); in Burgundy, Lyons and Mâcon (councils in 570, 581, 585); at the extreme end of this zone, Paris (councils of 552, 573, 614). The bishops who attend these councils come mostly from the provinces of Sens, Bourges, and Lyons. The bishops coming from the provinces of Trier, Rouen, Arles, and Vienne are much fewer. On the whole there seems to have been a kind of contraction of religious life into the middle of Gaul; if one wants to look for focal points of religious culture, it is there that they ought to turn up.

Unfortunately, there are none to find. One cannot point to a single center of ecclesiastical culture in this period except in Burgundy: there is a very busy *scriptorium* at Lyons, but it seems to have had no influence on the contemporary bishops of Lyons. The only regions where one senses a religious culture are those of Autun and Auxerre, at least under Syagrius, one of the rare bishops who had any relations with Pope Gregory the Great, and under his disciple Aunaire, who became bishop of Auxerre. The latter, we may note in passing, received a priest from Africa and asked him to write a *Life* of St. Germain in verse, and another *Life* of St. Amator. It is possible also that Jerome's martyrology was revised at Auxerre, and that already at that period a collection of canons was compiled there.

Outside these Burgundian centers, there is nothing. This does not mean that our Merovigian bishops are not educated. They are men of letters, but in the ancient manner. They are poets. Fortunatus has rivals in Felix of Nantes, Bertram of Bordeaux, Sulpicius of Bourges. They polish their style, they value the opinion of educated critics. At the council of Mâcon, in 585, the bishops pass judgment on the prose of Pretextat, the *orationes* this bishop had composed during his exile; some, says Gregory of Tours, loved these works, others criticized them as artistically weak. Thus we see the council of Mâcon turning itself into a literary academy. Gregory of Tours himself is very uneasy about his readers and quite sincere in the many excuses he makes for himself: he has not pursued a course of study, he is merely offering material that other men who are better trained may utilize. Gregory of Tours moreover takes it for granted that bishops have studied the liberal arts. Recall the concluding passage of his *History of the Franks:* "so thou, God's bishop, hast studied the seven Arts of Martianus Capella . . ." and there follows a list of the seven Arts. This view is quite the opposite of that of Caesarius of Arles, who recognized Biblical culture alone, rejecting all humanist culture.

These characteristics of the Church of Gaul are due, obviously, to the way in which its bishops are recruited. The bishops are former lay officials, born of great senatorial families, who come to the bishopric late in life. "Clergy", complains Gregory of Tours, "rarely arrive at a bishopric". The bishops are selected by the king for their administrative capacity, for their qualities as men, rather than for their understanding of theology or exegesis. If a bishop happens to have risen from the lower clergy, he is not likely to have much religious culture. The episcopal schools we hear of at Bourges, Poitiers, Clermont, Lyons, etc., are still very modest centers; they offer a professional training; they teach one how to read the scriptures, to sing psalms and hymns, how to administer the sacraments; they add the rudiments of canon law, and that is all. There are no exegetical studies; the Bible is read but there is no attempt to interpret its deeper meaning.

Can one find centers of religious culture in Southern Gaul, "Roman" Gaul, by turning to the monasteries? There was a great surge of monasticism in Provence at the beginning of the 6th century: the customs of Lérins were adopted at Arles, at Tarnat, at Grigny, at Lyons, at Condat, and possibly at Uzès. But these monasteries are primarily centers of spiritual life, of asceticism; they do not deserve to be called centers of culture. The monks read the Bible, the works of Cassian, the rules of Antony and Basil, mainly to perfect their personal spiritual development. Even when these monks copy manuscripts, they do it not from any desire to transmit knowledge, they do it as an ascetic task, just as the Eastern monks made baskets. Gregory of Tours makes this very clear in speaking of a monk at Tours who prepared parchment and copied manuscripts in order not to be idle and thus open to temptations. Again, the conditions of monastic recruitment, in the latter half of the 6th century, are not such as to favor the setting of important centers of study. The late Christian Courtois, at an earlier Spoleto conference, gave us a picture of monasticism prior to the arrival of St. Colomban, showing how monasteries took in children who had no vocation, and political prisoners. Monasticism was certainly in a critical condition before the 7th century. The only monastery more open to humanist culture at the end of the 6th century is that of the Holy Cross at Poitiers. The case is unique, due only to that extraordinary friendship between St. Radegonde and Fortunatus; after Radegonde's death there is no trace of culture at Poitiers. Thus we have no monastic centers in Gaul comparable with those of Spain at Dumio, Seville, Agalí, Servitanum; we are forced to the conclusion that there were no organized centers of ecclesiastical culture at all. It seems as though the surviving ancient culture hems the clergy in, prevents them from inventing any new type of religious culture.

What do we find if we turn now to barbarian Gaul? Northern and Eastern Gaul suffered greatly from being invaded and occupied. There, the fusion between the Gallo-Roman and Frankish populations came about much more rapidly than in the South. To be sure, at the end of the 5th century there were pockets of resistance. Among the friends corresponding with Sidonius we meet Rémi of Rheims, who wrote rhetorical exercises known as *declamationes;* we find Auspicius of Toul, Arbogast of Trier. We find a good many inscriptions at Coblenz and Trier. But no reorganization of culture could emerge from little resistant islets of Roman culture. It might well have been predicted that the political unification of Gaul would lead to disaster, to a total obliteration of culture, for the Franks were much less prepared for Romanization than the Burgundians; if, for example, one compares the Salian Law and the Burgundian Law, one sees that the Salians were primarily warriors and cattle-raisers, and still more or less pagan. What actually occurs is the reverse of any such prediction. The culture of Southern Gaul is not destroyed, not Germanized. And "Roman" Gaul helps to rebuild the culture of Northern Gaul. We have conclusive evidence of this. The Frankish aristocracy or at least a part of it, an elite—we are speaking throughout of elite culture—adopted the civilization of the written word. For example, it began to draft wills, a practice encouraged by the Church, which was the chief beneficiary. Some Franks adopted the custom of using written deeds as a record of donations, and written contracts of sale; slowly but surely Roman law advanced into these regions. Besides, the kings have some administration, embryonic, to be sure, but operative; to help them in it they call on educated southerners. Theodebert has Gallo-Romans in his service who, according to Gregory of Tours, still have a remarkable knowledge of classical culture. Parthenius, the grandson of Bishop Buricius, of Limoges, who had studied at Ravenna, becomes Patrician of Provence and soon after enters Theodebert's service. He meets a tragic death at Trier as a result of trying to levy a direct tax on the inhabitants. Gontran, too, takes men into his service who still have some classical culture; this is indeed reflected in the style of 6th-century royal diplomas. Andarchus, that slave who worked with his master Felix of Marseilles, is found at the side of Sigebert of Austrasia. Many Austrasian officials come from Provence; educated Provençals were able to exercise considerable influence in Austrasia.

Let us not forget that Austrasia annexed not only Auvergne but also the cities of Avignon, Aix, Vence, and half of Marseilles. Through Fortunatus, who travelled in these regions, we know there were cultivated men in high places; it is through him that we are able to assess the advance of culture in Frankish milieux. In about the year 565 Fortunatus journeys from Northern Italy up the Rhine valley, arrives at the court of Metz and is well received by the prince. He arrives just as Sigebert and Brunehaut are to be married, and composes a nuptial poem for them in the style of antiquity. He makes friends, among whom mention should be made of Gogo, Mayor of the Palace, who has left us a few letters with some coloration of ancient rhetoric. Thus we find three sorts of influence in Austrasia: Italian influence, through Fortunatus; Visigothic influence, through Brunehaut; and Provençal influence through officials in the service of the Austrasian kings.

In Neustria, too, under Chilperic, we find some attempt to organize centers of culture. If Chilperic has a bad reputation, it is mainly the fault of Fredegonde. In Chilperic we find a prince who fancies himself as a poet and a theologian. There is no question that if we compare his learning with that of Sisebut in early 7th-century Spain, there is a great gulf of disparity between the two men. In spite of this we should recognize the efforts that Chilperic made, crude barbarian as he was, to acquire a smattering of culture and to imitate the emperors: he tries to imitate them not only in holding races and fights in the arenas of Soissons and Paris, but in writing a theological treatise on the Trinity, and even in his talk of reforming the alphabet. These Merovingian princes, then, want to be cultured. It seems that they are already telling themselves that they are the heirs of the companions of Aeneas, to give themselves a noble ancestry. All this is perhaps rather feeble, yet when one thinks of the Germanic past of the Franks, it is nevertheless important.

The Austrasian and even the Neustrian courts are still very modest centers of culture in the 6th century. When unification is achieved under Clothar and Dagobert, in the first half of the 7th century, the court undeniably takes on a certain brilliance Today, however, this Merovingian court has a very bad name; it is regarded as a place of vice and debauchery. But we have probably relied too much on the word of hagiographers who wanted to show their heroes resisting evil customs or fleeing temptations. Doubtless all is not pure in the Merovingian court, for it swarms with young men eager to enjoy life. We know that the court is a center of fusion between the Germanic and the Gallo-Roman aristocracy. In the 7th century we see people there who have come from Aquitaine (Didier, Bonnet, Aredius) from Neustria (Dado, who is the future St. Omer), from Austrasia (Arnulf, Léger); these young men know and appreciate each other. Not a school in the academic sense of the term, this court is, however, a school of leadership, it gives a kind of training to youths who will serve as officials or become army leaders. They come to court at the age of puberty, that is, when they have had some elementary education, or even secondary education, if we can call it that. They are immediately entrusted to the Mayor of the Palace, who acts as director of the young palatines and is at the same time in charge of the education of the king's sons. The young men learn the duties of officials, of notaries, or even, as Aredius, Ansbert and

Dado did, of the chancellor. They probably learn shorthand and perhaps some law. Let me remind you, in this connection, how Marculf at the age of about seventy set to work to give a certain bishop named Landry a collection of deeds from models drafted earlier by young apprentice notaries. The stay at court left pleasant memories in the young men's minds. Let me cite only one piece of evidence of this, a passage from a letter of Didier's: "How I should like, if time were kind enough to permit it, to meet with you as we did of old when we were laymen and in the following of the most serene prince Clothar and used to divert ourselves in gossiping of trifles". It is safe to say that men at the Merovingian court under Dagobert learned the art of living. This court had a certain renown, since the widow of Edwin of Northumbria had sent her sons there to be educated.

In Dagobert's time the court was also a center of religious culture; it is at the court of Dabogert that the message of St. Colomban was first received. Laymen in the king's service were won over by St. Colomban's spirituality, and the court served as a relay station for spreading the religious ideal of the Irish monks. Above, I described a religious culture that was dying away for lack of renewal. The renewal came, at the beginning of the 7th century, from Ireland. Colomban and his disciples certainly shocked people, at first, by their dress, the form of their tonsure, by their liturgical customs and by the general unconventionality of their behavior, but it is clear that religious culture was strengthened by their invigorating contribution. St. Colomban, very quickly attracted the laity, both men and women; a spiritual revival spread through Northern Gaul. A spiritual, not a humanist, revival, for if Colomban himself was perhaps a humanist, he did not try to make Luxeuil a center of learning. The only study carried on there was the study of Holy Scripture. Luxeuil is a focal point of spiritual life and asceticism and so also are its daughter monasteries at Remiremont, Grandval, Rebais, Faremoutiers. The Columbanian monastery, at the beginning, is a nursery of ascetics and missionaries who go out to live among the peasants and convert them; it is this that led to the evangelization of Northern Gaul. The Columbanian expansion is for a long time limited to the territory north of the Loire; up to about 630, the only regions affected by the missions are Neustria, Austrasia, and the north of Burgundy, regions through which St. Columban himself travelled. The Columbanian monks who become bishops are installed at Tournai, Vermand, and Thérouanne, that is, in the northern regions. It is only under the second abbot of Luxeuil that the first Columbanian monasteries are established on the edges of Southern Gaul, in Berry and Nivernais. It is only thanks to the influence of Dagobert's court that Columbanian monasticism moves into the South. Didier, Eloi, and Dado were converted, as young laymen, by Columbanian monks. They lived on at court, in the world, but as monks, praying and studying. They founded monasteries even before becoming bishops. Eloi founds one at Solignac, in Limousin, the first Colum-

Figure 2. Centers of culture at the end of the 7th century.

banian monastery south of the Loire. When Didier becomes Bishop of Cahors, he too introduces the Celtic rule of the Columbanians into his diocese. Southerners who come to court are in turn spellbound by the religious zeal of the Irish. Examples are Philibert, from Eauze, who becomes a monk at Rebais before founding the great Norman monastery of Jumièges; St. Remaclius, a Limousin, who founds the monastery of Stavelot; St. Amand, from Berry, who founds monasteries in the south of what is now Belgium.

Thus by about 640 the whole of Gaul is won over by this spirituality. A veritable network of monasteries is created, a network through which new blood circulates and reinvigorates religious culture. And this monastic network is bound into the great western network which starts in Ireland, crosses England, and leads on to Bobbio, in Italy, where St. Colomban died in 614. There are exchanges between the different countries. Exchanges between Ireland and Gaul: St. Gertrude of Nivelles has scholars brought over from Ireland; Agilbert, after a period of study in Ireland, ends up as Bishop of Paris; Dido of Poitiers who, for political reasons, took Dagobert II to Ireland, was able also to profit from the Irish influence. Exchanges between Italy and Gaul: in 641 Jonas, an educated monk of Bobbio, went to spend three years in the monastery of St. Amand in Elmone and went on to Arras, to Faremoutiers, to Moutiers-St.-Jean. Exchanges between Gaul and Italy: before founding their Norman monasteries, Wandrille and Philibert spent some time at Bobbio. Bobbio is also a stopping-point for pilgrims on their way to Rome.

The monks who return to France from Italy do not come empty-handed; they bring books, and among these books they may have brought the Rule of St. Benedict. The first Benedictine monasticism known in Southern Gaul is that of *Altaripa,* in the diocese of Albi, about 620–630. But from the first diffusion of Irish monasticism, we find the Rule of St. Benedict associated with the Rule of St. Colomban at Luxeuil, Solignac, Fleury and Besançon. Thus, paradoxically, it is the Irish who introduced, or at least spread, the Benedictine rule in Gaul. And this is a decisive point in the history of culture: from this date Benedictine monasticism, or Benedictine-Columbanian if one can use the term, will take on, as it establishes itself, a quite new character.

Finally, to round out this sketch of cultural relations between monasteries of different countries, let us not forget that from the second half of the 7th century it is not only the Irish but also Anglo-Saxon monks who are settling down in Gaul. Queen Bathilde, a former Anglo-Saxon slave, founds Chelles and Corbie. Young Anglo-Saxon princesses are educated at Jouarre. Anglo-Saxons cross Gaul to follow Benedict Biscop and Wilfrid into Italy. It is interesting to trace the routes that these Anglo-Saxon travellers to Italy take: they start either from Quentovic or from the mouth of the Seine, then proceed via Paris, Auxerre, Langres, Lyons, and the Alpine passes, not by the Provençal route, which is by then abandoned; they might even, like Wilfrid, start from Frisia and follow the Rhine up to Coire and then climb up to cross the Septimer.

The establishment of Irish and Anglo-Saxon monks, the adoption of the Benedictine Rule, exchanges between different countries, all this contributed to give monasticism a new character, and to make possible the creation of centers of culture. Monasteries are no longer huts, they are huge buildings; monks have specialized functions; some are copyists or writers. Towards 680–700 we are on the verge of what is called "the Carolingian Renaissance". This revival is not peculiar to Gaul. There is a kind of awakening all through the West from Northumbria to the Lombard kingdom, due in part to these cultural exchanges between Ireland, England, Gaul, and Italy. In the new seats of culture in Northern and Central Gaul, and even in Southern Gaul, abbots are encouraging scribes and painters in the *scriptorium:* the first manuscripts from Luxeuil date from 669; the date of the *Lectionary* there is 700. At Corbie the first illuminated manuscripts appear about 704; Echternach has its famous Gospels by about 690. In the sphere of letters we find similar activity, directed to the writing of saints' lives: at Nivelles the *Life* of St. Gertrude, at Rebais the *Life* of St. Agilius, both in about the year 670; at Remiremont the *Life* of St. Amatus, at Laon the *Life* of St. Albert, in about 707. These coincidences are not fortuitous. There is a similar start on good hagiography at Fonte-nelle. And even at Coutances, in far-away Normandy, which had hitherto shown no sign of cultural life, the bishop finds a poet who writes an in-scription to be graven on the altar of Ham.

Southern Gaul, too, sees the rise of centers of monastic culture, in-fluenced by the Irish but responsive also to ancient traditions. At Méobec, an abbey in Berry, around 678, a monk who knows Gregory the Great's *Homilies* and the Irish texts is writing the famous *Vision of Barontius*. At the monastery of St. Maxentius the monk Ursin undertakes the *Life* of St. Leger. In Auvergne, at Volvic and at Manglieu two hagiographers who have read Jerome, Sulpicius Severus, and Gregory the Great and are familiar also with Caesar and Virgil, write saints' lives in a style that is astonishingly good. There is a similar improvement at Rodez, where lives of St. Dal-matius and St. Amand are written. This dipping into the classics for stylis-tic models rather worries the more austere monks at other places in Aqui-taine. A chapter on what to read, which Defensor of Ligugé includes in his *Liber Scintillarum,* a collection of excerpts from the Church Fathers, consists almost entirely of Isidore of Seville's advice to monks not to read "the lies of poets". If Defensor feels it necessary to repeat this injunction, is it not because an interest in humanism has to some extent infiltrated the monasteries of Aquitaine?

Yet this revival of culture in Southern Gaul is abruptly halted. The principate of Charles Martel and the reign of Pepin the Short were un-happy times for the regions where Roman culture had found a refuge. Aquitaine, which was tending to detach itself from the Kingdom, was ruined by the Arab invasions and again by the reconquest campaigns of the early Carolingians, into the age of Pepin the Short. By the mid-8th cen-tury there is not a single center of culture in Aquitaine. The only educated men of the region we know are found in Italy: three abbots of Farfa, not far from Spoleto, were from Aquitaine. Provence, too, whose great centers of culture had already died out, was laid waste by Charles Martel's troops. Burgundy and the region of Lyons were similarly ruined by Arab invasion and by civil war. Autun was destroyed in 731, its archives burnt. Lyons was retaken by Charles Martel in 733. Auxerre was occupied by Austrasian war-riors under Pepin the Short. It is not until his reign that Lyons can resume any cultural activity. On Figure 3, I have marked the episcopal seats and monasteries which were represented at the council of Attigny (760–762).

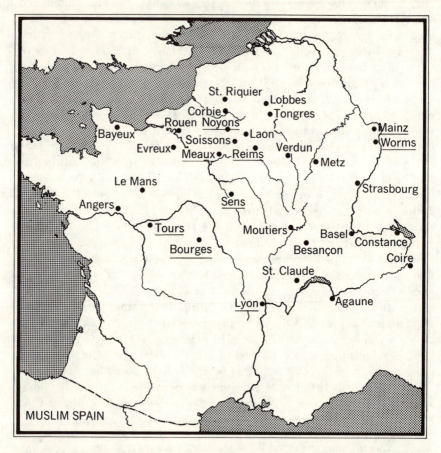

Figure 3. Centers represented at the Council of Attigny (760–762). Places
from which bishops were sent to Rome in 769 are underlined.

Among this council's signatories we find the bishops of Rheims, Sens, Soissons, Le Mans, Meaux, Noyon, Vermand, Metz, Mainz, Worms, Strasburg,
Basel, Constance, and the abbots of St. Riquier, Corbie, Lobbes. There are
no bishops or abbots from south of the Loire save from Tours and Bourges.
The map seems to be symbolic, it shows a vacuum which signifies the collapse of culture in Southern Gaul.

The only centers of culture under Charles Martel and Pepin the Short
are found north of the Loire, in Neustria, or in Austrasia. Essentially these
are great monasteries. This period is often spoken of as one of barbarism
and sterility. Certainly, the laity became illiterate and the clergy were
victimized by the social and political turmoil of the age; but the monks

found islands of refuge in the monasteries. The monks in the great monasteries are the only lettered men; the *scriptoria* are continually enriched. At Corbie, under Abbot Leuchar, in the middle of the 8th century, the *scriptorium* is already hard at work. At Laon it is enlivened by Anglo-Saxon scribes; copies are being made of the works of Origen, Augustine, and Orosius. At St. Wandrille, under Abbot Wando, who died in 747, the library is similarly growing, through activity in the *scriptorium;* the catalogue is no longer extant. At Fleury and St. Martin of Tours there are centers of culture which have perhaps benefited by receiving educated refugees from Arab Spain; these brought manuscripts into Southern Gaul, especially to the parts bordering on the region of the Loire. Finally, we must assign a special place among these great monasteries to St. Denis. St. Denis, a monastery under the protection of the Merovingian kings and the early Carolingians, was Charles Martel's choice as a school for Pepin the Short; Charles Martel did not entrust his son to a tutor, as had been the custom of the Merovingian kings, he entrusted him to monks. This signifies a change of outlook, it marks the opening of a new age. Pepin retained happy memories of his years at St. Denis; it may have been he who gave the abbey a set of books sent by Pope Paul I—works in Greek, and on grammar and geometry—for among them are the books attributed to Dionysius the Areopagite, who was regarded as the apostle of the Gauls. It is at St. Denis, in the early part of the 8th century, that the *Liber historiae francorum* was written; it is at St. Denis that the Gelasian Sacraments may have been compiled. The cultural level at St. Denis was definitely high. The monks may well have improved the style of the royal diplomas. Indeed, from Pepin the Short's time, the chancery acts are written in a much purer and more correct Latin than those of the Merovingian period. Should we not give the monks of St. Denis credit for this change?

The monks of 8th-century Gaul were equally well able to contribute to the moral and spiritual reform of the clergy and consequently to their intellectual reform. For there was no way of restoring the dignity of the clergy save by imposing on them a rule of life modelled on that of the monks. Chrodegang, Pepin's councillor, saw the solution very clearly; his Rule for canons is modelled on the Benedictine rule. The clergy of Metz live a communal life, practise poverty, devote time to reading, and learn liturgical chant. Metz becomes a center attracting foreigners; we find a friend of Alcuin's, Sigulf, even preferring to go to Metz rather than to Rome. In drafting his rule, Chrodegang was only going back to the example set by Caesarius of Arles, and indeed by Augustine, who had tried to give the clergy a way of life that was essentially monastic.

Little by little, thanks to the example of the monks, the Frankish clergy recover the taste for study. In 769 Stephen III asks Pepin to send to Rome "bishops instructed and versed in the divine scriptures and the institutions of holy canons". In these words the Pope does homage to the ecclesiastical reformation. And let us take one more look at Figure 3. The bishops who are sent to Rome are those of Noyon, Meaux, Sens, Tours, Bourges, Mainz, and Worms. Only two are sent from south of the Loire, the bishops of Bourges and Narbonne; besides, it may be that the Bishop of Narbonne was living in the north, for Septimania was not yet in a state of peace.

Thus we have traced the shift of centers of culture between the 6th century and the middle of the 8th. The situation at the start was the inverse of the situation at the end. It is no longer in the Mediterranean zone that one finds centers, but near that new Mediterranean, the North Sea and the English Channel. It is there that communication springs up and cultural exchanges occur, between England, Ireland, and Northern Gaul. Through the migration of Irish and later of Anglo-Saxon monks, a new Christian culture arises in monastic centers. Finally, though the centers of culture in Gaul were perhaps more modest than those of England or those of Spain, they were to prove more enduring. They last on as the solid points of support which make possible in the Carolingian age, a successful renewal of the intellectual life and art of the West.

19

Lotharingia as a Center of Arabic and Scientific Influence in the 11th Century

MARY CATHERINE WELBORN

Western European astronomers before the end of the tenth century were greatly handicapped in their work because of the lack of proper instruments for making observations. Up to that time their principal instruments were the Greek armillary sphere and the sun-dial. In reckoning the dates of Easter and the other movable feasts, and the lengths of years, months, and days, they depended upon Easter cycles or tables which were founded upon those made at an earlier time by the Alexandrians. Although for quite some time before the tenth century they had realized that their calculations were not correct, they were unable to improve upon them because they had not yet received from the Arabs better astronomical theories and instruments.

Towards the end of the tenth century knowledge of the Arabic astrolabe began to penetrate into the Latin West. From the manuscripts which have so far been discovered, this astrolabe must have been used first by Lotharingian geometers and astronomers. Professor J. W. Thompson has already discussed the question and has concluded that "Arabic science was introduced into the schools of Lorraine and was cultivated there before Gerbert", and ". . . that the schools of Lorraine in the last half of the tenth century were the seed-plot in which the seeds of Arabic science first germinated in Latin Europe, from which the knowledge radiated to other parts of Germany—witness Hermann Contractus in Reichenau—to France, and especially, owing to the preference of Knut the Great for Lotharingian churchmen, into England".[1]

It is not strange that the schools of Lotharingia should have been the

Sketch map of Lotharingia (950–1050).

earliest centers in Western Europe north of the Pyrenees in which Arabic learning was fostered, because in comparison with the famous schools of the tenth century, such as Reichenau, St. Gall, Reims, Paris, Chartres, and Cluny, those of Liége were especially outstanding for their real love of scientific subjects. Although this particular interest became evident first in Liége, it was also present in Gorze,[2] Cologne, Prüm, Lobbes and other Lotharingian cities. Throughout the latter part of the tenth century and during the eleventh, there was a lively exchange of letters and manuscripts on scientific subjects among the scholars of these cities, and from the latter to other places just outside Lotharingia, such as Reichenau.

The interest in astronomy at Liége started in the time of Euraclus, a Saxon,[3] who was bishop from 959 to 971. According to Reinerus (c. 1190), Euraclus had studied first at Cologne under archbishop Bruno, brother of Otto I, and then under Ratherius, the famous bishop of Verona. When he became bishop he immediately began to improve still further the schools in his diocese.[4] Due to his influence, interest in scientific subjects increased rapidly. That he himself was no mean astronomer is evident from the story of his expedition to Italy with the troops of Otto I in 968. On December 22 there was a solar eclipse and Euraclus was able to calm his frightened troops by assuring them that this was only a natural phenomenon, and that the sun would soon reappear. Reinerus says that he got his astronomical ideas from "Pliny, Macrobius, and Chalcidius, and many others, astrologers as well as compotists".[5]

At the death of Euraclus, a better known scholar, Notger, became bishop (971–1008) and under his direction Liége became one of the most important intellectual centers of Europe.[6] Notger had been educated at St. Gall, where astronomy and other sciences were of great importance, and from his youth he had given promise of becoming a great scholar. He has been called "the second founder" of Liége, because he built so many churches, monasteries, fortifications, hospitals, and imported various kinds of artistic objects from many countries. But above all he devoted great attention to the schools of Liége and encouraged even more vigorously than his predecessor, the study of mathematics and other scientific subjects.[7]

While Notger was bishop, there were several astronomers at Liége, for instance Englebert of St. Lawrence, a compotist, who investigated the number and movements of the stars, the sun and moon, as well as the causes of earthquakes and tides.[8] An interesting contemporary of Englebert was Radolf. Very little is known about the life of Radolf except that before he became one of the teachers in the cathedral school at Liége he had studied with Fulbert at Chartres. That he too was interested in mathematical subjects may be learned from his correspondence with his friend Ragimbold, master of the schools in Cologne (c. 1025). These letters deal chiefly with questions of geometry and arithmetic but Letter V does contain one very precious bit of information concerning astronomy. In this letter Radolf says that he has an astrolabe and continues, "I would willingly send it to you in order that you might examine it, but it is my model. If you wish to know what it is, come to the festival of St. Lambert, you will

not be sorry for it. It would be useless for you just to *see* an astrolabe." [9]
Radolf would undoubtedly not have been so eager for Ragimbold to see
his astrolabe if it had been of the ordinary Greek type. Unfortunately he
does not give us a description of the instrument nor does he tell us where
he got it; however from other manuscripts found in this region it is certain
that Lotharingian astronomers were by this time using an Arabic type of
astrolabe. Also there is no evidence from the writings of either Gerbert, or
Fulbert of Chartres, or Abbo of Fleury, all outstanding teachers of that
period, that they were using Arabic astrolabes in their schools.[10] So that
Radolf must have found his model in Lotharingia.

In the second part of the so-called *Geometria Gerberti*,[11] there are
several chapters containing descriptions of a quadrant astrolabe, a type
developed by the Arabs and used for surveying. According to Tannery and
Clerval this second part of the *Geometria* was assembled after the time of
Gerbert. They also say that Ms. 7377c in the Bibliothèque Nationale is the
oldest copy yet discovered which contains this collection, and most important to note, the article on the astrolabe is in that group of treatises written
in Lotharingia in the eleventh century. Might not John of Gorze, who had
been in Cordova, a center of Arabic learning, have brought back an
astrolabe or a treatise on the subject? [12] Although Radolf does not tell us
what kind of astrolabe he had, it might well have been this same type as
his principal interest was in geometry and this instrument described in the
Geometria was used by geometers and surveyors.

Although there are one or two very early anonymous treatises on the
astrolabe,[13] the first ones concerning whose author we have any definite
information, are those of Hermann Contractus, the lame monk of Reichenau.[14] Hermann, the son of Count Wolverds II of Alshausen, was born
in 1013. About 1020 he was sent to the monastery where he remained during the rest of his life. The master of the monastery school in the time of
Hermann was the great Cluniac scholar Berno.[15] We know practically
nothing of the life of Berno until the year when he succeeded Immo as
abbot of Prüm. That he studied under Abbo of Fleury before going to
Prüm has been claimed by some but is not at all certain.[16] He was a re-
nowned poet, musician, philosopher and theologian, and his abilities as a
scholar and leader finally attracted the notice of Henry II who in 1008
made him abbot of Reichenau. Berno took with him to his new monastery
many books, and under his influence the monks became extremely interested in music and mathematics. His most cherished student was Hermann
Contractus whose first enthusiasm for these subjects undoubtedly came
from Berno.

Hermann probably wrote two treatises on the astrolabe, the first being
the *De mensura astrolabii* [17] (c. 1048) which he wrote at the request of his
friends who were very curious about this instrument, and especially to
please a certain B. who was quite possibly Berno. In this work Hermann

discusses the method of constructing the type of astrolabe called by Latin writers *Walzachorra*, which is an improved form of the planisphere (*plana sphaera*) described by Ptolemy in the *Almagest* (II, 8). At the end of the article, Hermann says that he intends later to discuss the use of the astrolabe. This intention seems to have been carried out in the *De utilitatibus astrolabii*,[18] although certain chapters cannot possibly be by Hermann. The type of astrolabe here described is the astronomical quadrant, which was made by adding a zodiac band, star positions, and scales to the composite quadrant which was a geometrical instrument like the one described in the so-called *Geometria* of Gerbert. The first book deals with such problems as the finding of the position of the sun on the ecliptic on any given day, and the positions of the stars at certain hours during any given night. In this, as in the other works of Hermann, many Arabic words are used for the parts of the astrolabe and for the names of the constellations. As Hermann undoubtedly did not know Arabic himself, he must have used Latin translations containing Arabic words. Bubnov has printed an anonymous fragment of a manuscript which mentions an astrolabe and contains two or three Arabic words, which he says was possibly in the hands of the author of the *De Utilitatibus*.[19] However, a comparison of the two treatises shows that this fragment could not have been the main source of the author's information, as it is more in the nature of a general discussion of the value of astronomy, music, and the other subjects of the seven liberal arts, while the *De utilitatibus* gives a very definite and detailed description of the construction and use of an astrolabe and contains many Arabic words.

It is much more likely that Hermann used copies of Latin translations of the *De constructione astrolabii* and the *De utilitate astrolabii* of Mâshâllâh as his principal sources.[20] So far no Latin translations of the works of Mâshâllâh have been discovered which were made earlier than the time of Hermann, but a Latin version of his *Secretorum astrorum* is mentioned in a twelfth-century catalogue of the monastery of Wessobrunn which was close to Reichenau.[21] It is possible that this manuscript had been in the library for quite some time before this catalogue was made, and that there were others in this same region. For several reasons it seems more than probable that Hermann had these translations; first because both his works and those of Mâshâllâh contain descriptions of the same type of astrolabe, the quadrant astronomical one, and because throughout all the chapters of all the works the same Arabic words are used,[22] with identical spelling, to describe each part of the instrument, and because the same ways of using an astrolabe are given.

The second book of the *De utilitatibus* is not a connected treatise like the first but is a collection of writings on various subjects. The first chapter deals with an instrument for telling time whose use Hermann wishes to explain to a certain brother Werinhar, presumably the one he mentions in the *Chronicon* as "a monk of Reichenau very learned and given to true religion",[23] who died about 1053 on a pilgrimage to Jerusalem. The next three chapters take up the question of the circumference of the earth according to the report of Macrobius, where Hermann uses the Archimedean proportional number $\frac{22}{7}$ to calculate the diameter. In addition he employs an indirect method which is also found in chapter 56 of Gerbert's *Geometria* (in the part which was probably assembled in Lotharingia), and in a letter of Ragimbold. According to Cantor, these fractions were not used by Bernelius, a student of Gerbert, and were not Greek; [24] thus we have another link connecting Hermann and the scientists of Lotharingia. This letter of Ragimbold was probably read by Meinzo of Constance,[25] a former student of Hermann, who then sent it to the latter who included it in book 2, chapter 3 of the *De utilitatibus*. This chapter also shows definite signs of Arabic influence. That the *Geometria* was one of the main sources for this second book is shown by the fact that Hermann also included two complete chapters of it.[26]

The influence of Lotharingian mathematicians and astronomers not only extended southward to Reichenau but also westward to England. From the time of Knut on, Lotharingian scholars were very popular in England. Before Knut died, Duduc, "de Lotharingia oriundus", was bishop of Wells; Hermann, another Lotharingian, became bishop of Ramsbury in 1045 and in the next year Leofric, who had been educated in Lotharingia, became bishop of Exeter. Under Edward the Confessor there was another group. All of these clerics were interested in learning and many brought books with them from their own country.

Earl Harold did more than anyone to encourage Lotharingian learning in England. He secured the appointments of Walter as bishop of Hereford (1061–79) and of Giso as bishop of Wells (1060–88). Harold had traveled extensively and had discovered that the schools of Lotharingia and the nearby German cities were not only much better than those of England but also than those of France or northern Italy at the time. He founded a college of canons at Waltham on the model of the system of secular colleges with schools originated by Chrodegang of Metz. For head *magister* he chose the learned Athelard who had studied in Lotharingia and Utrecht.

During the time of William the Conqueror and William Rufus, Lotharingians were still being brought to England. The Conqueror invited to his court Robert of Lorraine, a distinguished mathematician, who was made bishop of Hereford in 1079. He was known for his work on the abacus and more especially because he brought to England the *Chronicon* of Marianus Scotus upon whose astronomical introduction he himself wrote a treatise. Another interesting scholar of this period was Thomas of Bayeux, who went to Germany and Spain to study the sciences and later, after he had spent some time with Odo of Bayeux, to Liége. After the Norman Conquest he went to England with Odo and in 1070 was made primate of York.[27]

Only a few of the many Lotharingian clerics who went to England in the eleventh century have been mentioned, but it is important to note that they were all interested in mathematics and astronomy. However it was not until the time of Walcher of Malvern that an astrolabe is mentioned in England.[28] Walcher was a Lotharingian who arrived in England about 1091. Thus we see that England as well as Reichenau was greatly influenced by Lotharingian mathematicians and astronomers, and that her first hint of Arabic science came from them.

NOTES

1 J. W. Thompson, "The introduction of Arabic science into Lorraine in the tenth century", *Isis*, vol. 12 (1929), pp. 184–94, at pp. 184 and 191.

2 *Ibid.*, pp. 188–9.

3 *Vita Euracli*, in B. Pez, *Thes. anec. noviss.* (1721–1729), vol. IV, part III, pp. 155–66.

4 Anselm, *Lectiones majusculis tradere*, p. 24, gives a delightful picture of Euraclus as a teacher.

5 *Vita Euracli*, chapter 24.

6 G. Kurth, *Notger de Liége et la civilization au Xe siècle*, Paris, 1905; H. Pirenne, *Histoire de Belgique*, vol. I (Brussels, 1909), p. 157; M. Manitius, *Geschichte der lateinischen Literatur des Mittelalters* (Munich, 1911–23), vol. II, pp. 219–28.

7 Kurth, *op. cit.*, I, pp. 130–69, 251–99.

8 Reinerus, *De claris scriptoribus*, bk. I, chapter 9, in Pez, *op. cit.*, vol. IV, part III, pp. 20–52.

9 P. Tannery and Abbé Clerval, "Une correspondance d'écolâtres du XIe siècle", in *Notices et extraits des manuscrits*, vol. XXXVI (1899–1901), pp. 487–543; M. Manitius, *op. cit.*, II, pp. 778–81.

10 In the list of astronomical instruments which Richer says that Gerbert used, he mentions only a solid sphere, an instrument of Greek, not Arabic, construction. See Richerus, *Historia*, in *MGH. SS.*, vol. IV, pp. 617–8. It is said that Fulbert knew the Arabic names for the constellations (C. Pfister, *De Fulberti Carnotensi episcopi vita et operibus*, Nancy, 1885). But there is no evidence in Fulbert's writings that he knew anything about an Arabic astrolabe. See L. C. MacKinney, "Bishop Fulbert", *Isis*, vol. 14 (1930), pp. 285–300. There are no Arabic words in Fulbert's brief notice on the calendar, in Migne, *PL*, vol. CXLI, col. 347. Nor is there any mention of an Arabic astrolabe nor use of Arabic words in the astronomical writings of Abbo of Fleury, the disciple of the astronomer Remi, of St. Germain of Auxerre. See M. Manitius, *op. cit.*, II, pp. 664–72.

11 Printed in Pez, *op. cit.*, vol. III, part II, pp. 37–82, as chapters 14–94. See also N. Bubnov, *Gerberti opera mathematica*, Berlin, 1899, and Tannery and Clerval, *op. cit.*, p. 542.

12 See J. W. Thompson, *loc. cit.*, pp. 188–90. None of the scientific manuscripts listed in an eleventh century catalogue of the abbey of Gorze has an Arabic title. See D. G. Morin, "Le catalogue des manuscrits de l'abbaye de Gorze au XIe siècle", *Revue Bénédictine*, vol. XXII (1905), pp. 1–14.

13 L. Thorndike, *A History of Magic and Experimental Science*, vol. I (New York, 1923), chapter 30; N. Bubnov, *op. cit.*, pp. 370–5.

14 See *Bertholdi Annales*, in *MGH, SS*, vol. V, pp. 267 ff; A. Holder, *Die Reichenauer*

Handschriften (Leipzig, 1906–18), vol. III, pp. 241–3; M. Manitius, *op. cit.,* II, pp. 756–77; M. Cantor, *Vorlesungen über Geschichte der Mathematik* (Leipzig, 1913), vol. I, pp. 885–9; P. Treutlein, "Intorno ad alcuni scritti inediti relative al calcolo dell' abaco", *Bull. di Storia d. Scienze Mat.,* vol. X (Rome, 1877), pp. 643–7.

[15] See Hermannus Contractus, *Chronicon, MGH, SS.,* vol. V, p. 119, and M. Manitius, *op. cit.,* II, pp. 61–71.

[16] It is denied in D. P. Blanchard, "Oeuvres attribuées à Bernon de Reichenau", *Revue Bénédictine,* vol. XXIX (1912), pp. 98–107. The story of Berno and Immo is important as it shows contact between Reichenau, Prüm, and Gorze at this time.

[17] Printed in Migne, *PL,* vol. CXLIII, col. 379–90, and in Pez, *op. cit.,* vol. III, part II, pp. 94–106.

[18] Printed in Migne, *op. cit.,* col. 390–403, and in Pez, *op. cit.,* pp. 110–39. N. Bubnov (*op. cit.,* pp. 109 ff.) places this first book among works doubtfully attributed to Gerbert, but for reasons given here it seems more likely that it was written by Hermann.

[19] N. Bubnov, *op. cit.,* pp. 109 ff.; C. H. Haskins, *Studies in the History of Medieval Science* (1927), pp. 51–3.

[20] Hermann's chapters 7, 8, and 11 resemble chapters 9, 12–13, and 8 of Mâshâllâh's *De utilitate.* For a 13th-century Latin text of the latter with an English translation see R. T. Gunther, *Early Science in Oxford* (Oxford, 1929), pp. 137–92. On Mâshâllâh (died c. 815–20) see G. Sarton, *Introduction to the History of Science* (Washington, 1927), vol. I, p. 531.

[21] G. Becker, *Catalogi bibliothecarum antiqui* (Bonn, 1885), p. 231.

[22] The scientific terms used in the anonymous fragment, in the works of Mâshâllâh and those of Hermann are printed in an appendix to the original version of this article.

[23] Migne, *op. cit.,* col. 262.

[24] *Op. cit.,* pp. 885–9.

[25] M. Manitius, *op. cit.,* II, pp. 786–7. For the letter see *Neues Archiv der Gesellschaft für ältere deutsche Geschichtskunde,* vol. V, pp. 202, 206.

[26] Hermann's book 2, chapters 6 and 8, on taking altitudes, is identical with chapters 21 and 82 of the *Geometria Gerberti.*

[27] See *Historians of the Church of York,* ed. J. Raine (Rolls Series, 1886), vol. II, pp. 98–228, and W. H. Dixon, *Lives of the archbishops of New York,* ed. J. Raine (London, 1863), vol. I, pp. 146–158.

[28] C. H. Haskins, *op. cit.,* pp. 113–7.

Medieval Unity

20

Medieval Unity and the Economic Conditions for an International Civilization

KARL W. DEUTSCH

In a world torn with nationalistic conflicts, men's minds are naturally turning to projects of international government and to hopes for a wider acceptance of international loyalties, language, and civilization. One of the last epochs in which a measure of such international unity can be said to have actually existed was the European Middle Ages. The following study of the conditions underlying medieval unity, therefore, may offer some information on a topic of present interest.

Accounts of the rise of modern nationalism frequently begin with a picture of the spiritual, linguistic, and cultural unity of medieval Christendom. Mr. Carlton Hayes speaks of "the traditional internationalism of civilized Europe" before the sixteenth and seventeenth centuries; [1] other authors similarly use the Middle Ages as a point of departure.[2] New forces are then pointed out, which in their rise toward the end of the Middle Ages broke up that unity into the present multitude of nations and sovereign states.[3] This useful method of exposition, however, suggests further questions. How did that "traditional internationalism" of medieval Europe come to exist? What were the conditions favouring its spread, and how durable was it likely to be under the law of its own growth? Can the medieval vision of cultural unity again be recreated on similar foundations?

Medieval unity was a transitory stage in history, destroyed by the growth of the same forces which had given it birth. All its major elements, the common Latin language of its intellectual life and written

247

records of trade and administration, its common legal and spiritual authority in the Popes and Councils of the Church, its common political head in Emperors like Charlemagne and the Ottos, its crusades, and its common style of Romanesque and Gothic art and architecture—all these were the achievements of a long process of growth. In the evolution of society they represented an adaptation to a particular set of circumstances and they could be expected to change, in the long run, with any fundamental change in the underlying conditions.

An analysis identifying these conditions may show more clearly why the international unity of the Middle Ages failed to last. Beyond this it may help the student of nationalism to add some new tools to his equipment; not a master-key to fit all times and countries, but rather a yardstick to note and measure some similarities and differences in their development. Understood with that limitation it may bring us another step forward in the development of a technique of analysis applicable to the problems of national and international unification in other times and places, including our own.

I

So far as the economic factor is concerned, much of the internationalism of the Middle Ages was rooted in a scarcity of goods and services, and in the scarcity of skilled persons. What is the connection between primitive internationalism and a certain stage in the scarcity of goods? As soon as any primitive agricultural economy has reached a minimum of labour productivity, some surplus becomes available for exchange. Owing to the primitive technical methods, the differences in regional resources play a great role; and owing to the simplicity of the local division of labour, only few goods and few varieties are available from any one place. As such economies produce few exchangeable goods, so they produce few incomes large enough to buy them. And as the few varieties of goods are so greatly determined by the resources of the region, there is little chance that there should be sufficient effective demand for them in the immediate neighborhood. Trade, therefore, will be small in bulk, but far-flung in distance. Few persons are engaged in it professionally, but their journeys are taking them all over Europe and beyond. The bulk of each people remain close to their villages, taking little part in any direct intercourse beyond their regions; the local peculiarities in their habits and ways of speech are tending to increase rather than to disappear. At the same time the traders have to carry on their business across many regions and languages. If these few traders can agree on a common language, better still, if most of them can be drawn from the same people or region, then they will be able to conduct their business more economically. Within the thin supernational web of trading communities the common speech, script, laws, habits, traditions, and perhaps family connections will represent the most economic adaptation complementing the local seclusion and paucity of exchange in a society of primitive agricultural communities.

What are the effects of a corresponding stage in the scarcity of skills? The simple division of labour gives rise only to few specialized skills. The bearers of the simple skills like baking, weaving, or cobbling remain within the local economy of household, village, or manor, taking part only indirectly, and only with a part of their products, in the processes of exchange and circulation. These simple skills can be developed locally almost anywhere. Their distribution throughout the economy presents no problem; once trained, rural artisans have merely to stay in their villages. But the specialized intellectual, technological, administrative, or business skills cannot be readily developed in any primitive agricultural region. They have to be produced, that is to stay, persons have to acquire them by training; or else they have to be distributed from an existing supply, that is, persons who possess such skills have to be brought to those places where their services are needed. Now in the medieval economy the production of complex skills was of necessity concentrated in a few regions. Scarce and almost indivisible factors in their production, such as teachers, schools, and hand-copied manuscripts, put a premium on the concentration of most specialist training in a few great monasteries, schools, and courts. The distribution of the supply of historically produced skills was not less unequal. Regions with social classes with a tradition of literacy were confined mostly to the Mediterranean. Similarly confined were the traditions of law and art, the higher skills of technology like building and engineering, and again the specific skills of business rationality. All these were traditional mainly in Greece, Italy, the Mediterranean cities which had become merged in their civilization, and among some nations of the Near East, such as Syrians, Jews, Arabs and others.

A similar limitation prevailed as to the skills of transportation. Almost anyone could be taught to ride a horse or row a boat. But only a few peoples of nomadic stock raisers like the Bedouins produced animals and men able to overcome the deserts of the Near East and Africa. Only few peoples of fishermen on the shores of the North Sea produced boats and men capable of sailing its waves and of floating down untamed rivers across Europe to keep up contact between the Baltic and Byzantium.

Military skills were naturally abundant on certain levels of economic life, such as pasturage and fishing, persisting in certain regions like steppes, mountains, and the rough sea-coast. From there their men would go forth to distribute themselves over societies less well supplied with the skills of war, which would either employ them or bow down to their conquest.

With the early feudal division of labor between peasant and horseman, the tiller of the soil and its defender, the production of military skills became to some extent decentralized over wide parts of Europe. Nevertheless, the comparative differences in military efficiency were still considerable enough to allow a skilled warrior people like the Normans to spread by service and conquest over large parts of Europe, contributing a great deal to the spread of the institutions of chivalry and to their international character.

So long as most of Europe remained on the level of scarcity which we have described, the effects of any local advances in a few countries had to be distributed at first by the same process of international stratification. Irish monks carried their learning far and wide over the continent; German knights went forth, more often bidden than unbidden, into Bohemia, Hungary, Poland; Flemish and German peasants and *locatores* brought more advanced techniques of agriculture and land reclamation into the Slavic regions north and east of eleventh-century Germany.[4] The spread of new ideas likewise had to follow the scant and wide-stretched network of intellectual centers, so long as there were only few persons in Europe able to read or interested in abstract thought, and even these few had little contact with the rest of the people.

In sum, there was from the end of the migration of nations through most of the Middle Ages very little mobility among the peasants and for the earlier part of the period among artisans. There was wider mobility among the noble bearers of military skills, especially when they possessed an important advantage against competing types of warfare, as in the tenth century when the Varangs ruled in Kiev and Novgorod. The highest horizontal mobility and interchange prevailed in the tenuous network of traders, and to some degree among the sparse layers of specialists, monks, scholars, and administrators, most of them part of the international organizations of monastery and church. It was this state of affairs which profoundly influenced the production and distribution of languages throughout early medieval Europe.

II

The primary distribution of spoken languages among the peasants of Europe was determined by the distribution of agricultural settlements at the transition from nomadic to sedentary agriculture. This transition took place at very different times in the different regions of Europe; and even where farming had already become fixed on the soil, the distribution of peoples and languages on the land was still liable to sudden change so long as new tribes of nomadic agriculturists were still coming into Europe, such as the Magyars in the tenth century, and clearing the land for their own settlement by driving out most of the earlier population. These invasions of farmers who drove out the former settlers in order to farm in their stead were different in their effects from the invasions of traders who settled in the midst of a people in order to trade with them, or from the conquest of warriors who spared the conquered in order to lord it over them. They brought immediate changes in the settlement of the land and with them sharp boundaries between very different, mutually unintelligible languages, such as between German and Magyar, English and Welsh, French and Breton, Spanish and Basque, and others.

In the beginning class differences were not sufficiently developed to prevent daily intercourse among practically all of the inhabitants in these communities which had just settled down to stable farming. Within each village the close community of life, the common dispositions regarding seed and harvest, tillage and fallow land, and the use of the common tended all to assimilate the language of any newcomers who did not deviate too far from the social level of the rest of the villagers; thus lower-class Magyars became Slovaks in the Slovak villages.[5] At the same time there was after the settlement very little intercourse between the bulk of the population from one peasant region to another. On the peasant level, therefore, the language frontiers soon hardened into stability with scarcely a change for centuries, winning for the peasants a reputation of being the most faithful preservers of nationality. The effects of rural immobility and seclusion went further, however. Originally common forms of speech became mutually unintelligible in widely separated regions, as in the classical case of the Romance languages. The peasant life preserved the Basque and Breton languages, but at the price of destroying their unity, breaking up each of them into a number of mutually unintelligible dialects.[6] Descendants of the same stock of Germanic settlers eventually found themselves speaking different dialects in the different valleys of the Austrian Tyrol.

Neighbouring peasant languages might be mutually unintelligible from the beginning, coming from greatly different stocks, so that they would appear automatically as independent languages; or their differences might slowly develop from a former common speech, so that they would appear for some time as mere dialects. Both dialects and "automatic languages" remained incomplete, however, so long as they lacked the words and concepts of urban life, that sociological development into all walks of life, carried on by several major social classes, which alone can elevate a spoken vernacular to the status of a full-fledged language.[7] In the absence of that sociological completeness the speech of the peasantry remained passively vegetating and slowly disintegrating from region to region, hidden below the international speech and civilization of their betters.

III

International languages of commerce, intellectual life, and, in many cases, administration represent an adaptation to a specific stage of economic and social development. This stage can now be defined. It is the stage where markets and long distance intercourse have already begun while no greater masses of the underlying population have yet been drawn into intensive personal participation in the exchange process. As this development was to some extent general in operation, we find in early medieval Europe the elements not only of one but of as many as five different international civilizations. Can we gain any indication from these five cases as to what are some of the factors underlying the aggressive strength and the long-run staying power of super-national civilizations of this kind?

In addition to the favorable stage in the economic development of the countries to be overlaid, the evidence points to a combination of several essential factors. A supply of manpower with a superior skill in transportation and warfare must be combined with a developed interest in long-distance trade and with adequate contact with an established center of superior skills of production. And these material elements must be welded together by a subjective effort. The opportunity must be utilized by the acts of men united by an idea, a myth, or a religion, calling them to action for a new way of life realizing the new potentialities.

With the ideas of state patriotism and Caesarism Greek and Roman civilization spread by road and galley around the Mediterranean; with the idea of monastic Christianity they penetrated along the trails and forest-paths of Europe. In Western and Central Europe it was the civilization of Latin Christianity with its script and language Latin, its center Rome, its laws and ethics those of the Roman Church, its routes of pilgrimage and trade centering in Italy. Next to it, in South-eastern Europe, we find the civilization of Byzantium, its script and language Greek, supplemented for purposes of missionary expansion by Church Slavonic, i.e., standardized Old Bulgarian; its center Constantinople, from whence it drew its architecture, art, and learning, and where its trade routes centered; and its Greek Orthodox Church, headed by the Emperor, reaching out into lands beyond the sway of the imperial administration. Caravans and horsemen, inspired by the faith of Islam, carried some of the high civilization of the towns of the Near East as far as central Africa, southern France, and the borders of China. Thus side by side with the blanket of Greek over the south-east, and of Latin over the north and the centre of Europe, there lay a blanket of Arabic speech and script, and of Moslem religion, civilization, trade, and upper classes over the peasants and townspeople whose descendants were to become the later Spaniards, Portuguese, and Catalans of the Iberian Peninsula.

Besides these three full-grown civilizations there were in Europe the elements of two others, carried by two other trading peoples, the Jews and the Vikings. The Jews had formed already before the Christian era a network of trading communities around the eastern Mediterranean; and now they were carrying on much of the commercial and financial life of Western Europe. The Jewish trading communities were further held together by a strongly unifying religion; by their Hebrew script and sacred language, supplemented by other special languages of their own like Judaeo-Spanish and Judaeo-German; and by their highly developed law laid down in the Talmud and its commentaries. They were rich in intellectual and trading skills, but they lacked man-power and, in spite of significant exceptions, military and productive skills. Since the destruction of the Temple at Jerusalem they had had no single spiritual or economic center. At one time there might have been a possibility of Judaism becoming the dominant faith in the network of Romance towns left abandoned with the remnants of their populations in the barbarian countries after the fall of Rome. That possibility was cut off not only by the early prohibitions of the Church and the new rulers against conversions to the Jewish faith, but also by the reluctance of the then prosperous Jewish trading communities to make mass conversions among the impecunious or the improvident, or to surrender to any large number of new converts their own valuable separate cohesion and identity so laboriously preserved through the centuries by the rigid prescriptions of their religion. Jewish civilization thus remained sociologically incomplete, although in a different way from that of the underlying peasant peoples.

The Vikings had seamanship, trading interests, fighting skill, and the fierce warrior's faith preserved in the Eddic poems. But the Vikings, too, lacked adequate contact with advanced skills and centers of production. In technology, agriculture, literacy, higher business skills, and written law they had little to offer. Their gifts were for commerce. But while we find a Viking chieftain buried in the Hebrides with the complete equipment of his civilization—sword, spear, battle-axe, and a pair of scales—these scales and the business they were used for can hardly be compared with the laws and the bookkeeping of the contemporary Arabs, Greeks, and Latins. Of economic goods the Vikings produced little more than transport service and raw materials. Most of their centers failed to last; those which survived soon lost their Viking character. Their common polytheistic religion and Runic script died away before the competition of Latin faith and letters. Their common Nordic speech, instead of becoming more firmly unified into a standard language as in the other civilizations, disintegrated into regional differences. In their unifying mission they had been themselves successors to an earlier trading empire in the North Sea, that of the Frisians. Now, in the tenth and eleventh centuries, they gave up their old civilization for that of Latin Christianity. Those of them who had settled

in Normandy accepted almost at once the French form of Romance language and civilization, while most of the trade in the North was taken
over by German merchants who had closer contacts with the new centers
of production in the German towns.

The pattern of primitive internationalism was not limited to early
medieval Europe alone. The Mongol horsemen of Genghis Khan and
Kublai Khan spread for a short time the contacts with the civilization
of China over central Asia toward eastern Europe, but no lasting economic advance was achieved nor was any idea or religion developed able
to maintain the new contacts and the new way of life. Unlike Christianity and Islam, it seems that the state philosophy of imperial China
has left as little of a lasting impression along the caravan trails as did
the state philosophy of imperial Rome. On the other hand, the Ottoman
Turks, combining Moslem zeal with Turcoman horsemanship in their
advance along the caravan trails and roads over Asia Minor toward the
Balkans, seem to have brought with them a greater increase in trade and
civilization than they have been usually credited with.[8] In all these cases
the fundamental pattern seems to be the same: an international blanket
spread over a host of primitive local economies.

IV

By the thirteenth century the five international civilizations of Europe
seemed to have given way to the single one of Western Christendom.
The Vikings had become its Norman crusaders; the Jews were being driven
from many of its main cities; the Arabs were being slowly pushed out of
Spain; Constantinople herself had been sacked by the Crusaders and
Venetians in 1204. As in other aspects, so also on the score of unity the
Thirteenth appeared as "the greatest of all centuries".

But the writers who drew this picture of solid unity must have found
it difficult to persuade that age to hold still long enough for its portrait.
Latin Christendom had triumphed. Its broad cultural base of Romance-
speaking peoples and Roman productive skills; its growing towns, multiplied by new ones springing up everywhere; the increase in its division
of labor and the new intensity with which people were drawn into its
markets and movements; the tightening and strengthening of the vertical
contacts from village to manor to town; the increasingly dense and rich
and varied life within each region—all these contributed to its victory.
But all these selfsame factors were bound to break up eventually the thin
shell of international Latin-speaking and writing unity which had rested
on their absence.

Early examples of medieval nationalism bear out the point. Out of
nearly sixty cases given in Mr. G. G. Coulton's article on "Nationalism

in the Middle Ages," [9] only twelve refer to events before 1200 A.D., while as many as twenty fall in the single century from 1200 to 1300, more than in any of the following centuries before 1500. While some of Mr. Coulton's examples refer to cases of regional or city patriotism rather than of allegiance to any nation, most of the remaining ones refer to situations where large numbers of newcomers or of members of rapidly growing groups such as Crusaders, monks, or townsmen entered into contact and some competition with each other or with established groups. It is from this pattern of the beginning break-up of an international civilization in times of intensified intercourse, as well as from its original rise in times of scant and extensive contacts, that a more general statement of the conditions of cultural assimilation and linguistic unity can be developed.

V

The following generalizations do not pretend to state inflexible laws. They seek to describe some fundamental quantitative relationships which seem to underlie the process of assimilation of men's speech habits, and possibly other slow-changing habits, to the established standards of another or wider community. These relationships seem to be present to some extent in all such situations of assimilation. In each individual situation, of course, peculiar factors may modify or even override the general pattern. After all, social sciences, like the medical ones, deal with people of flesh and blood, not with formulae. A general knowledge of the quantitative conditions for the balanced growth of individuals or communities should aid our diagnosis of each single case; it can never replace it.

Within these limitations, these seem to be the conditions of linguistic unity: 1. *The rate of assimilation must exceed the rate of entry.* That is to say, the rate at which persons acquire a common language must be greater than the rate at which persons habitually speaking other languages enter the zone of intensive intercourse in the community. "Entry" in this sense is brought about not only by immigration, but also, more often, by the extension of intensive intercourse to persons previously largely isolated. The condition applies therefore to the relationship of assimilation to immigration as well as to that of assimilation to the growth of intercourse accompanying economic expansion and progress. In the long run it is mainly with the effect of economic development on the rate of entry that assimilation has to keep step.

2. *The rate of assimilation increases* with (*a*) the similarity of the common language to the previous language of the new entrants; (*b*) the intensity of their contacts with the common language; (*c*) the willingness of persons to acquire the common language, and hence with the material

rewards and opportunities gained by its acquisition, as well as (*d*) the strength of the assimilating and unifying emotional and spiritual incentives, faiths, beliefs, and symbols current in the community; (*e*) the extent of the available educational facilities and existing skills and aptitudes for the teaching and learning of the common language, and hence with the smallness of cost, time, and effort needed for its acquisition; (*f*) the absence of social, political, or religious group emotions among the newcomers against the common language, as well as (*g*) the absence of any appreciable material advantage or privilege for them contingent upon their retention of a separate language and cohesion of their own; (*h*) the newcomers' lack of contacts with their previous language, and therefore also with their distance from its other speakers and with the fewness in numbers of the latter; and finally (*i*) the absence of institutional or emotional obstacles against the full assimilation and acceptance of the newcomers by the speakers of the predominating language.

3. *The rate of entry* of persons speaking other languages into the zone of intensive intercourse within the community *increases* with: (*a*) the growth of the zone of intensive intercourse itself, that is with the degree of the division of labor and the consequent amount of intercourse and contacts necessitated by the prevailing forms of production, technology, and economic life. It increases in particular *with the numbers of opportunities or positions* open in those social strata or professions where maintenance of contacts by speaking or writing make up a large part of the work, such as the organization of production, the recruitment and supervision of labor, the activities of commerce, the professions, administration, education, etc., and with the growth in the numbers of persons reached directly by any or all of these agencies. The rate of entry grows, in other words, with the growth in the social and economic demand for personnel in these contact services and for the forms of labor served by them, *constituting together the gross demand for new entrants.* The rate of entry grows also with (*b*) *the scarcity of available entrants from the predominant language group* at the level of rewards offered at this stage of economic development. The fewness of entrants from that group is determined among others by the smallness of its numbers, the lack of mobility between its occupations and social strata, and the extent of preferable alternative occupations open to its members. The gross demand together with the scarcity of available "fellow-speakers" determines the remaining *net demand for entrants from other language groups.* And finally the rate of entry increases with (*c*) the numbers and mobility of qualified members of other language groups, and with their lack of preferable alternatives, resulting in the *net supply of entrants from other language groups.* This supply may come both from outside or from within the country, but in either case from outside—and usually from below—the social classes of the dominant language group, which were making up, till then, the zone of intensive intercourse.

VI

The general method of analysing the conditions of linguistic unity in a changing society has here been developed from the observation of international integration in the relatively primitive economies of the European early and high Middle Ages. It can be applied to similar problems in other times and places. What services are to be expected from its application?

First of all, it can be used to isolate the economic factor more carefully from the political and emotional forces which interact with it in the making of national diversity and national conflict. Of the nine main factors listed as important for the rate of assimilation, three are economic: the intensity of the new contacts (2b), and the economic advantages and disadvantages of assimilation (2c and 2g). One factor is strictly linguistic: the similarity between the old language and the new (2a). Another one is largely dealing with given facts of history: the distance, dispersion, and fewness in numbers of the remaining unassimilated speakers of the previous language under consideration (2h). The remaining four points deal with emotional, political, and institutional factors which can be changed, in time and within limits, by political, propagandistic, or educational action (2d, 2e, 2f, and 2i). One factor operating on the rate of entry is largely economical: the gross demand for new entrants (3a). The two others, covering the mobility and availability of new entrants from both the dominant and the other language groups are determined partly also by political and emotional factors within the framework of economic conditions (3b and 3c); if desired they can be broken down into their component elements. All factors, of course, can be influenced to some limited extent by organized and sustained efforts of the political will. The vocabularies and grammars of kindred languages can be brought closer together or farther apart. The intensity of contacts with either the old or the new language, and even the economic rewards and opportunities for entry and assimilation can be influenced by deliberate statesmanship or the strength of aroused mass emotion. Applied to actual problems of nationalism the type of analysis outlined here may help to clarify the conditions under which statesmanship in each individual case would have to seek for a solution.

Secondly, our analysis can be applied to other not physically inheritable national characteristics besides language, such as accents, habits, traditions, peculiarities of character, and others. In most cases our information, if enough of it can be collected and organized, will show first of all the *latent national diversity* determined by the original settlement and later changes in the composition and speech of the agricultural population in and near the territory under observation. It will then show what effect historical and economic factors were having on the development of the rates of entry and of assimilation, and thus on the resulting *effective national diversity* visible in the zone of intensive intercourse.

At this point we reach one of the limits of our analysis of linguistic and cultural diversity. Whether any distribution of unassimilated people from different stocks in the fields of intensive intercourse will lead to national conflicts, seems to depend to a large extent on the relations, harmonious or antagonistic, prevailing among the different occupational groups, and on the degree of competition among persons within any of these groups. If economic and social conflicts between different classes, or competition within one or several of them, are intense—and would be intense also in the absence of national or language differences—then national diversity is likely to become one way of accentuating and dramatizing them. Under such conditions national differences will appear as a secondary factor in influencing the course of social conflicts and in contributing to their further intensification. Where such a development has been going on for some time, there the conspicuous and durable marks of language and nationality often eventually supplant earlier symbols and alignments of group conflict, until conflict in terms of religious or territorial allegiance gives way to conflict in terms of language and descent. In many countries modern nationalism has taken today the place of the religious communalism and territorial patriotism of earlier stages. A study of nationality can tell us here why men came to adopt the battle-cry of nationalism instead of the older ones for their conflicts; but we have to call on all the social sciences in asking for an explanation of the growth of the conflicts themselves.

VII

A specific study of the factors which have brought about till now such a development of growing national diversity and conflict may also indicate those factors, the strengthening of which would tend to weight the balance over to the side of decreasing conflicts and quickening unity. It may reveal in the interplay of largely impersonal forces at each stage the limiting or broadening of opportunities for statesmanlike action in favour of economic, political, and educational adjustment.

Such adjustments may be sought for the purposes of short-range politics, domestic or international. Political leaders may seek that balance of assimilation against expansion and entry which will prevent the accumulation of serious tension, while at the same time seeking the path of least resistance among the pressure groups. On the other hand, such adjustments may be pursued with a view to their long-range effects; in this case we are likely to find ourselves asking for a long-range perspective. Our analysis seems to lead to two such perspectives.

NOTES

[1] Carlton J. Hayes, *The Historical Evolution of Nationalism* (1931), p. 3.

[2] See for example Royal Institute of International Affairs, *Nationalism,* (1939), pp. 7–9; Hans Kohn, *Nationalism* (1938), p. 13; W. Mitscherlich, *Der Nationalismus, Die Geschichte einer Idee* (1929), pp. 63–73, 112–4.

[3] See Carlton J. Hayes, *Essays on Nationalism* (1928), pp. 30 ff.

[4] R. Koebner, "The Settlement and Colonisation of Europe", in the *Cambridge Economic History,* vol. I, esp. pp. 83–5.

[5] Otto Zarek, *The History of Hungary* (1939), p. 98.

[6] W. J. Entwistle, *The Spanish Language together with Portuguese, Catalan and Basque* (1936), p. 15.

[7] The concepts of "automatic language" and the criterion of sociological completeness for a full-fledged language are developed in H. Kloss, "Sprachtabellen", *Vierteljahreschrift für Politik und Geschichte,* vol. I, no. 2 (1929), pp. 107–8.

[8] William L. Langer and Robert P. Blake, "The Rise of the Ottoman Turks and its Historical Background", *American Historical Review,* vol. XXXVII (1932), pp. 468–505.

[9] *Cambridge Historical Journal,* vol. V (1935), pp. 15–40.

Looking at medieval unity, we found it based on a low rate of entry, on the scarcity of intercourse, the slowness of economic growth. Yet there are those who would recommend to us again that medieval unity as a model for today and tomorrow. If we are willing to pay the price, we may try to have it again. We may attempt to abolish ultimately national conflicts by erecting again international continent-wide or world-wide super-civilizations, based on the throttling down of the entry of the diversified and unassimilated majority of mankind into the world of intensive intercourse. This would have to be accomplished by the slowing down of economic progress and expansion to the limits set by the pace of gradual assimilation. Stretched above such a stagnating or extremely slowly growing world we then could again have a wide-flung shell of one or more international civilizations, based on a secluded upper caste of uniform language, traditions, and possibly ethnic or "racial" descent. A good deal of the enthusiasm of some German writers for the "Hochkulturen" of the past would fit in with such a perspective.

Or, on the other hand, we may realize that we will not return to the internationalism of scarcity of the early Middle Ages. Rather we may hope to abolish finally national conflict by speeding up economic growth and intercommunication everywhere until all mankind with all its secluded peasant masses will have entered the field of intensive intercourse. This would mean that *the unity of mankind will have to be sought through a* *intermediate period of still more increased diversity*. Instead of viewing cultural aspirations of small or hitherto submerged nations with i tience or alarm, we should greet their languages as vehicles of progr might find it even worth while to "lend-lease" philologists, gram teachers, and printers to some of the world's backward people not yet developed a written language from their daily speech. own countries, only in their own languages can the herit technological and scientific civilization be brought with countless villages and peasant families who still compr mankind. But having learned to read and write, hav quen communication with the rest of the world, th will be exposed to the forces of assimilation as nev all obstacles to assimilation will be reduced ar spiritual symbols as well as material opportur tion will be increased, then we may hope ultimately even linguistic unification of r to bottom and from land to land—a ta scope that it is barely beginning in ou conceivable.

Both these perspectives can b national civilization of the Midc

Looking at medieval unity, we found it based on a low rate of entry, on the scarcity of intercourse, the slowness of economic growth. Yet there are those who would recommend to us again that medieval unity as a model for today and tomorrow. If we are willing to pay the price, we may try to have it again. We may attempt to abolish ultimately national conflicts by erecting again international continent-wide or world-wide super-civilizations, based on the throttling down of the entry of the diversified and unassimilated majority of mankind into the world of intensive intercourse. This would have to be accomplished by the slowing down of economic progress and expansion to the limits set by the pace of gradual assimilation. Stretched above such a stagnating or extremely slowly growing world we then could again have a wide-flung shell of one or more international civilizations, based on a secluded upper caste of uniform language, traditions, and possibly ethnic or "racial" descent. A good deal of the enthusiasm of some German writers for the "Hochkulturen" of the past would fit in with such a perspective.

Or, on the other hand, we may realize that we will not return to the internationalism of scarcity of the early Middle Ages. Rather we may hope to abolish finally national conflict by speeding up economic growth and intercommunication everywhere until all mankind with all its secluded peasant masses will have entered the field of intensive intercourse. This would mean that *the unity of mankind will have to be sought through an intermediate period of still more increased diversity.* Instead of viewing the cultural aspirations of small or hitherto submerged nations with impatience or alarm, we should greet their languages as vehicles of progress. We might find it even worth while to "lend-lease" philologists, grammarians, teachers, and printers to some of the world's backward peoples who have not yet developed a written language from their daily speech. Only in their own countries, only in their own languages can the heritage of modern technological and scientific civilization be brought with any speed to the countless villages and peasant families who still comprise the majority of mankind. But having learned to read and write, having entered into frequent communication with the rest of the world, these diverse multitudes will be exposed to the forces of assimilation as never before. If at that time all obstacles to assimilation will be reduced and all aids and incentives, spiritual symbols as well as material opportunities, for world-wide unification will be increased, then we may hope for the eventual cultural and ultimately even linguistic unification of mankind in its entirety, from top to bottom and from land to land—a task so long in range and so wide in scope that it is barely beginning in our own time to become at all seriously conceivable.

Both these perspectives can be derived from a study of the great international civilization of the Middle Ages. Both are real with us today.

NOTES

1 Carlton J. Hayes, *The Historical Evolution of Nationalism* (1931), p. 3.

2 See for example Royal Institute of International Affairs, *Nationalism*, (1939), pp. 7–9; Hans Kohn, *Nationalism* (1938), p. 13; W. Mitscherlich, *Der Nationalismus, Die Geschichte einer Idee* (1929), pp. 63–73, 112–4.

3 See Carlton J. Hayes, *Essays on Nationalism* (1928), pp. 30 ff.

4 R. Koebner, "The Settlement and Colonisation of Europe", in the *Cambridge Economic History*, vol. I, esp. pp. 83–5.

5 Otto Zarek, *The History of Hungary* (1939), p. 98.

6 W. J. Entwistle, *The Spanish Language together with Portuguese, Catalan and Basque* (1936), p. 15.

7 The concepts of "automatic language" and the criterion of sociological completeness for a full-fledged language are developed in H. Kloss, "Sprachtabellen", *Vierteljahreschrift für Politik und Geschichte*, vol. I, no. 2 (1929), pp. 107–8.

8 William L. Langer and Robert P. Blake, "The Rise of the Ottoman Turks and its Historical Background", *American Historical Review*, vol. XXXVII (1932), pp. 468–505.

9 *Cambridge Historical Journal*, vol. V (1935), pp. 15–40.